232

THIRD EDITION

SOCIAL
WORK
RECORDS

D0024132

201-2 efficiency

THIRD EDITION

SOCIAL WORK RECORDS

JILL DONER KAGLE
SANDRA KOPELS
UNIVERSITY OF ILLINOIS AT URBANA-CHAMPAIGN

WAVELAND

PRESS, INC.

Long Grove, Illinois

For information about this book, contact:
Waveland Press, Inc.
4180 IL Route 83, Suite 101
Long Grove, IL 60047-9580
(847) 634-0081
info@waveland.com
www.waveland.com

Copyright © 2008 by Waveland Press, Inc.

10-digit ISBN 1-57766-546-5
13-digit ISBN 978-1-57766-546-5

All rights reserved. No part of this book may be reproduced, stored in a retrieval system, or transmitted in any form or by any means without permission in writing from the publisher.

Printed in the United States of America

7 6 5 4 3 2 1

CONTENTS

v

ACKNOWLEDGMENTS

The authors wish to acknowledge, with thanks, the following contributions to *Social Work Records:*

- Grants from the Lois and Samuel Silberman Fund in the 1980s made possible the breadth and depth of the research that forms the foundation of the book. The entire grant committee, especially Lois and Jayne Silberman, Thomas Horton, and Ellen Winston, were strongly committed to the project. Buddy Silberman generously shared his genuine interest, wide knowledge, and unfailing good advice.
- The Zellerbach Family Fund, which supported research at University of California-Berkeley School of Social Welfare in 2002.
- Colleagues at the University of Illinois at Urbana-Champaign, who shared their special knowledge and expertise, notably John Poertner and the late Shirley Wattenberg.
- Hundreds of direct-service workers, supervisors, and administrators from more than 300 agencies in 25 states who participated in wide-ranging interviews, surveys, and workshops and provided access to agency forms, policies, and records.
- Graduate students at the University of Illinois at Urbana-Champaign and the University of California at Berkeley who assisted with the research and editing, especially Philip Carey (Joel Sinai), MSW, research assistant on the Records I Project; Janice Hays Chadha, PhD, research associate on the Records I Project; Mei-O Hsieh, PhD, research assistant on the Records II Project; Cynthia Ozar, MSW, research assistant on the Records II Project; Woochan Shim, PhD, research assistant on the Records III Project; Hyun Ah Kang, PhD, research assistant on the Records III Project; Cindy Le, MSW candidate, research assistant on the Records III Project.
- Jonathan Kagle, Microsoft Corporation; Matthew Kagle, video game consultant; and Steven Kagle, Professor Emeritus of English, Illinois

State University, who provided their support and unsparing advice on all three editions.

- David M. Jameson, University of Hawaii; Stewart D. Griffeth, Jr., MSW; and Carol L. Gordon, PsyD, CADC, who provided their ongoing support and unwavering belief in the book's completion.

- Thousands of social work students and practitioners whose questions and meaningful examples have helped to fine-tune explanations of how law applies to social work practice.

JDK and SK

INTRODUCTION

Recording has always been an integral part of social work practice. The content and structure of records have changed through the years, but the rationale for keeping records remains. Social workers routinely document their services to demonstrate accountability to their clients, agencies, funding sources, communities, and profession. Records have many uses. Early in the history of the profession, Mary Richmond (1917) based her important study of practice, *Social Diagnosis,* on case records. Later, Gordon Hamilton (1936, 1946) showed that records were useful not just in the development of practice knowledge but also in enhancing services to clients. Today, records that document the purpose, goals, plan, process, progress, and outcome of services continue to play an important role in practice. They facilitate case continuity, enhance communication among professionals who are delivering services to the client, support practitioners' evaluation of their own practice, and serve as a basis for supervision, consultation, and peer review. Records can also serve as a practice tool, augmenting other forms of communication between worker and client.

Records are crucial to the operation of social service agencies and departments. They are the primary repository of information about clients and services. Records are used in claiming reimbursement for services and in seeking and maintaining funding for service programs. Records inform case, caseload, and agency management. Social workers use information from records in deciding how to allocate resources, and in evaluating the quality of services and their efficiency and effectiveness. Information culled from records is used to demonstrate practitioner and agency adherence to organizational policies, legal requirements, and professional standards. Records are used in accreditation reviews, managed care contracts and oversight, and internal and external studies of quality of care and service utilization. Should practitioners or their agencies be accused of malpractice or fraud, or if social workers are called to testify in court, records may be crucial in demonstrating professional credibility and integrity.

The multiplicity of uses for records in an increasingly complex service environment encourages social workers to keep thorough and inclusive

1

records. Records must be sufficiently detailed to document information about the client-need-situation[1] and the service transaction. This information justifies the need for services, describes how services were provided, explains how services were tailored to client needs and preferences, shows that services were selected in accordance with professional standards and best practices, and describes the services' impact on the client-need-situation. In deciding what to include in their records, workers must consider not just current but also potential future uses for information. Will a piece of information that seems inconsequential now turn out to be significant later? Is the record comprehensive enough to justify decisions and actions if the case were to undergo investigation? Sometimes practitioners are simply unsure about what to include in their records. Without clear guidance about what is important to include and about how to focus the record's content, they may overdocument to avoid being faulted for leaving out something significant. Social workers keep comprehensive records, then, to demonstrate accountability, justify decisions and actions, and manage risk.

At the same time, practitioners must deal with competing pressures to simplify recording and avoid unnecessary documentation. The most important of these pressures are time and cost. Recordkeeping is time-consuming and therefore expensive. Restricted funding for social work services means that agencies and practitioners must constantly look for ways to economize. Time freed up from recordkeeping is available for other activities, most notably for providing services to clients. Moreover, practitioners are justifiably concerned about protecting their clients' confidentiality, which is at greater risk in detailed records. Of course, professional ethics and privacy laws limit the flow of information into, within, and out of social service organizations. However, practitioners are well aware that a wide audience claims legitimate access to information in client records. Records are accessible to professionals and nonprofessionals within the organization as well as to most clients and others acting on their behalf. Information from records is transmitted to government agencies and other funders, and may be passed on to employers and advertisers, directly or via large databases. Moreover, despite new privacy laws and technological advances, practitioners worry that personal information in records might be released publicly as a result of system problems or errors in judgment, or accessed illegally by unscrupulous individuals. Whenever possible, then, social workers seek to limit recording in an effort to control costs, manage their time, and protect client privacy.

Social workers today face high demands for accountability while serving large caseloads of clients with complex problems and few resources. Indeed, recordkeeping, which never was a favorite activity, has become especially burdensome. Practitioners seldom have enough time to fulfill their practice responsibilities, so they may let their recordkeeping fall behind. They may rush through or delay recording, and play "catch-up" long after the work has been completed. As a result, their records may not reflect the quality of thought and action they have invested in the service transaction. In addition, in many agencies, recording has become more an administrative than a practice activity. Standards for records focus on information that managers need; practitioners no longer see the record's relevance to their practice. Unfortunately, records can also become a source of conflict between managers and practitioners, a lightning rod for performance criticism by managers and job dissatisfaction by workers. When practitioners fail to keep up with their recordkeeping, their supervisors sometimes fault them for being unprofessional or "resistant." Yet managers recognize that practitioners seldom have sufficient time for recording. They cite three major recordkeeping problems: records are incomplete and not up-to-date; workers have insufficient time for recordkeeping; and record-keeping takes too much time (Kagle, 1991). Practitioners, in turn, recognize the need for accountability, but believe that managers have unrealistic expectations.

The introduction of computers into recordkeeping offers some promise of reducing costs and practitioners' workload. However, many agencies have found computerization to be more expensive than expected. For practitioners, automation of records is often accompanied by increased demands for documentation, offsetting any workload reduction. New laws and regulations, most notably the Health Insurance Portability and Accountability Act (HIPAA), set new standards for the management of records and the protected health information they contain. These and other changes add to the complexity of recordkeeping and records management in today's professional social work environment.

Unfortunately, social work education has not always kept abreast of changes in recordkeeping or prepared students adequately for this important professional responsibility. With undergraduate and graduate curricula tightly packed with requirements, social work educators often fail to introduce recordkeeping in the classroom, where it should be integrated with theory and practice. Instead, they rely on agencies to teach recordkeeping in the field, where students may pick up idiosyncratic recordkeeping habits through their exposure to their field instructor's or field agency's distinctive way of keeping records. In addition, many social work education programs continue to require process recording in the field, an approach that does not equip students with the summary recordkeeping skills they will need as practitioners.

For most of the twentieth century, recordkeeping, like other components of the practice curriculum, was taught by the case method. Social work students and practitioners learned recordkeeping by studying sample records and through feedback on their own records from their field instructors and supervisors. They, in turn, had learned recording from their professional mentors, many of whom came into the profession when the expectations for recordkeeping and accountability were far less complicated than they are today. Gordon Hamilton (1936), whose historic writings formed the basis for the theory and practice of recording, wrote:

"It is not the recording," as a wise case worker once said, "which is difficult; it is the thinking which precedes it. If we can think clearly about the client's needs, his circumstances, and the treatment proposed, the record will shape itself easily and simply." (p. 207)

Certainly, clear thinking remains essential today, but it is no longer sufficient.

Social work practitioners, managers, and educators are rethinking their assumptions about recordkeeping, and developing new policies and procedures that respond to the current practice environment. Recordkeeping today, like the practice it documents, involves many difficult decisions, ranging from choices about agency-wide policies to the selection of information for each client's record. These choices are complicated, and involve balancing valued goals against each other. Accountability and risk management, for example, must be balanced against efficiency, cost, and client confidentiality. Recording, then, is not just a practice skill; it involves critical professional judgment at all levels of the organization and in every case.

Social Work Records is intended to assist social workers in balancing these valued goals and making these critical professional judgments. First published in 1984 and revised in 1991, *Social Work Records* has now been completely revised for its third edition, and includes a great deal of new material. For example, chapters 8 and 9 are entirely devoted to records and the law. These chapters include a thorough analysis of the privacy policies and regulations in HIPAA, and provide detailed guidance regarding subpoenas and the use of records in court. The third edition also includes new material on demonstrating cultural competence, systematic assessment, managed care, computerization, and record security as well as other topics.

Social Work Records presents an overview of the current status of recordkeeping in social work. It describes the process of recording but focuses on the product, the record. It delineates many of the issues facing social workers at all levels of the organization and suggests solutions that fit with the realities of today's practice. It proposes guidelines for improving agency-wide recordkeeping policies and procedures, and for selecting and organizing information in each record. It presents a number of forms and formats that may be adopted as is or adapted to suit a practitioner's or agency's needs. It presents a thorough discussion and analysis of the laws and regulations that apply to social work records.

Social Work Records describes an approach to recordkeeping that is congruent with contemporary practice and can accommodate future change. This approach is based on 12 underlying assumptions:

1. In setting agency standards and preparing records, social workers seek a balance among four competing goals: (a) accountability, (b) supporting and improving practice, (c) efficiency, and (d) client privacy.

2. Accountability is the primary goal of documentation.

3. Records demonstrate accountability by documenting compliance (or presenting the reasons for failing to comply) with agency policy, legal standards, practice guidelines, and professional ethics.

4. Records demonstrate accountability by documenting the rationale for, and the client's participation in, all judgments, decisions, and actions.

5. Records demonstrate accountability by documenting the purpose, goal, plan, activities, progress, outcome, and impact of services.

6. Records demonstrate accountability by correcting, amending, and clarifying previous entries whenever additional or contradictory information becomes available.

7. Records support practice when they are used in planning, monitoring, and evaluating services and their impact on the client-need-situation.

8. Records improve practice when practitioners have time to prepare them carefully and promptly.

9. Optimal recordkeeping standards are clear, reasonable, and explicit.

10. Optimal recordkeeping standards seek to limit the size of the record and the time spent in recording and retrieving information.

11. Agencies and practitioners can draw upon five mechanisms to protect client privacy: confidentiality, abridgement of information, client access, security, and anonymity.

12. Social work clients are at high risk of having personal information disseminated if it appears in the record.

These assumptions are revisited throughout the book, and can serve as a framework for understanding and analyzing recordkeeping policies, procedures, problems, and practices.

Chapter 1 introduces the 15 principles of good records, outlines the functions of records, presents a history of recordkeeping in social work, and describes current issues in the field. It discusses the varied uses for records in practice, the organization, and the service network. The chapter describes the development of the social work record and traces contemporary issues in recordkeeping to their roots.

Chapter 2 presents an overview of the content of social work records. It describes the Service-Centered Record, a model for selecting a record's content from the array of available information about the client-need-situation and the service transaction. It then outlines the elements of content, from intake through follow-up. Finally, the chapter describes in some detail each element of the content of a record, including social history, assessment, goals, plans, updates, outcome measures, and the closing summary.

Chapters 3, 4, and 5 focus on the structure of the record, describing and analyzing a wide range of approaches, formats, and forms used in selecting and organizing information. Each of these chapters includes examples of records based on actual practice. Chapter 3 presents three approaches to recording used primarily in social work education: process recording, the Teaching/Learning Record, and Essential Recording. This chapter also suggests ways for improving education for recording. Chapter 4 focuses on clinical records, and includes a discussion of the narrative summary format, Problem-Oriented Records, monitoring movement, and Goal Attainment Scaling. Chapter 5 presents a number of forms, using both fixed-choice and open-ended fields, that may be used in the documentation of clinical and management information.

Using a question and answer format, chapter 6 responds to questions practitioners ask. It includes discussions of client memoranda, the benefits of recording for the practitioner, recordkeeping in private practice, and record-keeping under managed care. It offers solutions to issues in practice from both the direct-service and the administrative perspective.

Chapter 7 has been substantially revised for the third edition. The first two editions focused on the key features of computer hardware and software, and their uses in social agencies. This edition assumes that the reader is familiar with computer technology, and that social workers and their agencies use computers for at least some of their recordkeeping functions. Using a question and answer format, chapter 7 now addresses questions that social work administrators ask. It includes discussion of the cost of recordkeeping, record security, uses of computers in social work agencies, and using records in research.

Chapters 8 and 9 provide a thorough analysis of records and the law. These chapters are new to the third edition of *Social Work Records*. Following a discussion of the five principles of privacy—confidentiality, abridgment, access, security, and anonymity—chapter 8 presents a brief history of federal privacy legislation. It then describes various federal and state laws that influence or control the handling of records and the information they contain. The chapter includes a thorough treatment of the privacy provisions of HIPAA, the relationship between HIPAA and state law, and privacy laws as they affect specific client populations. Chapter 9 focuses on records and their use in legal proceedings. After discussing why records would be used in court, the chapter presents legal issues pertaining to subpoenas, records, personal notes, and privilege, and the impact of federal and state law on social workers' responses. The chapter next looks at record retention under the law and presents content on how statutes of limitation influence retention. The chapter concludes with a discussion of expungement of records.

Social Work Records is designed for a wide audience of students, practitioners, and managers. It serves as a resource for beginning social workers who want to develop their knowledge and skill in recording and for experienced practitioners and managers who want to bring their policies and practices up-to-date and compliant with the law. Although not specifically written as a textbook, it can be successfully integrated into courses on direct service and administration, and it should be particularly valuable as a companion to the field practicum and in integrative seminars. Practitioners in all types of settings and at various levels of experience will find the review of familiar concepts, new approaches to recordkeeping, and guidelines for evaluating and improving records useful. For the profession as a whole, it provides a critical reappraisal of recordkeeping policy and practices in light of new technology, laws, and financial arrangements that have fundamentally changed the way social work is practiced and records are managed. In an environment of scarcity and skepticism about the very existence of our clients' needs and about the relevance of our services, it is vitally important that our records, which we must rely upon in practice and in the organization, keep pace with changing times.

Jill Doner Kagle
Sandra Kopels

NOTE

[1] Throughout *Social Work Records*, the authors use the term "client-need-situation" to describe the focus of the record. Adding "need" to "client-situation" suggests that records should focus on information about the client-situation that gives purpose and direction to the service process, rather than including all information about the client-situation that the worker comes to know.

CHAPTER 1

THE PRINCIPLES, FUNCTIONS, AND HISTORY OF RECORDS

Recordkeeping is an important component of social work practice. Recording has both clinical and administrative functions. Social workers keep records to document and retain information about client-need-situations[1] and about the process and progress of services. Records are used in planning, implementing, monitoring, and evaluating services to clients. Information from records is used to assess the quality, appropriateness, and impact of services. Records are also used in case, caseload, personnel, and agency management. The record is a focal point for accountability to the client, organization, community, and profession.

Social work records vary widely. This diversity reflects the breadth of social work practice. The content and structure of records varies from agency to agency because of differences in institutional mission, organizational structure, accreditation standards, personnel, service approach, and clientele. For example, records in child welfare agencies are quite different from records in hospitals and clinics. Even within a field of practice, records vary due to differences in accountability standards, funding sources, and inter-agency relationships. Social work records vary because they are intended to highlight the special nature of each service transaction. Different content, focus, and styles of recording are appropriate for different service patterns, practice approaches, and client-need-situations.

Social work records are diverse in content and structure, but have a common focus, scope, purpose, and function. Their focus is to describe and evaluate the special and shared characteristics of the client, the need, the situation, and the service transaction. Their scope is to link assessment of the client-need-situation, resources, service options, and client preferences to the purpose, goals, plans, decisions, activities, progress, impact, and outcome of services. Their purpose is to facilitate the delivery of services and document practitioner and agency accountability. Records function both as a process and a product. Through the recording process, which involves selecting, reviewing, analyzing, and organizing information, the practitioner comes to a better understanding of the client-need-situation. The record itself is the product; it serves as a repository of information about the client-need-situation and the services that have been provided.

FIFTEEN PRINCIPLES OF GOOD RECORDS

Good records adhere to the following 15 principles:

Principle 1: *Balance valued goals.* Good records balance four valued but competing goals: accountability, supporting and improving practice, efficiency, and client privacy.

Principle 2: *Mission focused.* Good records focus on content relevant to the mission of the agency and the goals of the service program.

Principle 3: *Manage risk.* Good records document compliance with or justify departure from agency policy, legal standards, practice guidelines, and professional ethics.

Principle 4: *Accountability.* Good records focus on service delivery, documenting the purpose of service; service goals, plans, and activities; and indicators of progress, impact, and outcome. Good records document the rationale for all service decisions and actions and compliance (or the reasons for failing to comply) with agency policy, legal standards, practice guidelines, and professional ethics.

Principle 5: *Abridgment.* Good records include no more information about the client-need-situation than is pertinent to the purpose, goals, and outcomes of service.

Principle 6: *Objectivity.* Good assessments are fair and impartial, and include four components: observation, sources of information, criteria used in judgment, and appraisal.

Principle 7: *Client involvement.* Assessments, goals, plans, and activities should be tailored to the individual client-need-situation. Good records document the client's role in all aspects of the service process, including decision making and action taking.

Principle 8: *Sources.* Information in good records is attributed to its source. The worker of record signs and dates each entry.

Principle 9: *Cultural context.* Good records document the cultural factors that influence the client-need-situation and service decisions, actions, and outcomes.

Principle 10: *Access.* Good records are written as if the client, those acting on the client's behalf, or those whose actions might oppose the client's wishes or interests were going to read them.

Principle 11: *Usability.* Good records include all pertinent information, are well-written, and form a coherent whole. The reader should be able to access important information about the client-need-situation and the service process over time. Good records are organized chronologically and by topic with cross-references to minimize redundancy.

Principle 12: *Currency.* Good records are living documents that are kept up-to-date. Records of long-term cases include periodic reviews and summaries.

Principle 13: *Rationale.* Good records provide the reasons behind and justifications for all service decisions and actions.

Principle 14: *Urgent situations.* Emergencies (e.g., hospitalization of a foster mother) and critical incidents (e.g., a client threatens a neighbor) are immediately and fully documented, with a report and plan of action signed by the worker and authorized by a supervisor or other administrator.

Principle 15: *Exclusions.* Good records do not include detailed descriptions of interviews or group sessions ("process"); speculation, unsupported opinions, judgmental language, gut reactions or intuitions; information about the client-need-situation that is unrelated to the purpose of service; or detailed descriptions of the worker's many activities on behalf of the client ("behold me busy" details [Bristol, 1936]). Good records exclude personal information about clients that is unrelated to the purpose, goals, or outcomes of service, as well as material that might be described as "inflammatory, demeaning or discriminatory" (O'Brien, McClellan, & Alfs, 1992).

FUNCTIONS OF SOCIAL WORK RECORDS

Good social work records are useful. That is, they include, in an accessible form, information that is necessary to fulfill the primary, secondary, and additional functions of recordkeeping in the agency or practice setting. The primary functions of social work records are to satisfy the expectations of accountability. These are: identifying and describing the client-need-situation and the need for service; describing and evaluating available resources; articulating the rationale for service decisions and actions; documenting compliance with standards; monitoring the process and impact of services; and claiming reimbursement. The secondary functions of social work records are to support practice, agency administration, and professional education and development. These include maintaining case continuity; communicating with other providers; sharing information with the client; supporting administrative oversight; facilitating the practitioner's professional development; providing information for accreditation review and other external oversight; serving as evidence in court; and educating students and other professionals. There are additional uses for records, most notably providing data for research and historical analyses.

IDENTIFYING AND DESCRIBING THE CLIENT-SITUATION AND THE NEED FOR SERVICES

Records contain information that identifies the client, describes the client-situation, and explains the need for service. They contain descriptions and assessments of the client-situation, which in some cases includes a psychosocial diagnosis; they describe the reasons for initiating service and the problems that are the focus of service. This information establishes the client's eligibility for service and specifies whether services were requested, offered, or mandated. In addition, records describe the relationship between the client-need-situation and the social environment. Sometimes workers prepare an eco-map (Hartman, 1978) to show visually the relationship between the client and various social systems. This information assists in case management and program management. When identifying information is pooled and analyzed, the organization can monitor trends in client characteristics, service needs, and program utilization.

DESCRIBING AND EVALUATING AVAILABLE RESOURCES

Records document the match between the client-need-situation and the programs, services, interventions, and resources that are included in the service plan. In their records, social workers scan the environment to identify the range of public programs, community services, interventions, and informal resources that might be suitable for the client-need-situation. They assess the quality, effectiveness, appropriateness, and responsiveness of various programs, services, interventions, and resources. Records also document limitations in resources that may hinder the service process or its intended outcomes. For example, services that might have been included in an optimal plan may be unavailable, inaccessible, too costly, or have long waiting lists; clients may be ineligible for or unwilling to participate in a program; or insurance may not cover some services. Descriptions and evaluations of available resources are continually updated and revised, and provide justification for the programs, services, interventions, and resources included in the ongoing service plan. This information also identifies barriers that may undermine the quality of services or their impact on the client-need-situation.

ARTICULATING THE RATIONALE FOR SERVICE DECISIONS AND ACTIONS

Records document the rationale for important decisions and actions in the case. Records are not just a repository of information about activities performed with and on behalf of the client, from opening to closing the case. They also provide an explanation for the selection of service goals, plans, and interventions. Records show, for example, how agency policy, client values and preferences, availability of resources, evidence of effectiveness, and other factors influence what services are offered, how they are delivered, and what impact they have. Records make clear the client's role in decision making and action taking. Records document workers' judgments based on observation, knowledge of human behavior, policy and practice guidelines, and legal and ethical constraints. They report on decisions and actions of other key professionals and agencies as well as family and community members who influence the service process and outcome. Providing a rationale for decisions and actions is crucial to accountability and sets professional records apart from mere reports of service activities.

DOCUMENTING COMPLIANCE WITH STANDARDS

An important component of accountability involves documenting compliance with agency policy, legal standards, practice guidelines, and professional ethics. Agencies generally outline their policies and procedures in manuals or online guides, and provide forms or formats for recording compliance. Such documentation might include, for example, client notification regarding agency policies on use and disclosure of personal information or parental consent to treat a minor. Records also document adherence to legal standards, such as reporting child or elder abuse to state agencies. Records are used to demonstrate that the practitioner has followed accepted standards of care in response to the client-need-situation. So, for example, a record would show that clients who manifested signs of substance abuse, depression, or other serious health and mental health problems underwent a thorough assessment. Records also document social workers' observance of their professional Code of Ethics, for example, by demonstrating respect for the worth and dignity of individuals, protecting client confidentiality, and practicing in areas of competence (National Association of Social Workers, 1999). In this way, the practitioner demonstrates accountability via recognition of and adherence to the important mandates and principles that guide competent practice. Moreover, this documentation may be crucial to risk management or in situations where the worker's or agency's actions are challenged in court (Reamer, 2005).

MONITORING THE PROCESS AND IMPACT OF SERVICE

The social work record is both a descriptive and an evaluative document. It is used not just for reporting but also for monitoring progress and reflecting upon practice decisions and actions. The record documents the initial contract between the worker and the client as to the purpose, goals, and plan of service. It also documents the process of service over time, assessing its impact on the client-need-situation and citing factors that may be facilitating or impeding progress. Throughout the service process, the record documents progress in implementing the plan, achieving goals, and accomplishing the purpose of service. Periodic review of records can signal the need for changes in service arrangements. Systematic measures can be used to gauge movement, and can be used by the worker and client as a basis for deciding whether to alter the purpose, goals, and plan of service. The record is useful to practitioners in assessing practice with individuals or groups of clients, as well as supervisors, consultants, and peers who seek to monitor and evaluate programs, practices, and providers.

CLAIMING REIMBURSEMENT

Records support requests for funding and claims for reimbursement. In agencies that receive grants or program funds, records are used to demonstrate that clients have been appropriately screened and selected, and that services have been delivered as agreed. In agencies that deliver services under managed care arrangements, records are used to document assessments, acuity (level of need) and treatment plans for preauthorization review, and ongoing process and progress information for continuing authorization. In most agencies, including those that receive fee-for-service reimbursement, records document not just each client contact, but also ongoing assessment of the client-need-situation, service goals and plans, evaluation of progress, and movement toward achieving goals. However, decisions about the specific information to document in a particular case may be dictated by the expectations of the funding source. The worker may document this information on special forms or via computer screens. To relieve the practitioner of a burden and centralize responsibility for this complex task, many agencies rely on clerical staff to collect and collate information from records, prepare written or electronic reports, keep up with changes, and ensure that varying requirements of different funders are met. Clerical staff may also be responsible for electronic data collection and transfer to receive reimbursement from such programs as Medicare and Medicaid.

MAINTAINING CASE CONTINUITY

Records that are up-to-date, well-organized, and clearly written assist the practitioner and others who are delivering services to the client in reviewing the case to date. Workers review their own records to recall events, find specific pieces of information, and review progress over time (Monnickendam, Yaniv, & Geva, 1994). Other practitioners rely on the record in an emergency or when the practitioner is unavailable. Information about the purpose, plan, process, and progress of service, as well as the rationale for decisions and actions in the case, are essential to case continuity when another worker assumes responsibility for the case, some time has elapsed since the previous contact with the client, or the client-need-situation is complicated and services continue over a long period of time.

COMMUNICATING WITH OTHER PROVIDERS

In interdisciplinary settings, as well as agencies in which services are delivered by teams of social workers, the record facilitates professional collaboration. Although the record can never substitute for team meetings and face-to-face discussions, it serves as an additional source of communication, coordinating individual efforts, making new information available to all practitioners, and reinforcing group decisions and actions. Information from social work records is used by other providers to supplement their own knowledge and understanding of the client-need-situation and the services clients are offered and receive.

SHARING INFORMATION WITH THE CLIENT

The record can be a direct means of communication with the client. Some practitioners choose to involve the client in the recordkeeping process. For example, a worker asks his client to keep charts documenting the circumstances under which a specific behavior occurs. These charts become a focal point of worker-client meetings, and part of the case record. Other practitioners share portions of the record with their clients. For example, at the beginning of each group session, a worker can distribute copies of her summary of the previous session to group members. Members then have an opportunity to comment on and correct the record. It also serves as a link between meetings. The record serves a therapeutic purpose, encouraging discussion of the service process and progress.

Most record sharing, however, is the result of federal and state laws or administrative guidelines. Clients often have access to their records as a matter of right rather than for therapeutic purposes. Privacy laws, ethical codes, and the policies of most social work agencies allow clients, or those acting on their behalf, access to some or all of their records. For example, federal and state privacy laws usually provide clients with the right to see, copy, and amend health, mental health, educational, and other public agency records.

The National Association of Social Workers' (NASW) (1999) Code of Ethics offers social workers meaningful guidance. It states that "social workers should provide clients with reasonable access to records concerning [them]" (1.08[a]). Moreover, with important exceptions like child abuse reporting, release of personal information to another agency or third party should, whenever possible, be based on the client's informed consent. This means that the client should be aware of what information will be released, where information is to be sent, and how it will be used. Practitioners are therefore obliged to describe the information in detail or provide clients with direct access to that information. The NASW Code of Ethics states that "social workers may disclose confidential information when appropriate with valid consent from a client or a person legally authorized to consent on behalf of a client" (1.07[b]), and that "social workers should inform clients, to the extent possible, about the disclosure of confidential information. . . . This applies whether social workers disclose confidential information on the basis of a legal requirement or client consent" (1.07[d]).

Of course, many social work clients do not read or receive copies of their records. However, an increasing number read portions of their records while they are receiving services or after services have been terminated. Records should be written as if clients or others acting on their behalf or even contrary to their interests may eventually read all or part of the record. The record can have an important role, either supporting or undermining the worker-client relationship and the goals of service. Whether or not workers intend them for this purpose, social work records are often a means of communication with the client.

SUPPORTING ADMINISTRATIVE OVERSIGHT

Records serve vital management functions. Records are used by supervisors and others to assist the worker in planning, implementing, and evaluating

their services. Supervisors often read records to gain an appreciation of a particular case or group of cases. Records supplement oral reports and direct observation, and can offer an in-depth and long-term perspective. Consultants may also
review case records before conferring about unique or problematic cases.

Records are used in supervision and other internal reviews to evaluate
compliance with agency policies and practice guidelines. Quality assurance
and peer review committees use information from records to assess the quality, timeliness, efficiency, and effectiveness of services. Automated recordkeeping systems enable practitioners, supervisors, and administrators to
analyze data from records for use not just in managing cases but also in
deploying personnel and anticipating changes in programs and services. For
example, information from records may be used to track clients through the
system, identifying service patterns, caseload and workload issues, and gaps
in resources. It may also be used to identify emerging client needs as well as
underutilized services. Some of the information used in managing the agency
comes directly from client records. Practitioners document additional information on forms, such as daily activity logs, and in regular or special reports.

FACILITATING THE PRACTITIONER'S PROFESSIONAL DEVELOPMENT

Records can play an important role in the practitioner's ongoing evaluation of her or his own practice. Records reveal the practitioner's knowledge,
skills, and values; the bases and consequences of the practitioner's decisions
and actions; and the practitioner's relationships with clients and others. Practitioners can use their records to reflect upon their approach to practice, monitor service processes and outcomes, and identify their strengths as well as
areas needing improvement. Supervisors, peers, consultants, and others who
support the practitioner's professional development can use the record con-
structively, to surface notable aspects of a particular case or the practitioner's
caseload. They can support the practitioner's efforts to identify patterns in
communication, hidden themes and implicit meanings, missed opportunities,
and unanticipated consequences. Records can be used to enrich supervisory
conferences, staff meetings, and case consultations, contributing to staff
development. Unfortunately, records are too often used punitively, to fault
practitioners for inadequate performance or poor recordkeeping.

PROVIDING INFORMATION FOR ACCREDITATION REVIEW
AND OTHER EXTERNAL OVERSIGHT

Records may be subject to review as a component of the agency's accreditation or as a means of external oversight. The Joint Commission
(www.jointcommission.org), which accredits health and mental health hospitals and agencies, and the Council on Accreditation (www.coastandards.org),
which accredits public and private child and family agencies, are two examples of organizations that set standards for documentation and review records
to assess compliance with those standards. Records may also undergo review

by state licensing authorities, the courts, funding agencies, and other organizations that seek to assess the quality and efficiency of an agency's programs.

SERVING AS EVIDENCE IN COURT

Privacy laws, agency policies, and professional ethics help maintain the confidentiality of client records. In addition, social workers' testimonial privilege, that is, the right to refuse to disclose confidential information in court without the client's consent, further protects such information from public disclosure (*Jaffee v. Redmond*, 1996). However, there are occasions when records are used as evidence in court. This may occur when clients are under court supervision (e.g., in cases involving child abuse or criminal activity) or when social workers serve as consultants to the court (e.g., by conducting evaluations of families in custody disputes). Records may also be used in court if the client authorizes their disclosure, if worker-client communication was not confidential, if the client sues the agency or worker, or if any of a number of exceptions to the privilege is invoked (see chapter 9).

EDUCATING STUDENTS AND OTHER PROFESSIONALS

Records have always played an important role in professional social work education. Until the 1970s, the primary approach to teaching social work practice was the case method. Social work education relied heavily on records in teaching casework, group work, and community organization practice. Today, records are sometimes used in the classroom to supplement didactic and experiential learning. They introduce students to a variety of client-need-situations, examples of communication and relationships, and processes of assessment, intervention, and evaluation. Many students, however, are first introduced to records in the field, where agencies use them to teach students and new workers about agency policies, procedures, and practices. Records demonstrate by example how clients are served and records are kept in the agency. For better or worse, records serve to perpetuate ongoing agency practices, as students and new workers seek to replicate what they read in records. Records also play an indirect role in educating clients, practitioners, and others about social work. What they read in social workers' records teaches them a great deal about what social workers do and how they do it.

PROVIDING DATA FOR RESEARCH AND HISTORICAL ANALYSES

In the early years of the profession, research was considered a principal reason for keeping records. Although it is not clear how often they actually were used for this purpose, records were considered an important and trustworthy source of data on human behavior, social needs, and the role of the social services. Narrative records were certainly influential in the formulation of social work practice theory (Richmond, 1917). More recently, large-scale studies using administrative data as a primary source have informed policy and practice in child welfare, for example Children and Family Research

Center, 2001; Courtney & Barth, 1996; Fanshel, 1975). Narrative records have also been the primary source for sociological and historical analyses of early social work practices (Margolin, 1997; Odem, 1995; Tice, 1998).

Today, records continue to be used in research; however, they are no longer considered a ready and reliable source. Practitioners, scholars, and students who wish to conduct research using agency records must undergo stringent prior review by institutional review boards to ensure that clients' rights are protected and ethical standards are met. Moreover, many agencies are reluctant to become involved in formal research due to the time and costs involved, potential for negative findings, and concerns about the burden of removing identifiable information as required by privacy laws. In addition, scholars question the reliability and thoroughness of agency records, which are often written retrospectively and for different purposes. Many prefer instead to use instruments tailor-made for the research. Nonetheless, records continue to be used in agency-based research. Practitioners, administrators, students, and university scholars conduct systematic studies of existing clients' needs, service outcomes, and more (see, for example, Stiffman, Staudt, & Baker, 1996). They use single-subject methods to monitor client behavior, interventions, and goal achievement. They pool data from records to assess the quality, efficiency, and impact of various programs and interventions.

Records are also used in historical studies and analyses. Agency records stored in national historical archives, most notably the Social Welfare History Archives at the University of Minnesota, offer scholars a glimpse into the records of diverse organizations and service provider agencies. Agencies themselves may retain administrative records and inactive case files. Barbeau and Lohmann (1992) argue that, despite high costs and technical difficulties, this practice offers an important resource to future administrators, practitioners, and social welfare historians.

A Brief History of Social Work Recording

The history of recordkeeping in social work reflects the history of the profession and its developing theories, methods, and roles. Over time, practitioners and agencies have adopted new approaches to practice that, in turn, changed the record's focus, content, and structure. As social work practice became more complex, records too became more varied, documenting the breadth of client problems, social programs and policies, and social work practices. As records became more important to the management of social agencies, they focused increasingly on demonstrating accountability. The development of recording throughout social work's history shows that changes in content and structure are linked to changes in social work practice and to the record's purposes and uses.

The first important book entirely devoted to case records, *The Social Case History: Its Construction and Content*, was published in 1920 by Ada Eliot Sheffield. She described the record, which had developed with the growth of social casework, as

> a body of personal information conserved with a view to the three ends of social case work; namely (1) the immediate purpose of furthering effective treatment of individual clients, (2) the ultimate purpose of general social betterment, and (3) the incidental purpose of establishing the caseworker herself in critical thinking. (pp. 5–6)

It is clear that in common practice of the day, the first of these purposes was dominant, since records were focused on demonstrating the relationship between the client's need and the treatment that was offered. Reflecting this purpose, the record was likely to contain

> a certain range of facts [that] has come to be generally accepted among case workers as uniformly having significance for their purpose. This range would include such items as usually appear on face cards: the client's name and address, the date and place of birth, the nationality, addresses of physicians, employers, and so on. (p. 20)

Recording this information called for "no act of judgment," but was the responsibility of a trained worker. The record would also include information requiring judgment, bearing upon the "client's prospects of successful citizenship: family history, health, employment, education, finances, character" (p. 21).

One senses that, like other authors who later wrote about records, Sheffield wished to move the record—and casework practice—to a new level. She suggested that the worker go beyond this "factual" information to "key conceptions which would give the facts significance." (These conceptions are precursors of today's assessments.) In further work with the client, the worker's aim was to "frame a hypothesis as to what a fact means, and then search for confirmation or disproof in recurrent instances" (p. 38). Sheffield also emphasized the role of the record in advancing knowledge and social betterment. The record was to be a social specialist's report, identifying typical instances of social maladjustment and relating them to defects in the social order.

In 1925, Mary Richmond described the reasons for keeping records. Her description of their uses is as pragmatic—"workers get sick"—as it is wide ranging. Records could be used in supervision, training, improving treatment, helping the public to understand social work, as well as in studying practice. In response to the question of whether checkings (checklists) could be substituted for narrative records, Richmond presented what she considered irrefutable evidence for narrative records. Not only had checkings been tried with "disastrous results," but her own work could not have been drawn from checkings: "How could these marks have made the sequence of events clear to any one else? Only the fullest and most careful recording made these apparent to me for instance" (p. 216).

In 1928, Ernest Burgess, a sociologist, suggested that caseworkers make their records useful for sociological interpretation by replacing selective narratives with full verbatim reports of the client's statements during interviews. This, he argued, would make the record more valuable to the caseworker and to the researcher by revealing the "person as he really is to himself . . . in his own language," and would make the record "really objective and open to anyone to interpret" (p. 527). Burgess suggested a very complete record, for it was to include

> a verbatim account of the family history, in both husband's and wife's versions; the conception of each regarding his [or her] role in the family and community, philosophy of life, ambitions, attitudes, and plans; attitudes of individuals and the group in family interviews; and interviews with such representative local persons as neighbors, employers, and landlords. (pp. 529–530)

In addition, the record was to include, in summary form, a diagnostic statement and a treatment plan, a closing case review, and any conclusions that might be applicable to similar cases.

It is not surprising that Burgess's proposal was met with a strong reaction. Several authors responded by pointing out that, contrary to his contention, verbatim records would be longer than summary narratives—and therefore more expensive to produce—and would necessarily involve selection. And this was not the only criticism of Burgess's proposal. Eliot (1928) argued that it required that "one . . . train and trust a recorder to remember passages supposedly most symptomatic of attitudes relevant to the situation or its solution, and this introduces another chance for bias: in the training of the recorder, in the recorder herself, or both" (p. 540). By asking "Can one be simultaneously scientific and sympathetic? Can one simultaneously experience and reflect? . . . Can one preserve objectivity in a subjective experience?" (p. 542), Eliot was raising a fundamental and persistent question in practice and in recording. Swift (1928) also differed with Burgess, his comments typifying the views of many of his contemporaries as well as those of many future practitioners. He stated that "as used by the caseworker, the ultimate purpose of a case record must be treatment . . . [and therefore the] emphases are not the same as they would be for research purposes" (p. 535). Nonetheless, despite these and other limitations, the verbatim or process record still is used today, for educational rather than for research purposes. The costs of preparing, transcribing, and reading process records prohibit their regular use in practice.

Whereas the use of records in research is a recurrent issue in the social work literature, research has never become a predominant function of such records. For the two decades following the publication of the Burgess article, the acknowledged purpose of the record was treatment. This focus is apparent in Margaret Cochran Bristol's *Handbook on Social Case Recording*, published in 1936. Here, as in Gordon Hamilton's (1936) *Social Case Recording*, the process of recording, as well as the record itself, has importance in assisting treatment. Bristol (1936) stated at the outset that the values in case recording are not confined solely . . . to those which are derived from the record after it is prepared. During the process of preparation, critical thinking and careful organization of material are stimulated and the worker is compelled to think through the situation and to make an analysis (or diagnosis) of the problems as she might not otherwise be impelled to do. (pp. 5–6)

Bristol emphasized the qualities of accuracy, objectivity, brevity, color, ease of reference, clarity, uniformity, and up-to-dateness of the record. In achieving these qualities, she recognized the difficulties in making records both objective and brief:

Without doubt, one of the most effective methods of shortening the record is by the careful selection of material. Although this procedure may decrease the objectivity of the record, it may increase its value, provided the caseworker has been objective in securing and selecting the material to present. (p. 59)

Bristol suggested that the records of the future would resolve this basic conflict, through the use of "more carefully defined terminology, which in turn will permit considerable abbreviation of records without a sacrifice in their objectivity" and through an "increasing emphasis . . . upon the responsibility of the worker to make and record interpretations competently and accurately without the necessity for extensive and detailed descriptions of minute objective phenomena on which her interpretations were based" (pp. 77–78). Bristol envisioned a selective, diagnostic record, not one that was descriptive.

Unlike Sheffield, who suggested that the record focus on common characteristics among clients, Bristol and Hamilton believed that the focus of the record should be individualization. What was unique about the client and the situation formed the core of casework and of the casework record. Both authors also recognized the close relationship between good practice and good recording.

Through Hamilton's (1936) work, these concepts became accepted principles of professional practice. For Hamilton, there could be no one prototype for the record that could be used as a guide by the practitioner. The content and the structure of the record were inherent in the case itself: "There is no such thing as a model record, no routines which will make the case inevitably clear, accessible, and understandable. Records should be written to suit the case, not the case geared to a theoretical pattern" (p. 2). Furthermore, according to Hamilton, recording skills could not be taught, but would be developed in concert with other practice competencies, reflecting the practitioner's maturing diagnostic judgment.

A good record would be that in which, issues having been apprehended early, there is a minimum of fact or thinking irrelevant to the problems under consideration. In the hands of the skilled practitioner, only such material, after the initial study, would be recorded as has bearing on shifts in the hypothesis, with more accurate interpretation and with cor-

responding developments or changes in treatment. In an ultimate sense
only the trained diagnostician can write a good record, for only he can
pluck from the unending web of social experience the thread of probable
significance. (p. 209)

The record was to be "the writer's attempt to express, as practitioner, the
meaning of the case" (p. 44).

Hamilton's themes, with variations, were further developed during the
1940s and 1950s. In both casework and group work, students and novice
practitioners would begin with the process record. They would try to reproduce, with as much accuracy as possible, their interaction with clients during
interviews and group meetings. Worker and supervisor would then carefully
study these records to find the essence of the client's communication and of
the treatment process. In this way, knowledge of the case and practice skills
were both being developed. Ideally, experienced workers would then move on
to diagnostic summary recording, returning to process recording only as an
aid to treatment in complex cases. In reality, this transition from process to
diagnostic summary records was sometimes difficult, and the resulting
records were of poor quality.

Three articles published in 1949 revealed the difficulties in moving individual workers and the profession as a whole from process to diagnostic summary recording. Little wrote that agency records were needlessly detailed,
and attributed this to the failure of schools of social work to prepare students
for their responsibilities as practitioners. She said that "the caseworker has
not been expected to formulate his tentative diagnosis and the direction of his
activities" (p. 15). Sytz proposed methods of teaching diagnostic recording
skills in the classroom, and of conceptually linking the process of recording
with casework and group work practice. Sackheim described the following
criteria developed in her mental health clinic for selecting information for a
condensed, diagnostic record: (1) meaningful data about the patient; (2)
movement in therapy; (3) activity of the worker and client; and (4) emotional
interaction between worker and client. "What further," she asked, "should be
included in a record that would not be excessive detail?" (p. 20). Despite
Hamilton's assurance that practice and recording skills would develop simultaneously, these authors believed that recording would improve if social
workers were educated in diagnostic recording and provided with guidelines
for selecting information for the diagnostic record.

Marguerite Munro (1951) placed more of the responsibility for trans-
forming records in the hands of supervisors and administrators. Early in a
practitioner's career, a worker with only "a limited degree of discerning, dis-
criminating skill" would need to record interviews in detail so that the
worker and supervisor could "evaluate together details of the interview's content. A more mature worker need illustrate the process with only enough content to provide meaning . . ." (p. 186). Munro envisioned what was then a
radical shift in responsibility for case decisions over time, from supervisor to
practitioner, with records becoming briefer and more selective, focused on

"the essentials needed in supervision" (p. 187). Such a shift would require administrative leadership and sensitivity since "it can be hard for a caseworker to assume new responsibilities, even though she wants them . . . and for a supervisor to give up responsibility, even though her primary interest is in the caseworker's development" (p. 197).

The attention directed to the record as a resource for teaching and learning agency-based practice and assessing and refining practitioners' diagnostic skills transformed the record. In the minds of many practitioners and supervisors, the primary purpose for recording was supervision—an assumption supported by some research findings. In their study of recording in two Chicago family service agencies, Frings, Kratovil, and Polemis (1958) found that records were being used most frequently in supervision. In 1960, Aptekar wrote that "in most agencies, records are meant to be read by the supervisor" (p. 16).

By the mid-1950s, the diagnostic record was firmly in place. Process recording was still used in social work education and beginning practice. However, the time and effort required to prepare such records was not suited to day-to-day practice. Rather, the record had become selective and analytic. The worker prepared the record for its primary audience, the worker's supervisor. The record was intended to show the supervisor the worker's diagnostic thinking and approach to the case. But, although in theory recording was to be a thinking-planning process, in practice records were often prepared long after the work had been completed. As a result, analyses were often retrospective reconstructions of, rather than prospective aids to, the worker's thinking processes.

The 1960s and 1970s brought major changes to social work and its environment. These changes had a significant impact on the form and function of the social work record. The community demanded broader accountability from all service professions. Not only were agencies to provide quality services; they were to demonstrate that their services "worked." In response to funding requirements, many organizations moved to supplement or replace diagnostic, analytic records with more systematic documentation of service activities and their effects. During the 1970s, many large and some smaller agencies and hospitals began using automated management information systems and other computer technology in their recordkeeping. New practice models that incorporated innovative recording procedures were introduced into the field. For example, behavioral intervention incorporated ongoing measurement and charting of target behaviors into their records. Family therapy used live supervision, as well as audiotaping and videotaping of sessions with clients, as a basis for improving practice and practitioner skills.

Concern for the confidentiality of personal information contained in health, social service, and educational records led to legislation to protect personal privacy. The Privacy Act (1974) and the Family Educational Rights and Privacy Act (1974), for example, established requirements for protecting client privacy in federally financed programs and public education. By the late 1970s, most states had enacted privacy legislation that extended those rights to many clients in health, mental health, and social service organizations. In general, these policies placed limits on information collection and dissemination and provided clients with access to their own records.

During this same period, the NASW (1975, 1979) revised and updated its policy guidelines and its Code of Ethics regarding the handling of confidential information. The social work literature in the late 1970s reflected professional concerns about changes in privacy policy (McCormick, 1978; Reynolds, 1976, 1977) and described the effects of new policies on record-keeping procedures in social agencies (Schrier, 1980; Wilson, 1978). Although the literature as a whole showed that professionals were apprehensive about client access (for example, see Prochaska, 1977), some authors described innovative, practical, and positive responses to client access in their own practice (Freed, 1978; Houghkirk, 1977).

New recording models that emerged during this period were dominated by concern for accountability and the documentation of client change. *Goal Attainment Scaling* (Kiresuk & Sherman, 1968) was developed for use in community mental health centers. This approach, which organizes accountability around program goals, offers a method of describing the intended outcomes of service concretely, linking goals to measures of client behavior, and evaluating client change and goal attainment through time. The *Problem-Oriented Medical Record* (Weed, 1968), which organizes accountability around a list of the patient's problems, was developed originally as an aid to medical education. Ideally, the health team generates a list of the patient's problems; then each member of the team organizes his or her activities and chart notes around these problems. However, the team component is absent in many of the health and mental health settings that have adopted the problem-oriented approach; each health professional may generate a problem list independently. In addition, the method of organizing progress notes is used more often than the problem list. The "SOAP" note organizes progress notes into four components: S = subjective information, O = objective information, A = assessment, and P = plan. Several articles introduced the Problem-Oriented Record, and the "SOAP" note, into the social work literature and suggested adaptations of the model for social work records (Hartman & Wickey, 1978; Johnson, 1978; Kane, 1974). Finally, time-series measures, an integral part of the behavioral model of practice, were introduced to a wider social work audience as a component of a new practitioner-researcher approach to practice (Bloom & Fischer, 1982; Jayaratne & Levy, 1979; Nelsen, 1981). Time-series or single-subject designs, which organize accountability around repeated measurement of target behaviors, thoughts, or feelings, have received strong support in social work education. These designs and measurement procedures have now also been widely adopted by agencies.

The social work record has always been an accountability document. Prior to the 1960s, the practitioner was accountable through the record to the supervisor, other professionals working with the client, and the organization. During the 1960s and 1970s, the record became a vehicle for accountability to a much wider audience, including accreditation, oversight and funding organizations, and clients and their families and advocates. Furthermore, the focus of accountability changed. Prior to the 1960s, accountability focused on the process of service and the quality of diagnostic thinking; during the 1960s and 1970s, accountability focused also on service activities and their impact on the client-need-situation. Kagle (1984b, 1991) developed the Service-Centered Record to assist practitioners in balancing accountability and support for practice with client privacy and efficiency. The Service-Centered approach, which is fully described and illustrated in chapter 2, focuses the content of the record on describing, monitoring, and providing the rationale for service decisions and actions.

The ability of social workers to respond to accountability requirements was greatly enhanced by the widespread introduction of computers into social agencies and social work departments. Automation began in the 1970s (Rein, 1975; Young, 1974a, 1974b) and accelerated in the 1980s. During this period, computers were not yet ubiquitous. Data entry and word processing were still considered special technical skills, and computers themselves were expensive and cumbersome. In many agencies, hospitals, and departments, social work practitioners did not have direct access to computers or terminals. Their recordkeeping continued to involve writing, typing, or dictating information that was then transcribed or entered into the computer by others. Records included narratives and forms that were generated by computers, but computers were not yet widely used interactively for recordkeeping or retrieval of information. However, computers supported practitioners' recordkeeping, and were used in many agencies to retain, access, and analyze information for case, program, and agency management.

The 1990s ushered in a new technological age, with widely available, inexpensive, fast, and easy-to-use personal computers. Many practitioners prepared their own reports, using their agency's or their own computers. Social workers newly entering the field had "grown up" with computers, were skilled in their use, and relied on them not just for recordkeeping but for interpersonal communication and searching for information. Some experienced practitioners followed suit, although many continued to keep notes and records in longhand.

By the beginning of the twenty-first century, social work records were largely computer supported. Hand-written notes still appeared in records, but required information was likely to be entered directly into computer systems or transcribed by computer. Records-management software offered practitioners and agencies recording applications that could support documentation of cases from intake through termination and follow-up, and included scheduling and billing functions. Decision trees and preformatted screens assisted practitioners in decision making and documentation. Devices and media like facsimile (fax) machines, cell phones, handheld computers, wireless modems, and the Internet supported access to and transfer of written and verbal communications. The federal government, state governments, and many large insurers encouraged or required electronic transfer of data in programs they funded.

At the same time, practitioners and the public worried about the confidentiality and security of data. The states and the federal government sought to strengthen privacy standards and regulate the handling of personal and confidential information in medical, financial, social service, and other records. The federal Health Insurance Portability and Accountability Act (HIPAA) of 1996, which encouraged electronic transactions, also required compliance with wide-ranging standards for the handling of medical records and "individually identifiable health information, whether electronically, on paper, or orally." HIPAA gave consumers access to their health records; required informed authorization for the release of information; required health agencies to have written privacy procedures, with training and monitoring, and to disclose their privacy policies to consumers; and offered special protections for psychotherapy notes. Generally, however, HIPAA was more permissive than many state privacy and records laws, for example, regarding patients' consent to release information. When such discrepancies occurred, practitioners were expected to comply with state laws.

The profession's concern about encroachments on client confidentiality and the privacy of records is reflected in NASW's (1999) Code of Ethics. The section devoted to "Social Workers' Ethical Responsibilities to Clients" provided additional guidance on confidentiality and the handling of records given new technology. While restating practitioners' overall obligation to safeguard personal information, the Code directly addressed the practitioner's ethical responsibility for the confidentiality of information "transmitted to other parties through the use of computers, electronic mail, facsimile machines, telephones and telephone answering machines, and other electronic or computer technology" (1.07[m]). Social workers were gratified by the U.S. Supreme Court's recognition of testimonial privilege for social workers in federal court (*Jaffee v. Redmond*, 1996). In its ruling, the Court acknowledged that all 50 states had established some type of privilege for psychotherapist-client communication. The privilege also extended to social workers' records of their counseling sessions.

In addition to innovations in computer technology, social workers in the 1990s and early part of the twenty-first century experienced the increasing penetration of managed care into the financing, delivery, and oversight of social work services. Managed care dominated hospital and agency-based health and mental health practice in the 1980s, and moved into private practice and child welfare in the 1990s. Under managed care, records, like the practice they documented, focused on brief, goal-directed practice that linked a specific client-need-situation with a targeted plan of service and well-defined, measurable outcomes. Such records came under full scrutiny by funding agencies, and in some cases were considered their property.

Services to clients were briefer than in the past, but the requirements for documentation were expanded. To be accountable meant to follow expected standards of practice. Practitioners sought to demonstrate in their records that they had thoroughly assessed the client-need-situation, identified appropriate interventions, followed procedural guidelines, and taken all warranted decisions and actions. Social work, like related disciplines, was gathering and using research on effects of different interventions on specific client-need-situations to guide practice (Reid, Kenaley, & Colvin, 2004). Practice guidelines, based on expert review and analysis of research findings, were sometimes available (Rosen & Proctor, 2000). Often, however, practitioners relied on agency "best practice" guidelines, supervision, and their own knowledge and experience. To be accountable also meant that clients were engaged as informed consumers of service, considering options, voicing preferences, and acting as partners in decisions and actions. The emergence of evidence-based practice (Gambrill, 2003) and the strengths perspective (Rapp, 1998; Saleeby, 2002) reflected these trends.

Many social workers practiced "defensive recording." To be accountable meant preparing records that went beyond reporting decisions and actions to justifying them. Records were tailored to meet bureaucratic, funding, and legal requirements, and limit practitioners' and agencies' potential liability. Workers sought to anticipate challenges to their judgment by showing, for example, that risk had been properly evaluated; all warranted actions, such as child or elder abuse reporting, had been taken; the least costly of suitable interventions for the assessed problem had been chosen; services had been authorized; and all forms had been completed and signed. Some practitioners complained that the real purpose of records, supporting practice by reflecting workers' evolving understanding of the case, had been subverted. Records no longer documented the complexity of client-need-situations, the dynamics of the worker-client relationship, or the art of practice. Rather, they had become focused on compliance with defined protocols and mandated processes. Over the decades, the principles of accountability became clearer. However, records continued to be a source of dissatisfaction for practitioners, and contention within agencies and in the field.

CONTEMPORARY ISSUES

The most pervasive, ongoing recordkeeping problem continues to be the lack of time and other resources needed to keep records complete and up-to-date. Social workers carry large caseloads and serve clients with complicated and entrenched problems. They are expected to work with clients to assess the need for services, identify meaningful goals, and achieve measurable outcomes quickly, while at the same time meeting accountability standards. Few practitioners have enough time to serve their clients' needs, let alone keep up with their recording. Moreover, many agencies simply do not have the means or have chosen not to invest in supporting recordkeeping. Recordkeeping is made more difficult and time-consuming when computers, software, or clerical staff are insufficient or unavailable. It is not surprising, then, that agencies have cited a litany of recordkeeping problems. A survey conducted in the late 1980s (Records II)[2] (Kagle, 1993) found that many of the most frequently cited problems were related to lack of time or other resources:

1. Insufficient time available for recordkeeping
2. Recording takes too much time
3. Workers resent or resist recording
4. Insufficient clerical help
5. Lack of storage space
6. Records not up-to-date
7. Records poorly written
8. Funding and accreditation reporting demands unrealistic

Unfortunately, these problems persist today. Too often records are poorly written, redundant, disorganized, or imprecise. Important information is missing, out-of-date, or hard to find. Records are difficult to use because crucial information is absent or buried in an excess of detail. Assessments and service plans are overly general, perfunctory, or formulaic. The focus of services is unclear, or there is no clear link between assessment, goals, service plans, and intended outcomes. Too often, accountability requirements exceed the available resources.

Although the expectations for accountability have become clearer, the recording process remains complex. Practitioners must find time to record when there is insufficient time even to respond to real and emergent client needs. Furthermore, in selecting information and preparing a record, workers are faced with a number of dilemmas. They must include sufficient information to meet accountability standards, but have difficulty identifying what is most important in each case, what is crucial enough to include, and what to leave out. They are sensitive to potential risk if important information is excluded, but are concerned about protecting the client's privacy and simplifying their own work. Many lack professional education and ongoing training for recordkeeping, moreover, the assumptions of accountability may not match their own practice theory or approach. Accountability standards assume that practice is linear, that is, that it moves in a direct line from assessment to goals, plans, and outcomes. Practitioners who follow psychodynamic, ecosystems, or humanistic theories, for example, may find it more difficult to fit their practice to these assumptions. Finally, practitioners may find that they are criticized by their agencies for the poor quality of their records but are not given adequate training, time, or resources to improve them.

Indeed, in many agencies, the practitioner and managerial culture actually seems to discourage good recordkeeping practices. Agency guidelines are outdated, unclear, or unrealistic. Computers, software, and clerical support are lacking. Practitioners are faulted both for what they record and for failing to record. Colleagues and managers, who respect time devoted to direct client services, may interrupt, devalue, or otherwise disparage time devoted to recordkeeping.

If records are to improve and workers are to be supported in this important task, practitioners will, at minimum, need:

1. Educational preparation.

Recording is especially difficult for practitioners who have not been adequately educated for the task. Some workers find that they do not possess the writing skills they need. For some of them, grammar, spelling, word choice, and punctuation are a problem. For others, the challenge is to write clearly and summarize important information succinctly. Because recordkeeping is usually taught in the field rather than in the classroom, social work students' experience with recordkeeping is often idiosyncratic. That is, students become familiar only with the recording style that they learn in their own field agency. Moreover, many students spend much of their time in the field learning process recording, which they will not use in practice, rather than developing the summary recording skills they will need. As a result, relatively few practitioners are well-prepared for recordkeeping. They end up having to learn recordkeeping "on the job," modeling their own records on the sometimes good, sometimes poor examples they find in their agencies. Many lack an overall understanding of the role records play in practice and the skills necessary to prepare high quality documents. No wonder practitioners often describe recordkeeping as their most difficult and unpleasant professional responsibility.

2. Explicit and reasonable guidelines.

If practitioners are to prepare well-written, timely, cost-effective, and useful records, they need explicit guidelines as to the appropriate content and structure of the record, and reasonable timelines for completing documentation. Agencies should develop manuals and other materials that clearly describe and provide examples of what, at minimum, should be included in the record, how that information should be organized, and when and how often that information should be documented. Standards should be sufficiently uniform to routinize the recordkeeping task, create order within each record, and encourage consistency among records. At the same time, standards should be sufficiently flexible so that workers can document the special nature of each client-need-situation and service process. In addition, standards should be reasonable and achievable, given workers' caseloads and other workload responsibilities.

3. Ongoing training.

When agency accountability requirements change, workers are informed via memo, during supervision, at staff meetings, or during in-service training. These communications usually focus on how to fill out forms, comply with standards, and implement procedures. Too often new requirements are simply added on to those that already exist, increasing practitioners' recordkeeping tasks and overall workload. Whenever possible, training and supervision should focus on ways to integrate new requirements with ongoing recordkeeping practices, substituting new requirements for old ones or otherwise simplifying the task. If recordkeeping demands are increased without altering other expectations, work stress and performance problems may result.

4. Adequate resources.

Good social work records depend on the agency supplying sufficient resources to support recordkeeping activities. At minimum, the agency should provide clerical services, equipment, and adequate time for preparing and using records. Unfortunately, budget constraints cause many agencies to skimp on clerical staff and defer purchasing, repairing, or updating computers, software, and other equipment. Budget constraints can also result in high caseloads and high turnover. These conditions undermine accountability. Workers may need to assume some clerical functions; practitioners have less time for recordkeeping; and records are seldom complete or up-to-date. If records are to improve, agencies need to address resource problems and reinvest to support recordkeeping.

5. Agency culture.

Even when practitioners are well-prepared and agencies provide adequate resources for recordkeeping, an agency's culture may formally or informally undermine good recording practices. Rather than blame practitioners for incomplete or poor quality records, they need peer and supervisory encouragement and feedback to prepare records that are well-written, meaningful, useful, and up-to-date. Practitioners also need to believe that others in the agency will value the time and effort they commit to preparing good records. The agency's culture should recognize recordkeeping as an important professional activity, not just bureaucratic busy work. For example, recordkeeping should take its place alongside other areas of practice as a focus for professional and organizational development. In addition, agencies should partner with practitioners in an effort to remedy ongoing recordkeeping issues, such as writing problems, resource deficiencies, or unrealistic expectations for accountability.

RECORDING AND PROFESSIONAL JUDGMENT

Recordkeeping involves much more than just skill; it requires complex professional judgments. In developing protocols for their agency's records, selecting, organizing, and analyzing information, and documenting each case, social workers need to exercise considerable discretion. They must constantly consider valued but conflicting goals. On the one hand, records should be concise enough to conserve resources, protect the client's confidentiality, and be kept up-to-date. On the other hand, they must be comprehensive enough to facilitate service delivery, justify service judgments, actions, and decisions, and meet accountability standards. Even with a clear sense of purpose and explicit guidelines for selecting information and organizing their records, social workers must make crucial professional decisions each time they record. The following chapters are intended to guide social workers in making these important judgments.

NOTES

[1] Throughout *Social Work Records*, the authors use the term "client-need-situation" to describe the focus of the record. Adding "need" to "client-situation" suggests that records should focus on information about the client-situation that gives purpose and direction to the service process, rather than including all information about the client-situation that the worker comes to know.

[2] Throughout the book, studies undertaken in conjunction with the first edition of *Social Work Records* are referred to as "Records I"; studies conducted for the second edition are called "Records II." These and other studies of social work records published prior to 1995 by Jill Doner Kagle were supported by grants from the Lois & Samuel Silberman Fund.

Chapter 2

Service-Centered Recording

Selecting content for the record is the most important recordkeeping decision social workers make. They must choose what is significant and relevant for the record from the array of details about the client-need-situation and the service transaction. They must try to balance the goals of accountability and supporting practice against the sometimes competing goals of efficiency and client privacy. If practitioners record too much information, they may leave too little time for other valued activities or fall behind in their recording. They may also compromise their clients' confidentiality. If they record too little, they may not document the information that is necessary for accountability or to support their own or others' practice.

In their records, social workers depict unique and shared characteristics of the client-need-situation and the service transaction from intake through termination and follow-up. They document what is unique about a case by individualizing the client-need-situation and showing how services were tailored to meet the special circumstances, interests, and preferences of the client. They document what is shared, that is, what the case has in common with others, by demonstrating that services were chosen and provided in compliance with agency guidelines, professional standards, and best practices. They rely on their knowledge of human behavior in the social environment, efficacious interventions for particular client groups, and agency and public policy to provide a rationale for how problems were identified, services were chosen and delivered, and the client-need-situation was influenced and changed.

Selecting content for the record is more than just a practice skill. It involves a high level of professional judgment. In preparing their records, practitioners are guided by the agency's mission, accountability structure, recordkeeping policies and procedures, funding sources, mode of service delivery, and clientele. At the same time, they know that what they record may become widely known by personnel in the agency, funders, and oversight groups; the client and those who are acting on the client's behalf; and those who might disseminate the information publicly or use the information against the client's wishes or interests. Each record, then, reflects the practitioner's distinctive approach to decision making, service delivery, professional values, and accountability.

This chapter assists social workers in the complex process of selecting and documenting content for the record. It describes *Service-Centered Recording,* an approach to recordkeeping in which the focus and primary criterion for selecting and documenting information in the record is its *relevance to service delivery.* The chapter outlines and describes in detail the information that should or may be included in social work records; it also identifies materials that should be omitted. It includes a thorough analysis of the key elements of the record's content and provides numerous examples of records based on actual practice.

THE SERVICE-CENTERED RECORD

A contemporary social work record should be, above all, a record of service. The Service-Centered Record, in which the primary criterion for selecting information for the record is its relevance to service delivery, differs from traditional approaches to recordkeeping. It shifts the focus of the record from information about the client and the worker-client interaction to information that is relevant for understanding and evaluating service delivery. Of course, Service-Centered Records include information about the client and worker-client interaction. However, this information is placed into the framework of the record's primary focus: documentation of service decisions and actions from intake through closing. The Service-Centered Record's purpose is to demonstrate how services addressed the special characteristics of the client-need-situation, were delivered in accordance with professional standards and agency policies, and were evaluated for their quality, efficacy, and impact. Service-Centered Records meet the expectations of accountability by highlighting the systematic description and assessment of the client-need-situation, available resources, service options, and client preferences and linking these assessments to the purpose, goals, plans, decisions, activities, progress, impact, and outcome of services.

Service-Centered Recording was first developed in the 1980s in response to changes in how records were being used, who had access to their contents, and how available agency resources were being deployed (Records I). Over time, social workers had become accountable to a wider constituency, and their records had become accessible to a much larger audience. The confidentiality of information in records had become a major concern. In addition, social workers and their agencies were coping with cutbacks in resources and reacting to increased demands for documentation.

Social workers had found that traditional approaches to recordkeeping no longer met their needs. Their records usually included long, detailed narratives or process recordings focused on the developing understanding of the client and the evolving relationship between worker and client. Given the demands of practice, such records had become too time-consuming to prepare, too cumbersome to use, too revealing to protect client confidentiality, and too speculative to meet new accountability standards. In addition, while these records included a great deal of information about the client and the service process, they often gave only cursory attention to the purpose of service and to service goals, plans, decisions, actions, and outcomes.

Service-Centered Records have a different focus than the "patient" or "process" records that many social workers are accustomed to. "Patient" records focus primarily on the "client" or "consumer." In selecting and documenting information for these records, practitioners are guided by the notion that the record is intended to be a repository for a wide range of information about the patient/client. "Process recording" focuses on the interaction between the worker and the client, with the goal of understanding the client and strengthening the practitioner's interpersonal, therapeutic, and analytic skills. Their purpose is to support the practitioner's or social work student's professional development through careful attention to worker-client communication via self-reflection and supervision. In preparing process records, practitioners are guided by the principle that they are to document everything they can recall, and in sequence. In contrast, Service-Centered Records focus on the bases for, substance of, and consequences of all decisions and actions taken in the course of providing services with and on behalf of the client. They incorporate a great deal of information about the client-need-situation in the context of providing a rationale for understanding the services that are offered, how services are delivered, and what impact services have on the client-need-situation and available resources. In addition to assisting the practitioner and agency in meeting contemporary expectations for accountability, the Service-Centered Record offers additional benefits. It assists practitioners in balancing the competing demands of accountability and supporting practice with client privacy and cost-efficiency.

Service-Centered Records focus on
information about the client-need-situation and available resources,
along with client preferences, agency standards, and best practices
that provide the rationale for
service decisions and actions, including the
purpose, goals, plans, and methods of service
and show what impact service has upon
the client-need-situation and available resources.

Service-Centered Records document the foundation for professional judgments and actions, and are intended to show the linkage between assessments, decisions, actions, and service outcomes. These records focus on how professional judgments are formed through observation and analysis of the client-need-situation and available resources. They document how such judgments and actions are influenced by policy and procedure, knowledge of human behavior in the social environment, the availability of resources, standards of practice, and client values and preferences. Service-Centered Records also document the client's role and contribution to decisions and actions affecting service at each step of the process.

The primary criterion for including information about the client-need-situation in a Service-Centered Record is its relevancy to service delivery. The best records fully document the bases, substance, and consequences of service decisions and actions. They document information about the client-need-situation that demonstrates why services were offered, how services were delivered, and what impact services have had. However, they limit information about the client-need-situation to what is clearly relevant to the purpose of service. Other information, however interesting, is not to be included. Documenting information about the client-need-situation that is unrelated to service delivery unnecessarily intrudes on the client's privacy, is time-consuming, and does nothing to further the goal of accountability.

To meet the expectations of accountability, Service-Centered Records document the reasons for and results of service decisions and actions over time. The record develops as the service transaction develops; its focus shifts as service moves from intake through termination. During the initial phase of service, when the worker and client are concerned with exploring the problem, need, and availability of services, identifying the purpose of service, and developing a service agreement, the record focuses upon such elements of content as:

- the reasons for initiating service;
- descriptions and assessments of the client-need-situation;
- descriptions and assessments of resources and barriers;
- risk and strengths assessments; and
- the client's views and preferences.

Once the service plan has been formulated, the record focuses upon implementation, documenting, for example:

- worker and client decisions regarding service;
- purpose and goals of service;
- plans;
- decisions and activities;
- progress; and
- assessments of movement and impact.

Finally, the process of termination changes the focus of the record to:

- reasons for termination, transfer, or referral;
- description and assessment of the client-need-situation at closing, including any potential risks; and
- evaluation of service and its outcomes.

Service-Centered Records are intended to be temporally linked to the practice they document. Records should be kept up-to-date, and should focus on the phase of service currently under way. As new information becomes available, the record should be updated to include any changes in the purpose, goal, or plans of service. The record should also include periodic updates of assessments, which change over time. Similarly, new information about available resources should be added as it becomes known, and the purpose and plan of service should be reformulated as necessary.

The need to update client information and alter the direction of service sometimes makes records (and the process of service) seem disorganized and unfocused. Why not wait to write records until after long intervals have passed or services have been terminated, when the direction of service is clear and the record can be more systematic? Retrospective recordkeeping may be feasible in some cases, especially when services are brief and relatively routine. However, records can only be accurate and useful in supporting practice if they are kept up-to-date, documenting changes in the purpose and direction of services as warranted. Records of long-term or complex cases that are written retrospectively may appear to be more organized and systematic, but such records may actually exclude important information, may serve only to justify the outcomes that were reached, or may not fully or accurately report what actually happened in the case.

In summary, the essential function of the Service-Centered Record is to describe, explain, and evaluate the service transaction it documents. To fulfill its primary goal, accountability, it should include content that is:

- selected to reflect the bases, substance, and consequences of professional decisions and actions;
- composed of observations and inference in the form of descriptions and assessments of the client-need-situation and the service transaction;
- grounded in the knowledge, values, and ethics of the profession; and
- grounded in the agency's mission, standards of care, and best practices.

The Service-Centered Record is also intended to facilitate ongoing service delivery. To do so, it must be a "living and working" document rather than a retrospective review of activities long past. Therefore, it should be up-to-date and linked in time to the practice it documents. The Service-Centered Record is also intended to protect client privacy and control costs. For these reasons, it limits content about the client-need-situation and service transaction to information relevant to understanding and evaluating service decisions, actions, and outcomes.

ELEMENTS OF CONTENT

The elements of content found in social work records are shown in exhibit 2.1 and discussed in some detail in this chapter. The left column of exhibit 2.1 outlines information that is basic to all records. The right column outlines elements of content that are appropriate to include in some records, depending on the purpose of service to the client and the accountability standards under which services are provided. Concepts that appear in exhibit 2.1 are *italicized* in the following discussion.

Exhibit 2.1   Elements of Content

Information to Include in All Records	Information to Include in Some Records
Opening Summary	
• Client demographics • Means and reasons for initiating services: presenting problem, need, impetus • Key actors: client, family, service providers, others • Eligibility for services • Informed consent to initial services	• Intake form or screen • Urgent situation • Referral • Previous services in the agency • Other agencies or providers serving the client currently or in the past
Data Gathering and Social History	
• Descriptions of client-need-situation • Information sources • Social history (see exhibit 2.2) • Ongoing and past relationships with medical, mental health, legal, social service, educational, work, other organizations and professionals • Resources, barriers, unmet needs	• Responses to requests for information by other agencies and providers • Personal information • Interpersonal relationships • Social information • Institutional connections • Physical environment
Assessment	
• Systematic assessments: observations, information sources, criteria used, worker's appraisal • Strengths • Cultural factors that affect services • Risk assessment • Specialized assessments • Worker's appraisal and criteria used in making judgments	• Personal and environmental assets, abilities, capacities, and skills • Child abuse/neglect • Elder abuse/neglect • Suicide, self-abuse • Domestic violence • Community violence • Substance use/abuse • Poverty, homelessness • *DSM* diagnosis (mental health) • Behavioral • Family dynamics • Functional behavior (school)

Decisions and Actions Resulting from Initial Assessment	
• Actions taken in response to initial assessment • Compliance with relevant policies, laws, and standards of practice • Referrals	• Child, elder abuse report • Tarasoff warning • Interventions to protect client and others

Service Planning	

Service Options	
• Options considered, client's role • Screening, eligibility for programs, services • Options rejected: unavailable, inaccessible • Criteria used for selecting among various options	• Costs, limitations, alternatives, potential risks and benefits, and possible outcomes • Potential for alleviating assessed problem or need • Services available, accessible; client eligible • Quality, evidence of effectiveness • Within agency scope, mission, expertise • Reimbursable • Client preferences

Purpose, Goals, and Plans of Service	
• Purpose • Goals • Plans • Indicators of movement toward completing plan, realizing goals • Agreements regarding termination of services • Client-worker contract	• Within scope and mission of agency • Referrals • Standards of care • Involvement of other agencies, providers, family, and community members • Potential risks, benefits

Interim Notes	
• Updates and new information about the client-need-situation • Indicators of movement • Assessment of the status of the client-need-situation • Descriptions of service activities • Assessment of the process and progress of services • Any changes in purpose, goals, plans, indicators	• Chart indicators • Chart all service contacts • Evaluation of the selected indicators • Barriers to service delivery and goal achievement

(continued)

Special Materials	
• Documents, forms • Consents • Critical incidents and emergencies, with decisions and actions taken • Periodic service reviews	• Records and reports from other agencies, practitioners • Accounting of disclosures of information
Closing Summary	
• Reasons for terminating services • Status of case at termination	• Brief review of client-need-situation from opening to closing • Review of service purpose, process, goals, and activities • Evaluation of outcomes and impact of services • Referrals or other planned activities • Follow-up

Of course, agencies and practitioners have considerable discretion about what information to include in records, and they may reasonably decide not to include even some basic elements of content. For example, records that document very brief services or cases that are closed after only one or two contacts because the client has dropped out might omit many elements of content. Further, information may appear in records in a different sequence than is outlined here, and some elements of content may appear again and again. For example, records may include several interim notes, documenting ongoing assessment, new information, changes in the client-need-situation, and new agreements about the purpose or process of services. In addition, some agencies and practitioners may label elements of content differently. For example, "interim notes" are often called "progress notes." Finally, elements of content that may be part of a particular agency's or practitioner's records may not be included here. However, every effort has been made to include representative content, based on principles that can be adapted to diverse social work practice environments, with examples that reflect actual practice.

OPENING SUMMARY

Client Demographics

Demographic information, which may appear on an *intake form* or *screen*, is usually entered into the record early in the service transaction. Some of this information may be gathered and recorded by clerical workers or by clients themselves prior to the first meeting between the worker and the client. This information is usually reported by the client or the client's family, and supplemented by information in public documents and other service records.

Demographic information is used in:

- determining eligibility for services
- delivering services
- accountability
- administrative planning
- identifying characteristics of clients served
- research

Clients (individuals, families) are identified by:

- name
- address
- phone
- date of birth
- sex
- agency case number

Records also typically include information about:

- level of education achieved
- current employment
- marital status
- family composition

Depending on the field of practice, service program, or funding source, some agencies document the following information:

- insurance, Medicaid, or Medicare coverage
- income
- health, mental health diagnosis
- tested IQ, functional behavior status
- military status
- guardian or other surrogate decision maker

In the past, such demographic information as:

- race, ethnicity
- religion
- citizenship, immigration status
- social security number

were routinely documented. Today, however, this information may be deemed private, imprecise, sensitive, or of questionable value. Practitioners and agencies are concerned about the accuracy of some categories (race, for example), and the potential impact on clients if some information were to become public (immigration status, for example). They recognize that placing a client in a demographic category may oversimplify her or his experience and identity (of religion or ethnicity, for example), and may undermine culturally competent service delivery. In addition, public policy has restricted the use and dissemination of certain unique identifiers, notably, social security numbers. As a result, agencies and practitioners are advised to limit documentation of this demographic information to cases in which they are directly linked to the purpose of service, required by policy, needed for eligibility determination or reimbursement, or otherwise crucial to service delivery or accountability.

Means and Reasons for Initiating Service

Clients seek or are offered, referred for, or mandated to receive services for a variety of reasons. The means or impetus for initiating service are documented because they offer a preliminary understanding of the client's perception of the agency and its services, and provide a rationale for the approaches used to engage the client and others in the service process. This information can also be used in evaluating how the agency is perceived in the community and how clients actually arrive at the agency.

The reasons for initiating services, which many social workers call the "*presenting problem*," are the client's or others' initial view of the need for or potential benefit of services. Sometimes the reason for initiating service is an *urgent situation*, such as a critical incident or emergency. In such cases, the practitioner would respond to the critical incident (for example, a threat of harm) or emergency (for example, a car accident) by moving quickly through the process of data gathering and assessment, and then take quick and decisive action with and on behalf of the client and others in the situation. The record should document not just the presenting problem, but a description of what occurred, an assessment of the situation, a plan of action, and frequent updates about the plan and the ongoing situation.

More often, the reasons for initiating services are ongoing problems rather than an urgent situation. Sometimes the client can articulate the reasons for seeking services and identify the most important needs or problems. Sometimes others in the client's or the service environment have defined the problem or need. If the client did not initiate contact with the agency but was referred, mandated, or offered service, it is especially important to document the client's perception of the situation. The reasons for initiating service should be clearly differentiated from the purpose of service. Although in some cases the "presenting problem" is the "problem to be worked," in many cases the purpose of service emerges only through careful exploration and discussion. As the practitioner and client work together to understand the client-need-situation, they define the purpose of service, which is often more complex and sometimes quite different from the "presenting problem." For example, a client is referred to an employee assistance program because she is frequently absent from work. After some exploration, the client reveals that she misses work after her husband punches her and causes visible bruising.

The worker and client agree to focus on finding alternative living arrangements and services for victims of domestic violence. In this case, then, the presenting problem is work absenteeism; the purpose of service is to assist the client in escaping domestic violence.

The means and the reasons for initiating services are stated succinctly in the opening summary. The worker describes the *presenting problem, need,* or *impetus* for seeking services. Whenever appropriate, the source of and reason for *referral* should also be documented.

For example:

> "Mr. D became a member of our cardiac patient group upon his admission for bypass surgery, 1/26/xx."

> "Agency initiated services after Mrs. B called our office. She said that she had been concerned for the past year that her daughter, Linda, was slow. Linda is three years, five months old; she does not speak or respond well to verbal cues."

> "Kelly will soon age out of foster care; she has no place to live."

> "The S family was referred for service by the juvenile court. Regina has been repeatedly truant from school in the past three months. On 8/2/xx, she was arrested for shoplifting at R department store."

Sometimes, the means for initiating services are immediately apparent, although the reasons are not. A client may be selected for outreach or preventive services on the basis of personal or social characteristics that place them at risk. In hospitals, for example, social workers may offer their services to all elderly clients diagnosed with dementia in recognition of the special needs this client group and their families experience. In such cases, practitioners educate the client and others about the availability of services, and help them anticipate and plan for future needs. Here, the means for initiating services is outreach; the reason is to educate and assess the client-need-situation to determine whether there is a need for and interest in receiving social work services.

Key Actors

In the opening summary, records identify key actors in the case. The record documents not just who is the client (the recipient or recipients of service) but also other parties who have an interest in and influence on the client-need-situation, such as household members or school and court personnel. Key actors are those who are directly or indirectly involved in identifying the client's service needs or providing information or resources. They may have a vested interest in the service process or its outcomes, supporting, or even in some cases undermining, the client's efforts.

Eligibility for Services

Early in the process of exploration, the client's general eligibility for services needs to be determined. For example, does the client reside in the area served by the agency? Is the client seeking the kind of services the agency offers? If the client does not meet such eligibility standards, he or she may receive a *referral* to another agency.

Informed Consent to Initiate Services

Today, many agencies and practitioners begin the service process by providing the client with information about the agency and how it conducts services. The client may be given documents that outline policies on confidentiality, billing, insurance, and about the frequency of client-worker contacts, for example. Often, the worker and client take time to discuss the clients' questions and concerns. Clients, or those acting on their behalf, are then asked to sign an authorization to initiate services. This document becomes part of the record.

The opening summary also may include information about, and references to, records of *previous services* received by the client in the agency, and information about *other agencies or providers* that currently or in the past have provided services to the client.

DATA GATHERING AND SOCIAL HISTORY

Services begin with an exploratory process. In the process of thinking and talking about the client-need-situation, the worker and client also come to know each other. Of course, exploration is ongoing, and practitioners continually gather and update information about the client-need-situation for the record.

Descriptions of the Client-Need-Situation

The social work record contains current and past information about the client-need-situation that places the client's problem or need in its historical and ecological context. This information is documented for a number of important reasons, among them to:

- afford the client, family, and significant others an opportunity to "tell their story," thereby reviewing and sharing their experiences;
- individualize the client, situation, and relevant environment;
- locate sources of problems and resources for resolving them;
- discover strengths and coping abilities as well as needs and limitations;
- identify cultural issues that may influence problems, needs, resources, services, or outcomes;
- focus attention and services on relevant issues and points of intervention;
- convey pertinent information to other service providers; and
- document the bases for social work decisions and actions, including services within the organization and referral for services elsewhere.

Information Sources

The worker may gather information from a number of sources. Of course, the client serves as the primary source of information. The worker may also consult family members and other members of the client's intimate social network, as well as the records of any previous or ongoing services in the agency. In addition, with the informed consent of the client or an authorized decision maker, the practitioner may gather information from:

- other service providers outside the agency, such as physicians, educators, psychologists, attorneys, and other social workers;
- records of services provided by other agencies;
- other individuals who play a significant role in the client's social environment;
- tests, reports, and examinations; and
- direct observation.

These sources vary in their knowledge, objectivity, motives, and point of view. Information may be freely given or offered under duress. The nature of the information and the circumstances of the case may encourage candor or concealment. For these and other reasons, it is important the worker identify the sources of information and the context in which the information was revealed. The record should describe the information provided by various sources, including any *responses to requests for information by other agencies and providers*. It also includes an evaluation of the information, weighing differences of opinion, alternative perspectives, and personal biases. By describing and evaluating various information sources, the worker gauges the quality of the information and shows the complexity of the client-need-situation.

For example:

> "Mrs. S reluctantly told me of previous calls to the police. She said that she would tell because I would find out anyway, but if her husband found out, he would probably hit her again."

> "Dr. R told me of a brief encounter with the F family shortly after the accident occurred."

> "Mrs. B said her English is not very good, and I told her I did not speak Phasa Thai. With her permission, I brought Ms. Ba, who works in accounting, to act as translator at our next meeting."

> "The interview took place in a crowded and noisy office; Mrs. W repeatedly referred to the fact that she did not want others to hear what she was saying."

> "Agency began investigation because of a report by the school. At first, Mrs. N would not let me into the house; after about 15 minutes she said that, since the neighbors might see us, I might as well come in. She said again and again that she would only tell me what she had to in order to get the school off her back."

> "The following information was collected from the record of an earlier admission to this program, 5/16/xx–10/18/xx."

"Mr. K described Mrs. K's reaction to the fire in detail. Later, Susan K gave a similar account."

"Thomas's school behavior was described by his teachers and his mother. I observed similar behavior during an hour in his classroom on 9/15/xx."

Social History

Many records include a social history, that is, a careful review of the client-need-situation over time. A social history may be brief or extensive. It may focus on a client's present situation and recent past, or it may delve into a family's history over one generation or more. A brief social history concentrates on personal, interpersonal, social, and environmental information pertinent to understanding the current client-need-situation, and placing it in its relevant ecological context. An extensive social history moves beyond these issues to seek historical antecedents, recurrent themes, and long-term patterns.

Exhibit 2.2 provides a comprehensive list of areas that may be covered in a social history. Although practitioners may wish to engage in an extensive social history-taking process, time constraints may limit the breadth of exploration. In contemporary practice, practitioners and clients often must move quickly to formulate a purpose of service, identify appropriate service approaches, and select goals and plans. They rarely have time during the initial phase of service for a full, historical exploration of the client-need-situation. However, such information often surfaces during the service process, especially when the client receives services over an extended period. The practitioner can then update the record.

The social history is both a process and a product. By discussing various aspects of the social history, the practitioner and client come to understand the various components of the current client-need-situation. As a process, social history-taking involves exploration of cognitive and affective content, allowing the worker and the client to review, sort through, and share significant events and circumstances. It provides essential information while contributing to the helping process. Clients find it beneficial to talk about their situations with an interested, thoughtful, and knowledgeable listener. As a product, the social history documents information about the client-need-situation that forms the basis for initial service decisions and actions. It is often used by other service providers in understanding the client's background and current circumstances.

The social history-taking process involves exploration of the client's experiential landscape. The client reviews familiar territory in a new way with a worker who is both guide and follower. The worker guides the client through areas of interest and concern and responds to information as it is revealed. The worker and client scan the entire client-need-situation for salient issues, needs, and resources. As new information surfaces, the worker and client seek linkages and explore the client's thoughts and feelings in some depth.

Exhibit 2.2   Social History Outline: Areas for Exploration during the Social History-Taking Process

Personal Information

   Cognitive and Physical Development: Specific milestones (e.g., rolling over, sitting, other motor activities); first word, language development; toilet training or other self-care, habits; critical experiences (e.g., mother's pregnancy, child's birth, illnesses); unusual family events (e.g., death, separations, divorce); development of siblings, other family members; important events and experiences in psychosocial maturation; client and family attitudes, expectations; tested IQ.

   Health: Current and past illnesses, accidents, disabilities; family history; signs, symptoms, complaints, diagnoses; previous hospitalizations, treatments, procedures, medications, prostheses; health behavior, including diet, exercise, substance use, sexual practices; attitudes, expectations, knowledge, beliefs; adaptation to health status.

   Mental Health: Current and past cognitive, affective, social and behavioral functioning; onset and duration of any current difficulties; critical events related to current status; current or past mental health diagnosis; previous hospitalizations, treatments, procedures, medication; attitudes, expectations of client, family, others in social environment.

   Problematic Behaviors and Patterns of Response: Problematic behaviors or patterns linked to current situation or of concern to client, family, or others in social environment; antecedents and consequences of those behaviors; controlling conditions, such as cues, reinforcers; distressing or stressful behaviors and habits such as substance abuse; running away; bingeing and purging; cutting or other self-abuse; antisocial behavior at home, work, school, or in community.

   Knowledge, Information, Cognitive Patterns: Client's and others' interpretation of current situation and of related events; knowledge, information, and beliefs regarding human behavior, social services, and so forth; current and recent efforts at problem solving; self-concept; insight; values, preferences regarding means and ends of service.

   Feelings, Emotional Responses: Client's and others' emotional responses to current situation, critical events related to situation; current level of anxiety, discomfort; motivation for change, action; commitment to service; attitudes toward future, potential for improvement in current situation; self-esteem.

   Education: Schools or other educational programs attended; level of performance, achievement; experiences, attitudes, expectations regarding ability, achievements, value of education, and credentials; desire for further education; behavior in classroom; study habits, level of basic skills.

   Employment: Paid, volunteer, and in-home work experiences; current employment, employer, position; critical incidents in work history; knowledge, skills, interests, aptitudes, attitudes, expectations; job-seeking skills, work habits.

   Finances: Current and recent sources and amount of income; savings, investments, holdings, assets; monthly outlay; financial responsibilities, debts; means of defraying costs of current situation, such as insurance coverage of hospitalization; attitudes, expectations, priorities regarding income, use of resources.

(continued)

Legal Issues: Current and past incidents involving police, civil court action, or criminal court action; past incarcerations; parole, probation status; involvement as perpetrator, victim, or witness to acts of violence or other antisocial acts; immigration status; custody, guardianship.

Interpersonal Relationships

Marital, Domestic, and Family: Current and past marital, domestic, and family situations, including descriptions of members of household, roles, responsibilities; relationship to absent parents, siblings, children, members of extended family, ex-partners; adoption and fostering; same-sex partnerships; milestones and critical events in marital, domestic, or family development; attitudes, beliefs, values regarding marriage, family, domestic relationships; relationship of family to neighborhood community, culture; family or domestic structure and function, such as child-rearing, intergenerational responsibilities.

Peer Groups and Informal Social Network: Description of informal peer relationships, including social, recreational, sexual relationships; membership and participation in formal organizations, groups; interpersonal behaviors, skills, concerns.

Work Relationships: Description of relationships within the work environment, including relationships with supervisors and others in authority, peers, subordinates; critical incidents in work relationships.

Social Information

Culture: Values, preferences, and expectations of behavior; issues of prejudice, discrimination; opportunity, access, availability of resources; attitudes toward services, service providers; language and custom differences from community; resources.

Community: Formal or informal resources; demography, economy, ecology, physical characteristics; critical incidents involving client and the community.

Institutional Connections

Relationships, if any, with schools and other educational organizations, employment and volunteer associations, religious groups, legal system, health and mental health practitioners and organizations, social welfare agencies and programs.

Physical Environment

Description of the physical environment, with special attention to the safety, adequacy, upkeep, and accessibility of housing, nutrition, clothing, community and neighborhood, transportation, work environment.

During the exploratory process, the worker's responsibility is not just to assist the client or others in scanning the client-need-situation. The worker guides the client through a focused exploration, examining in some depth the specific factors that knowledge and experience indicate may be of critical importance to the client's particular need-situation. Sometimes these factors are suggested by the agency's social history form, which guides the worker to particular areas that are to be explored and documented.

Focused exploration is also guided by:

- the client's characteristics, and the means and reasons for initiating services;
- the client's interests and expressed concerns;
- theory and research on factors that cause, maintain, remediate, or are in other ways linked to the problem or need;
- knowledge of service processes, available resources, and the potential effects and outcomes of different approaches to service; and
- best practice guidelines for services with this client group.

Familiarity with current knowledge about the client-need-situation is essential to competent social history-taking and social work assessment. Informed by such knowledge, the social worker uses focused exploration to develop, and then substantiate or refute, hypotheses regarding critical factors that may influence the client-need-situation and may be relevant in developing a service plan. Once the worker identifies these critical factors, he or she can use them in formulating an assessment.

Two Examples of Brief Social Histories.   In the two social history examples that follow, the worker and client discuss specific information relevant to understanding the "presenting problem" and the emerging purpose of service. In the first example, two school-aged children have been returned home after a brief stay in protective custody following reports of parental abuse and neglect. As part of the remediation plan, the parents have been referred for counseling services in a family agency. The purpose of this social history is not to investigate whether abuse or neglect occurred. Rather, the social history-taking process explores factors known to be associated with child abuse and neglect, to assess their relevance in this particular client-need-situation.

The social history is guided by knowledge that child abuse and neglect may be linked to a history of:

- socialization to violence;
- substance abuse;
- parent-child attachment problems;
- scapegoating of one or more child;
- situational stress, such as job loss or economic hardship;
- structural inadequacies, such as the lack of affordable child care;
- skill deficiencies, such as inadequate parenting skills;
- knowledge deficiencies, such as lack of information about child development and children's developmental needs; and
- social isolation.

Although very brief, the following social history identifies key issues in the client-need-situation. Following a discussion of family dynamics, the social worker offers an initial appraisal of the situation and outlines a plan for continuing services.

"Family Dynamics: Mr. M has been staying at home most days since he was laid off. He watches TV and drinks beer. By evening, he is often drunk and 'ready for a fight,' according to Mrs. M. She feels that he is a good man down on his luck—and if the court takes their children, Terry and Jerry, he'll 'take it real bad.' Although she did not volunteer the information, Mrs. M has also been the target of abuse.

Impression: Based only on information from Mr. and Mrs. M, it appears that the immediate cause of abuse is linked to Mr. M's job loss seven months ago. Mrs. M is working while he is home all day drinking. No one member of the family is the target of abuse; rather, all have been targeted.

Plan: Mr. M is now involved in a job search program. He has been referred to AA but has not yet attended. Both Mr. and Mrs. M were referred to a parenting skills group, which she is attending. Terry and Jerry have been enrolled in a socialization group at school. I will continue to meet with Mr. and Mrs. M twice a month for the next three months. Will continue to urge Mr. M to go to AA and attend parenting group."

In the second example, an elderly client is experiencing dementia. The client's physician has asked the social worker to interview the client's daughter, who is providing information from her own perspective. The purpose of the brief social history is to investigate personal, social, and environmental factors that may be linked to the client's cognitive deterioration. Here, the worker's familiarity with dementia helps to guide social history-taking and initial assessment.

Exploration in this case focused on these issues:

- onset of symptoms;
- changes in the client's physical environment;
- misuse or interactions of medication;
- malnutrition;
- infection;
- physical trauma;
- emotional trauma, such as the loss of a loved one; and
- depression.

The record documents Mrs. H's perspective, followed by the worker's initial assessment of the client-need-situation.

"Mrs. H (daughter) reports that Mrs. O has had poor memory for two years. She first noticed it immediately after her father, Mr. O, died. Mrs. H described her mother as changing from a cheerful, active person to an old woman 'overnight.' Although they do not live in the same part of town, Mrs. H visited her mother several times a week during the first year after Mr. O's death. She found her mother absentminded, complaining, and uncaring about her home or appearance. Finally, after being 'yelled at once too often,' Mrs. H stopped visiting regularly. She would occasionally take her mother shopping, but she hired a housekeeper to do most of the work around the house, the marketing, and so forth. Although she visits infrequently, Mrs. H reports that she and her brother have, in the past year, taken over all finances and watched their mother lose interest in herself and others.

Specific Causes: Mrs. H is aware of no illness or physical trauma, although she thinks that her mother may have fallen without anyone knowing about it. In addition, medication and nutrition have not been supervised or supported by others. Loss of husband, role, and relationship with daughter is evident.

Impressions: Factors that may be contributing to Mrs. O's mental status and quality of life: over- or under-medication; poor nutrition; depression; isolation; loss of family and other social contacts.

Plan: Interview scheduled with Miss T (Mrs. O's housekeeper) on June 14. Following that interview, I will meet with Dr. F about these findings and impressions."

The social history-taking process is guided by the agency's or program's accountability structure, clientele, field of practice, and mission. It is also influenced by who will use the information and for what purpose. In schools, for example, social workers may collect, evaluate, and document a thorough review of a child's family background and social and developmental history. This information may then be used by social workers, teachers, family members, administrators, and others in determining eligibility and planning for the child's needs for special education and related services.

Some agencies leave the selection and organization of information to the discretion of the worker, who may document it chronologically or topically (see exhibit 2.3). However, many agencies have found this approach too time-consuming and idiosyncratic. To ensure that information necessary for accountability appears in the record and is easily accessed, many agencies now use outlines, forms, and screens to guide the collection, analysis, and documentation of background information (see exhibit 2.4) In addition, some use decision trees and other protocols to guide *risk assessments*, for example, of child or elder abuse and neglect, and for *specialized assessments*, for example, in mental health diagnoses, using the current version of the American Psychiatric Association's (APA) *Diagnostic and Statistical Manual (DSM)*. Their goal is to ensure that all necessary areas of the social history are explored and documented, and that assessment follows agency guidelines and best practices.

Exhibits 2.3 and 2.4 show the documentation of one case using different forms. In exhibit 2.3, the worker used an open-ended narrative style; in exhibit 2.4, the worker used a brief history form provided by the agency. The exploratory process was the same, but the records are quite different.

Exhibits 2.3 and 2.4 document the case of a client who was experiencing schizophrenia. At the time that the social history was taken, the diagnosis had already been made. The worker's responsibility was to assist the client in developing a service plan that could help maintain him in the community. The worker focused the process on factors that are known to support or undermine community participation by clients with this diagnosis, and on the client's strengths, capacities, and resources as well as needs and limitations. The social history-taking process explored:

- early social development and adaptation;
- age and stage of first symptoms or episodes of severe dysfunction;
- educational history and experience;
- social and vocational skills;
- work history and experience;
- family history;
- quality of current and past family relationships;
- sources of stress, satisfaction, and social support;
- history of hospitalization, treatment, and medication; and
- history of community participation.

Exhibit 2.3   Social History of a Client with a Severe and Persistent Mental Disorder (Open-Ended Narrative)

Background Information: Mr. C, who is now 29-years-old, was first known to this community mental health center when he was 22-years-old (August 20xx). He had been discharged to the community from Lorall State Hospital following a four-month stay. He was hospitalized after locking his parents into a bedroom and setting the house on fire. At the time of discharge, his diagnosis was "paranoid schizophrenia," and he was treated with thorazine. Upon his return here, he moved into a basement room of his older sister's farmhouse. After a few weeks with the sister (Mrs. W) and her family, he moved out.

For the next three years, he lived alternately with his sister, two aunts, in supervised housing, and on the streets. He received SSI benefits, which were delivered to his sister's house. He attended the clinic irregularly for medication checks and to talk with his case manager. He also was rehospitalized on four occasions. Case notes indicate that, upon discharge from inpatient treatment, he would attend the medication clinic and meetings with his case manager. However, within two or three months, his attendance would become irregular, his behavior would become increasingly disturbed and troublesome, and, eventually, he would stop coming to the clinic. This would be followed by readmission to Lorall (for one to three months), usually through the emergency room at Ranger Hospital.

His last contact with this clinic was in June 20xx. Following readmission to Lorall (8/xx–10/xx), Mr. C returned to his sister's house for a week; following a fight, he left town. What happened subsequently is unclear. He reports that he traveled "out West," was hospitalized briefly on two occasions, and "lived on the street." He returned to this community in March.

Current Situation: Mr. C was treated at Ranger Hospital from 4/28/xx to 5/19/xx, when he was discharged to supervised housing and the outpatient treatment program. He has had no contact with his sister or his mother since his return to town, although he believes his sister "spotted" him in town. His father is now deceased.

Family and Developmental History: According to the extensive materials collected when he first came to the clinic, Mr. C is the fourth of five children and the only son. He was born when his father, a disabled farm laborer, was 57 and his mother 38-years-old. His next older sister (Mrs. W) is 14 years his senior. According to Mr. C's father, his wife's parents, sister, and nephew all were "feebleminded" and "had nervous breakdowns." Mr. C was described by everyone in the family as shy and fearful. He was physically abused by his father throughout his childhood. At age nine, he was given a BB gun for Christmas. After that, he spent many hours in the woods shooting at birds and small animals. He never brought friends home or visited other homes. His only significant peer relationships during his childhood appear to have been with his cousins, many of whom live in this county.

Mr. C attended school until age 16, when he dropped out in the ninth grade. His grades in school were poor, and he was held back twice, in grades four and six. His school records indicate that he was a "loner," but he was not troublesome in the classroom or in conflict with his peers or the community. He indicates that he does not read or write well.

There is little information available as to whether Mr. C has ever had a job. This is a very sensitive topic that Mr. C avoids discussing. Mr. C was visibly upset when Mr. V (the vocational counselor) described his role in the home program during Mr. C's first group home meeting. Mr. C attempted to leave but was told that he must remain until the end of the meeting.

Areas for Further Exploration:
1. What are Mr. C's feelings toward and experiences with work?
2. Is it appropriate to reconnect Mr. C with Mrs. W and Mrs. C? How could they be a resource for Mr. C?
3. What serves as a trigger for medication noncompliance and withdrawal from services?
4. What is Mr. C's reading level? What is his vocational potential?

Initial Impressions: Mr. C has a cyclical history of good adjustment and medication compliance, followed by noncompliance and deterioration. Clearly, his sister has been an important resource in the past, although there has been no contact in three years. Vocational development may be a problem, since his social skills and language skills appear to be very limited. Perhaps more important, he experiences even the discussion of work as stressful.

M. Grover, BSW
5/20/xx

Exhibit 2.4   Social History of a Client with a Severe and Persistent Mental Disorder (Brief Form)

Wesson County Mental Health Center (WCMHC)
Brief History Form

Client Name: Darryl C   #83-4291   DOB: 3/12/xx
Date: 5/20/xx   By: M. Grover, BSW
Information from: Darryl C, WCMHC records
Initial Diagnosis: Paranoid schizophrenia, 8/xx
                       Lorall State Hospital, B. Benton, MD
Hospital Admissions: Lorall State, 19xx, 19xx, 19xx, 19xx
                         Ranger Hospital, 19xx, 19xx, 20xx, 20xx

WCMHC:
Current: Supervised housing
Medication clinic (thorazine)
Case management
Past: Nine reopenings, 19xx–20xx
Services: Medication clinic; thorazine maintenance; case management
Status at termination: No show, medication noncompliance
Benefits: SSI *reapply*_____   DPA _____   DVR _____

Brief History:
Father:	Wolfgang C, deceased. Farm laborer, was disabled. Much older than his wife. History of abusing Mr. C throughout childhood.
Mother:	Myra C, 67-years-old. History of "feeblemindedness" and "nervous breakdowns" in her family. No contact since 20xx.
Siblings:	Four sisters, three older and one younger. Greta W, next older sister (14 years older), has allowed Mr. C to live with her family in the past. No contact since 20xx.
School:	Dropped out at age 16, in ninth grade. School grades poor; failed fourth and sixth grades. Described as a "loner," a "poor student," but not a discipline problem.
Work:	No work history available.
Marital:	Not married.
Children:	None.
Housing:	Lived briefly with Mrs. W and family; otherwise, has lived on the street, in shelters, or in hospitals. Currently living at The Haven (supervised housing).

Ongoing and Past Relationships with Medical, Mental Health, Legal, Social Service, Educational, Work, and Other Organizations and Professionals

Most clients who seek or are offered social work services have current or past relationships with service agencies or professionals who have sought to assist them with health, mental health, legal, social service, educational, work, or other special needs or problems. The identified needs or problems and the services offered or received should be carefully explored and documented in the record. This information may be used in:

- identifying current and past needs and resources;
- identifying sources of information;
- planning and implementing services;
- avoiding duplication of services;
- identifying potential for coordination among services and providers;
- understanding the client's perception of the current client-need-situation; and
- understanding the client's views and experiences with services and practitioners.

Resources, Barriers, and Unmet Needs

In response to the problems and needs identified during the exploratory process, the worker and client consider resources and services that are needed, available, and accessible. These resources, as well as potential barriers and unmet needs, should be carefully documented in the record. The client may already have an established relationship with formal or informal resources, such as a church, self-help group, or social service agency. In addition to services offered by the worker's agency, the worker and client may discuss other service options, some of which the client may have already considered or tried. In addition, barriers such as costs, transportation, eligibility, wait-listing, and the client's own and others' experiences must be weighed. When resources are available in other agencies, the worker, with the client's consent, may initiate a referral. In addition, the worker may need to develop new resources or advocate for the client in new or established service relationships. It is important to document what agencies and services were considered, what referrals were initiated, what services were unavailable or inaccessible, which services the client had tried or rejected, and what other barriers may prevent access to existing services.

This information is useful in:

- engaging the client in planning and implementing services;
- demonstrating accountability to the client and the organization;
- providing a rationale for service goals and plans;
- understanding the impact of services; and
- documenting emerging needs and inadequacies in community services.

The following example describes barriers to needed resources:

> "In the past week, Mr. and Mrs. L's attempts to find suitable services for Mickey have been met with a series of disappointments. Marymont, the local outpatient treatment program, has lost funding and has closed intake indefinitely. (There are indications that half of their clients will have their cases closed or transferred to

Cold River, 80 miles away.) They also found that respite care has a four-month waiting list."

ASSESSMENT

Throughout the record, observations, descriptions, background information, and updates of the client-need-situation and the provision of services are usually accompanied by assessments of the information presented. In assessments, the worker analyzes critical factors in the client-need-situation or the service transaction using a specific and explicit frame of reference or a set of criteria. Assessments show the worker's thinking process and the bases for service decisions and actions. Assessments are used in:

- planning, implementing, and evaluating service;
- supervision, peer review, and quality assurance;
- demonstrating accountability to the client, the organization, accrediting bodies, and funding sources; and
- communicating with others in the organization who are also offering services to the client.

In the best records, the worker's views are clearly separated from descriptions and observations and are labeled to show that they reflect the worker's appraisal or impressions. In addition, the sources of information used in formulating the assessment are always clear. These may include, for example, client self-report, direct observation by the worker, medical records, court documents, family meetings, or information provided by other agencies or providers. The criteria used as the basis for professional judgments in assessments are stated explicitly. These criteria, which reflect agency policies, procedures, and practices as well as the worker's knowledge and skill, may be drawn from:

- theories of human behavior in the social environment (e.g., the behavior of social systems);
- assumptions underlying a particular approach to practice (e.g., stages of group development or the concept of reinforcement);
- classifications of behavior developed for use with specific client groups (e.g., as in the *DSM*);
- social policy and agency procedure (e.g., guidelines for Medicare reimbursement for skilled nursing facilities or application procedures and eligibility standards for Medicaid); and
- previous experiences with this and other clients with similar problems, needs, and situations.

Finally, the worker's appraisal of information about the client-need-situation and available resources is thorough, fair, and nonjudgmental. Appraisals of the client-need-situation acknowledge strengths and resources as well as problems and unmet needs. Likewise, appraisals of the service process identify when there is deterioration in the client-need-situation, when the service plan stalls, and when the client's motivation flags as well as when there is progress and improvement.

In poor records, descriptions and assessments are admixed, so it is not clear to the reader what the worker has observed and what he or she believes or has inferred. Information sources are not carefully documented. The criteria against which observations and other information have been judged are not made explicit, although judgments may be couched in professional-sounding jargon. Appraisals may be vague, judgmental, or unrelated to the information provided. Sometimes they are overly general, as in what have been called "Aunt Fanny" assessments (Kadushin, 1963); that is, assessments are so universal that they could apply to just about anyone . . . even your "Aunt Fanny."

Here is an example of a poor assessment, which can be improved by separating the worker's impressions from the information on which they are based.

Poor:

"Mr. F described the first time that Randy was picked up for shoplifting. Mr. F received a call at work and immediately went to the police station. Randy and Mr. F decided not to tell Mrs. F about the incident, so that she would not be upset. This is one of many instances in which Mr. F colludes with Randy, implicitly suggesting to Randy that what mother does not find out about is okay. Mr. F felt that he had done all he could in handling the situation. He 'read Randy the riot act' and told him that if this got out it might be trouble for him in his job." [Mixes description with analysis; criteria are implicit.]

Better:

"Mr. F described the first time Randy was picked up for shoplifting. Mr. F received a call at work and immediately went to the police station. Randy and Mr. F decided not to tell Mrs. F about the incident, so that she would not be upset. Mr. F felt that he had done all he could in handling the situation. He 'read Randy the riot act' and told him that if this got out it might be trouble for him in his job.

Impressions: This appears to be one of many instances in which Mr. F allies with Randy in keeping an important secret from Mrs. F. He seems to be protecting Randy from some of the consequences of his actions, and is implying that Randy's behavior is not serious enough to justify upsetting Mrs. F. Need to explore possible problems between Mr. and Mrs. F. [Separates description from assessment.] It appears the ties between Mr. F and Randy may be the result of difficulty between Mr. and Mrs. F and may be undermining the generational structure of the family." [Makes criteria explicit.]

The following is an example of an overly general assessment. It does not adequately describe or contribute to our understanding of the client-need-situation. In the interest of accountability, clarity, and efficiency, it should either be revised and developed or omitted.

Poor:

> "*Impressions:* The client appeared to be anxious during the first interview, although no more anxious than most clients who are coming in to see a social worker for the first time. After about 15 minutes, she seemed to relax." [Overgeneralizes.]

Better:

> [Omit; avoid extraneous observations.]

Systematic Assessments

The centerpiece of a good record is systematic assessment. *Systematic assessments* provide the underlying justification for decisions and actions in the case. They highlight the key components of the client-need-situation, available resources, and the process and progress of service. Systematic assessments document not just the practitioner's professional appraisals of the client-need-situation and the service process, but also the observations, sources of information, and criteria used in making those appraisals.

Unfortunately, practitioners too often fail to document thorough and systematic assessments. Instead, they record their own or others' views, beliefs, or judgments of the client-need-situation or the service process. They fail to identify the observations, sources of information, and criteria used in making those judgments.

Here are some examples of inadequate documentation:

> "Mr. K is a good parent."

> "The teacher encourages Joseph's disruptive behavior."

> "According to the nurse, Mrs. V is only cooperative when the doctor is around."

> "The J family is enmeshed."

> "Raquela is depressed."

> "Raquela is less depressed than she was on her last visit."

> "Therapy is going well."

In these examples, the practitioners' and others' views have been presented as if they were systematic professional assessments. They are not. What is missing are the bases on which the worker made these judgments. Did the worker base these judgments on "gut feelings" or a systematic review of the available information? Further, the criteria used in making these judgments are not documented. What is a "good parent"? What behaviors lead to the judgment that a family is enmeshed? Because the record has not documented the information or the criteria upon which these judgments were based, it is not clear how these conclusions were reached. Even when such views are couched in professional-sounding language, they do not fulfill the expectations of accountability.

Systematic assessments begin with *observations* of the client-need-situation, the service environment, or other elements of content that are central to decisions and actions in the case. They contain specific and relevant descriptions:

> "Mr. K arrives at Ms. N's home most days at 6:00 PM to fix Bakiri's supper and give him a bath."

> "I observed Joseph in class for about 30 minutes today. At least 4 times, Joseph jumped up during reading group and went to talk with other children who were sitting in their seats. The teacher warned him that he would get a 'time out' several times, but did not follow through."

> "Raquela cried on and off, and paused for long periods. She said it was hard to talk about how mean the other girls, especially T and V, treat her. She said she comes to school but skips class and hides out in the bathroom to avoid them."

Systematic assessments also document other *information sources* that have been used in the assessment. In arriving at an assessment, social workers may use information that is:

- provided by the client or others in the client's social network;
- provided by other providers in and out of the service agency; and
- found in records, reports, or other documents.

Here are some examples of how information sources may be documented:

> "The children looked at the floor when Mr. J said that he was not drinking any more."

> "Today Chrissy called to say that she wanted me to know that Michael came home last night 'smelling foul of beer and smokes,' like he used to. 'He'll get me if he knows I told.'"

> "Dr. P's notes indicate no change in Mrs. V's status since her last exam."

Systematic assessments should also include references to the *criteria used* in evaluating the available information and formulating appraisals. Among the criteria that social workers use are:

- knowledge of social policy, agency procedures, and the availability of social resources;
- knowledge of human development, health and illness, and mental health;
- classification systems, such as the *DSM*;
- theories of human behavior in the social environment;

- knowledge of practice concepts, principles, and interventions;
- standards of practice and best practices;
- evidence of positive effects of specified interventions for the client-need-situation;
- professional values and ethics; and
- client resources, as well as access to services and preferences.

The criteria used may be documented formally. For example:

"According to *DSM-IV-TR*, Raquela does not meet the criteria for major depression but may be experiencing dysthymic disorder."

"The teacher says she is using behavioral principles that are 'not working.' She warns Joseph, but does not follow through with consequences (time out) when he fails to remain in his seat. Her warnings may actually serve as positive reinforcement, encouraging this behavior."

They also may be mentioned informally. For example:

"At least in my experience, Mr. K is an exceptionally attentive and reliable noncustodial parent."

"The children's nonverbal behavior (looking at the floor) suggested that they did not agree with what Mr. J was saying: that he was no longer drinking."

Systematic assessments conclude with the *worker's appraisal*, which is a synthesis and analysis of the information that has been presented. At least initially, the worker's appraisal should be stated tentatively, since conclusions drawn early may be revised as new information emerges. The appraisal should also take into account contrary information, differing points of view, and alternative hypotheses, and should identify steps that will be taken to gather additional information to raise confidence in or alter the initial assessment.

"In the 17 months since his son's death in an accident, M has had difficulty sleeping, reexperiencing his coming upon the accident in nightmares and intrusive thoughts. He says that things have gotten worse lately. He continues to work but says he just 'goes through the motions.' He refuses to go to church, and is angry with the minister, with God. He stays mostly to himself now, going out only to work, watching TV rather than eating with the family. He says that G used to 'bug' him about church but she lets him alone now. 'I get angry, jumpy when I see people I know so I don't go places where I would run into somebody.' In the first two sessions, M refused to discuss use of medication, alcohol, drugs. These issues will be the focus of the third session. Plan also to ask M to invite G to fourth session.

Preliminary Assessment: PTSD: numbing, avoidance, and sleep difficulties have been observed. It is unclear yet whether M is experiencing hypervigilance or flashbacks. Possible substance abuse."

"Mrs. B, aged 85, was admitted with severe abdominal pain, confusion, and weight loss. She was diagnosed with cancer of the stomach, but surgery was ruled out due to her fragile condition. She is confined to bed and requires full nursing care. Dr. P has discussed the diagnosis and prognosis with the family, and recommended discharge to a nursing facility with hospice care. Mr. B is adamantly opposed. He wants to take her home (a one-bedroom apartment) and care for her himself; he feels that this is what she would want and would do for him.
Assessment: Mr. B is mentally alert but frail. His son, the nurses, and the physician have been unable to persuade him that he could not lift her, etc., and that her condition would worsen if he took her home. He has not accepted the seriousness of Mrs. B's condition, her prognosis, or his ability to care for her at home."

Completing systematic assessments may require several contacts with the client and others over a period of days or weeks. The record should note that the assessment is incomplete, and that additional contacts with the client and others have been scheduled.

For example:

"*Reason for Social Work Referral:* Teacher asked for evaluation of home situation. Student is having school adjustment problems.
Background: James transferred to Metropolitan High School in October. He and his mother left St. Louis in May to look for work in the Chicago area. When she could not find work, she moved on to Detroit and then to Cleveland. James and his mother moved in temporarily with her sister and her five children. James says that there is little food and too much noise. Mrs. K and her sister argue frequently. James, born 3/11/xx, is placed in a class two years below his age level. His teacher indicates that he comes to school poorly dressed, is not clean, and has not eaten.
Assessment: It appears that James and his mother are homeless or nearly homeless. Because they are new to the city, Mrs. K may be unaware of the services available in this community. Among the emergency services for which they may be eligible are: family shelter, school breakfast program, food bank, food stamps, and job service.
Plan: Appointment scheduled with Mrs. K on February 2. Once immediate needs are addressed, I will discuss James's educational history and performance with her. I will observe him in the classroom this week."

Assessing Strengths

Following the work of Weick and colleagues (1989), Saleeby (1996, 2002), and others, social workers have recognized the importance of assessing and developing clients' strengths, not just addressing their problems, needs, and challenges. Regardless of whether practitioners adopt a "strengths perspective" in their practice, their records should include a description and assessment of the client's *assets, abilities,* and achievements; motivation and commitment; competencies and *capacities;* positive relationships and interpersonal *skills;* as well as family, social, and community resources.

Assessing Cultural Factors That Affect Services

Cultural factors often play a key role in clients' views of themselves and others, and their definition of need and the situation. Culture affects relationships with family, community, social network, and resources; willingness to seek and accept services; expectations of services and outcomes; interaction and communication with service providers; and much more. Cultural factors should be documented in the record whenever they are relevant to the client-need-situation or the purpose, process, and impact of services. Race, gender, national origin, religion and spirituality, disability, sexual orientation, and regional custom, for example, can strongly influence how the client and others define their problem or need and what service options they find acceptable.

In recognition of the core role culture plays in mental health, the *DSM-IV-TR* (APA, 2000) includes in Appendix I an "Outline for Cultural Formulation and Glossary of Culture-Bound Syndromes." The outline assists the practitioner in developing a cultural formulation for the client, and in assessing the potential impact of culture on diagnosis and treatment (Munson, 2001). This outline has some weaknesses, notably failing to recognize a range of individual identities within a culture and cultural factors that can enhance service delivery and effectiveness. Nonetheless, it is a good starting point for cultural assessments in mental health and other fields of practice. The Joint Commission on Accreditation of Healthcare Organizations (2001) now includes specific references to spiritual assessment in its standards of care. Although limited in scope, it too can encourage practitioners and clients to begin a dialogue on important spiritual and cultural issues.

In addition to cultural factors that affect the client-need-situation, it is important to note differences in culture between the practitioner and client that may surface at any time during the service process. The record should also document the worker's efforts to bridge those differences and guard against prejudgments or stereotypes that can result in misunderstandings and mistrust.

Social workers can demonstrate cultural competence in their records by:

- recognizing the role of culture in the client-need-situation;
- showing knowledge of and respect for the client's culture, community, tradition, and values;
- outlining the role culture plays in the client's definition of the need-situation, acceptable service options, and available resources;

- describing special efforts to overcome language or other communication barriers;

- describing special efforts to overcome cultural barriers in the relationship, agency, or environment;

- noting when the client has had opportunities to discuss her or his preferences and values;

- showing how the client's preferences and values have been incorporated into service arrangements, goals, plans, and referrals; and

- illustrating continuing efforts to identify cultural barriers and assets as well as monitor services for cultural biases and strengths.

Risk Assessment

Social workers assess clients for risk of danger or harm in compliance with the law, agency policies, and standards of ethical and competent practice. Even if the risk does not fall within the agency's mission or the purpose of service to a client, social workers have an ethical, and sometimes legal, obligation to assess and respond to the risks that vulnerable clients face. For example, a social worker who is providing services to a client seeking housing assistance may find that the client is at risk of *suicide* or *domestic violence*. Although this is not his agency's mission or the purpose of service to his client, this social worker should assess these risks, and work with the client in developing and implementing a plan. Of course, in all fifty states, regardless of setting, social workers have a legal responsibility to assess and report suspected *child abuse and neglect*.

Sometimes agency protocols require that all clients with certain characteristics be assessed for risk at intake. For example, social workers in health settings may screen all elderly clients who have injuries for risk of *elder abuse or neglect* by caregivers. Social workers in child welfare often assess parents for risk of domestic violence. Social workers as well as other mandated reporters assess children in schools, health, and community organizations for risk of abuse or neglect. Sometimes the "presenting problem" or issues identified during the initial assessment suggest potential risk. For example, clients may seek help for depression or show signs of despair during an interview, signaling the need to assess risk of suicide.

> "Ms. P called our Crisis Line on 2/15/xx. She said that she had just broken up with her boyfriend and was thinking of suicide. Susan R spent over an hour talking with her; after assessing the risk of an imminent suicide attempt, Susan R determined that an emergency admission would not be needed. Ms. P agreed to come in for an appointment on 2/16/xx, and to call back immediately if the situation got worse."

Sometimes records of past or ongoing services indicate the potential for risk. For example, a client's record may reveal a history of *substance abuse*. Sometimes a risk of danger or harm emerges only after the worker and client have established an ongoing relationship. For example, clients may reveal their illegal drug use or risky sexual behavior only after they have developed a sense of trust in the worker. Sometimes risk becomes apparent only after the worker observes the client's personal circumstances or social environment directly, thereby discovering, for example, a family's *poverty and homelessness* or the potential for violence in their community.

Assessment of danger or harm, along with strengths and protective factors, should follow best practices, using validated standardized diagnostic instruments or protocols, whenever possible, to supplement careful, individualized interviewing. For example, documentation of risk of substance abuse might include the MAST (Michigan Alcohol Screening Test) or another screening instrument. Documentation of risk of suicide should include a thorough review of factors associated with lethality, including any previous attempts, critical precipitating events (job loss, health crisis), substance use, social isolation, hopelessness, plan and intent, and availability of means. Clients should be assessed for risk of suicide following stressful life events and during important transitions in care, for example, from hospitalization to outpatient mental health treatment (Bongar, 2001). Practitioners should document their appraisal of the level of risk and carefully spell out the rationale for all actions taken as well as those not taken or deferred (Callahan, 1996).

For example:

> "Mr. L has a long history of depression and suicidal ideation. He says that he has never actually made a suicide attempt, although he has intrusive thoughts about driving his truck into a tree. Since his recent two-week hospitalization, which followed his decision to stop taking his depression medication, he continues on his medication. Based on my interview with him, and the findings of a BSSI (Beck Scale for Suicide Ideation), I find his risk to be moderate at this time. His therapy will focus on his job frustrations, family difficulties, and suicide ideation. I do not think he is in need of rehospitalization at this time, but will continue to assess his situation and risk."

Documentation of assessment of risk for child abuse and neglect, domestic violence, or other danger or harm should include:

- observations and descriptions;
- sources of information, including prior records of social work or other intervention;
- use of standardized protocols;
- criteria for judging information;
- worker's appraisal;
- justifications for actions taken and not taken;
- recommendations for next steps; and
- actions taken and planned.

Any such risk should be taken very seriously. Generally, other activities should be suspended until the risk is thoroughly assessed, various options are carefully considered, and a plan of action is in place. Of course, this information should be immediately documented in the record. Whenever possible, a supervisor or someone else representing the agency should sign off on the plan to demonstrate agency as well as practitioner accountability.

Specialized Assessments

Social work records sometimes include specialized assessments associated with a field of practice, client-need-situation, or approach to intervention. Such assessments are based on information collected via formal interview protocols, standardized checklists, direct observation, client self-report, or other sources, and rely on the practitioner's special knowledge and expertise in a particular field or practice method. Specialized assessments contribute directly to the formulation of social work goals and plans, and influence decisions and actions of other professionals in the agency.

For example, practitioners in mental health agencies or those whose clients exhibit mental health difficulties may document an assessment and diagnosis using the APA's *Diagnostic and Statistical Manual*. In recent years, a *DSM diagnosis* has often been a requirement for authorization and reimbursement for services provided under managed care and other public and private insurance programs. Practitioners who adopt a behavioral approach to practice may conduct and document a *behavioral assessment*, which includes, for example, the contingencies of specific behaviors. A family therapist might assess *family dynamics*, observing and assessing the family's patterns of verbal and nonverbal communication. A school social worker may conduct a *functional behavioral assessment* (FBA) for a child with special needs (Witt, Daly, & Noell, 2000).

In most records, practitioners document an initial assessment at the end of the data gathering process. Here, the record documents the *worker's appraisal* and *criteria used in making judgments* about the information collected during the early phase of the service process. It is important to note, however, that practitioners document additional assessments throughout their records, for example, in interim notes, service reviews, and closing summaries. To ensure that these ongoing assessments are systematic, practitioners should include in them not just their appraisals of the client-need-situation and the service process, but also the information, observations, sources, and criteria on which these appraisals are based.

DECISIONS AND ACTIONS RESULTING FROM INITIAL ASSESSMENT

Decisions and Actions Taken

The record should document responses to each issue identified in the initial assessment. Some of these issues may require urgent and immediate action. If, for example, indicators of *child or elder abuse* or *risk of suicide* surfaced, the practitioner would report the abuse or take action to prevent the suicide. Any risk, crisis, or urgent situation that is identified during the initial assessment process requires some action (or the decision to take no action), in *compliance with relevant policies, laws, and standards of practice.* Of course, if such situations are identified at any time during the service process, they require similar action and documentation. The record should fully document all decisions and actions, including reports and *referrals* to other agencies, *interventions to protect the client and others,* and descriptions of services provided or planned. Whenever decisions or actions differ from customary policy or procedure, or involve special circumstances or potential agency liability, the practitioner should consult with agency administrators and get their "sign off" in the record for the service decisions, actions, and plans. For example, unless such actions explicitly adhere to agency policies, practitioners are advised to consult with agency managers, and perhaps legal counsel, before breaching client confidentiality to issue a *"Tarasoff warning"* (Kagle & Kopels, 1994; Kopels & Kagle, 1993) or to undertake other forceful measures.

SERVICE PLANNING

Service Options
Other issues identified in the initial assessment call for a deliberative process, through which the worker and client identify available resources and consider various service options. The record should document the rationale for all service decisions and actions, including the service *options that were considered* and the *reasons for selecting among various options.* It is important also to document the *role clients have played* in evaluating and choosing among various service options. The NASW (1999) Code of Ethics states that "social workers should provide services only in the context of a professional relationship based . . . on valid informed consent" (1.03[a]). Social workers are expected to "inform clients about the purpose of the services, the risks related to the services, limits to services because of the requirements of a third party payer, relevant costs, reasonable alternatives and clients' right to refuse or withdraw consent" even when clients are "receiving services involuntarily" (1.03[a], [d]). Evidence-based practice takes this ethical obligation a step further. Not only are clients asked for informed consent for service; they are to be "involved as active participants in the decision-making process," and their preferences and expectations are to take precedence (Gambrill, 1999, p. 346). In evidence-based practice, practitioners seek out and appraise available evidence on the efficacy, appropriateness, and impact of various interventions in the context of the client-need-situation. They then share this information, as well as the fact that some evidence may be lacking, with their clients (Gambrill, 1999).

Even when clients come to an agency with an identified problem and for a specific service, the practitioner has the responsibility to discuss *costs, limitations, alternatives, potential risks and benefits, and possible outcomes* with them. Moreover, assessment may indicate that clients need different or additional services along with those the client initially sought.

Screening may show that clients do not meet *eligibility* standards for particular programs. Further, some service options may not be considered or may be *rejected*. Sometimes desired services are unavailable, for example, when an agency is not accepting new clients. At other times services are inaccessible, for example, because of transportation problems or because an agency is not physically accessible. All this information, and the client's response to it, should be documented in the record, along with the *criteria that are used for selecting among various options.*

Of course, the primary criterion for selecting among service options should be *quality, effectiveness,* and *potential for alleviating the assessed problem or need*. Each option should also be evaluated for its *availability* and *accessibility,* the client's *eligibility*, and whether services are covered by the client's insurance or are *reimbursable*. The *client's preference* for a specific agency or practitioner because of its reputation, cultural values, convenience, or familiarity should also be noted, as should any recommendations by the practitioner or others.

> "Because the S family situation is not classified as emergency status, they were offered two options: wait listing (six to eight weeks) or referral to the NCH outpatient program. They chose wait listing but will call if an emergency arises or if they decide on an alternative service."

> "Ms. H asked to be referred to a Christian counselor. She had received counseling from her pastor in Jefferson Parish before the evacuation."

Information about service options is used in:

- planning, implementing, and evaluating service;
- supervision;
- demonstrating accountability to the client, accrediting bodies, and funding sources; and
- evaluating service outcomes and impact.

Purpose, Goals, and Plans of Service

Social work records document the purpose, goals, and plans for all services delivered with and on behalf of the client. The purpose of service is the reason for providing services, and should be derived from the assessment of the client-need-situation and available resources while considering the client's preferences and expectations. Service goals and plans are more specific statements of what services are intended to accomplish and how they will proceed. It is important to record not just the purpose of service, goals, and plans, but also the anticipated benefits and any possible unintended outcomes or risks that may be associated with receiving services, realizing goals, or implementing plans. The record should also document any factors that may stand in the way or otherwise affect the kind, quantity, and quality of services to the client.

This information is used in:

- implementing service and evaluating its impact;
- documenting adherence to accepted standards and procedures;
- promoting continuity of service; and
- accountability, supervision, and peer review.

Purpose of Service

Clarity of purpose gives structure to the service transaction and to the record. The purpose of service is a statement of its overall objectives. To demonstrate accountability, the worker must ensure that the purpose of service falls *within the scope and mission of the agency* and the service program. Arriving at the purpose of service may involve mediating among the views of the client, influential people in the client's environment, the agency, funding sources, and others in the community. It may involve reconciling various views with what resources are available to the client. The purpose of service, then, describes what is to be accomplished within the context of the client-need-situation and the agency's or program's mission.

A statement of purpose unifies the record and forms the basis for:

- locating appropriate points of and approaches to intervention;
- establishing a plan of service;
- communicating with other professionals who are also involved in service delivery; and
- evaluating the impact of service.

Unfortunately, this element of the record is often absent from social work records. Even when it is included, it may be stated in vague terms or by describing the process that will be used in providing services.

Poor:

"Improve social functioning." [Vague]

"Act as advocate in the client's attempt to get the landlord to comply with city ordinances." [Process]

"Improve communication among family members [Vague] through the use of family therapy." [Process]

Better:

"Improve client's employment potential and relationships with extended family."

"Improve client's housing conditions."

"Assist the family in adopting more direct patterns of communication."

Goals

Goals are specific statements of intended outcomes. Goal statements should be clear, meaningful, and attainable. Whenever possible, they should reflect the client's priorities and be stated in the client's own language.

> "W's goal is to find employment; his dream is to work as a cook in a restaurant."

> "W's goal is to reestablish a relationship with his mother and sister."

> "The goal: within two months, M will be in suitable housing. Either her landlord will comply with city ordinances or M will find a better place."

> "Change the family's pattern of communication, typically blaming and withdrawing, to making explicit requests and using responsive listening."

Plans

The service plan specifies the actions the worker, the client, and others will take to fulfill the purpose of service and realize the stated goals. The records should explain how the plan falls within accepted agency practices and professional *standards of care*. The plan may involve *referrals* to *other agencies and providers*, and may be formulated in concert with other agencies, as well as *family and community members*. A detailed statement of the plan is particularly useful in maintaining continuity of service when the worker is absent and another service provider takes over the case or when services are delayed or episodic.

The plan is also used in:

- demonstrating adherence to agency policy and procedures;
- facilitating supervision, consultation, and peer review;
- communicating with others who are providing service to the client; and
- evaluating service implementation.

A plan of service may, for example,

- Describe agency or program referrals:

  "Refer Mrs. T to Family Service for homemaker service."

- Suggest issues for exploration and intervention:

  "Discuss John's current development and changing needs for parental guidance with Mrs. K."

  "At next meeting, encourage Carl to ask the group for suggestions on how to deal with conflict with his roommate."

  "Discuss school situation in depth with Rachel; avoid direct confrontation, but explore what others want her to do and compare with what she wants."

"Following its success in the classroom, teach Mr. and Mrs. M how to use time-out whenever Tom has a tantrum."

- Outline a sequence of steps to be taken by worker, client, and others:

"a. Meet with Mr. and Mrs. T to assess their awareness of Mr. T's long-term care needs; meet with Dr. Q if needed.

b. Explore financial and employment situation, home environment, available individuals, and resources if Mr. T returns home.

c. Discuss possible discharge arrangements and preferences with Mr. and Mrs. T.

d. Recommend interviews with nursing homes, home health agencies, and meetings with physical therapy and nurses."

"By next interview, Mr. N will have polled residents of house to see if they are having problems with the landlord and if they are willing to attend a meeting. Worker will locate a meeting place and will find out about building code and procedure for reporting complaints."

- Suggest contingencies:

"Mr. P and I have agreed to meet again on 8/28. If he has not by then been recalled for his job, he will enroll in the training program."

"If a place in a group home is available, begin preparation for move. If not available, place name on list, seek temporary support from respite care, family members, and their church."

Some interventions and practice approaches lend themselves to detailed planning, while others do not. When service calls for action in the environment, group activities, or cognitive-behavioral intervention, for example, the record can clearly show when, how, and who will undertake each step in the process. In contrast, a plan for services using a psychodynamic or other insight-oriented approach may describe only the critical issues the worker and client will explore over time.

The record of the plan of service is most useful if it:

- is up-to-date;
- covers the ongoing and subsequent phases of service;
- is specific enough to be implemented by another service provider, if needed; and
- is open to review and evaluation.

Indicators of Movement toward Completing Plan, Realizing Goals

It is important at the outset of services for the worker and client to decide not only on the direction services are to take but also on how they will assess whether services are moving forward and in the intended direction. The worker has an important responsibility in identifying the particular indicators that will be used to evaluate change or movement in the client-need-situation. Such indicators should be tailored to the specific purpose, goals, and plans in the case. Indicators should accurately measure the intended outcomes of service; contribute to the service process; and be meaningful, feasible, and acceptable to the client. The client and others in the client's environment may also play important roles, such as selecting and endorsing the goals and measures to be used and documenting indicators over time. For example, a client and worker may choose to monitor the client's thoughts, behaviors, and feelings to assess movement in alleviating depression; the client may complete a self-anchored scale prior to weekly meetings with the worker. A school may wish to improve the classroom environment for students with disabilities; a second-grade teacher may monitor children's behavior toward and acceptance of a disabled classmate before and after they complete a curriculum on the topic. A worker and family member may monitor the implementation of a plan to find suitable housing and support services for a client who is to be discharged from a hospital.

In situations where particular services or interventions may pose *risks* as well as *benefits*, practitioners should make sure that specific indicators are in place to monitor potential problems as well as movement toward achieving goals. For example, a child or adolescent who is being treated with antidepressants should be regularly monitored for suicide risk. Indicators of movement are to be systematically documented in interim notes. Because they are used to evaluate the progress of service, it is important for the practitioner also to assess whether indicators actually measure what they are intended to and if they are being documented consistently, honestly, and fairly.

Sometimes clients are involved in programs or services where similar goals or indicators of movement are established for all clients. For example, in a substance abuse treatment program, eliminating the use of alcohol and other drugs and preventing relapse may be goals for all clients. Even in such programs, however, it is important to establish individual client goals and select indicators of movement that reflect each client's special situation. For example, one client may wish to improve her parenting skills, while another may need employment coaching.

In selecting indicators, it is useful to include:

- more than one indicator for each goal;
- more than one source of information;
- measures that gauge intermediate changes as well as ultimate outcomes; and
- milestones in the implementation of the service plan.

Using a variety of indicators and sources of information can help surface movement or stability in complex client-need-situations from varying perspectives. Indicators might include:

- direct observations of the client's performance in specific environments (e.g., a teacher's observations of a child's behavior in the classroom or a coleader's observations of the client's participation in group meetings);

- the client's self-report of thoughts, feelings, or attitudes;
- brief instruments in which the client responds to queries about a specific symptom or pattern of behavior (e.g., level of anxiety in social situations);
- client memoranda about their thoughts, feelings, or actions in their natural environments (e.g., each member of a family describing their reactions to a family event); and
- the practitioner's impressions of the client's responses (e.g., the client's developing insight).

Using a variety of indicators can also be beneficial as services evolve. One indicator may be more significant at one phase of the service process while another may be more useful at another phase. For example, measures of subjective feelings of well-being may show crucial changes early in the process, while measures of specific behaviors, social functioning, or changes in the social environment may become more important later (Lueger et al., 2001).

Monitoring intermediate goals and milestones in implementing plans can provide direction for continuing services or changing the plan, time frame, approach, or ultimate goal. Of course, practitioners are actively involved in identifying indicators, and in monitoring and evaluating movement and change. But clients who participate in monitoring process and outcomes by reviewing records and other documents can benefit in various ways. Those who see the evidence that they have accomplished intermediate goals may be more optimistic and committed to working on ultimate goals. For example, a client who sees that he has been successful in changing a cognitive pattern may be more committed to change other long-standing patterns. Similarly, those who reach milestones in implementing a service plan may be more motivated to complete it. At the same time, clients who see evidence that their situation is not changing, is getting worse, or that they are running into barriers that impede progress may be motivated to renew their commitment to existing goals and plans or to rethink them.

Agreements Regarding Termination of Services

Initial and subsequent discussions and agreements about termination should be documented in the record. Discussions about termination provide the client with important information about how long service may last and how service may end. Indeed, such discussions may actually prevent clients from terminating services prematurely. Services may be time limited, for example, because of third-party coverage or program length, or they may be open ended, with decisions about termination made as plans unfold and goals are met. Agreements about termination can always be altered, as goals and plans change. For example, a client may decide to focus on more limited goals or stop short of completing plans. Circumstances may interfere with the service process, or clients may need additional services. For example, a client may lack transportation to group meetings or wish to seek additional services after third-party coverage ends. In such cases, the worker is ethically obligated not to abandon (NASW, 1999, 1.16[b]), but to assist the client in making arrangements for alternative or additional services. Unfortunately, too often services end prematurely, when clients simply stop coming for services. Discussions and agreements about termination, and contracting for achievable, short-term goals, may help to prevent clients from dropping out (Kagle, 1987a).

> "The B family has agreed to come for family interviews on Wednesday afternoons for six weeks. We will work on parenting skills, especially discipline, and M's school attendance. During the sixth session, we will look at what progress is being made, and decide about whether to continue or terminate services."

Client-Worker Contract

Mutual decisions regarding the purpose and process of service are sometimes formalized in a client-worker contract (Barker, 1986; Hepworth, Rooney, & Larsen, 2004). The contract usually includes general agreements as to the goals, plans, and methods of service as well as specific agreements regarding, for example, the scheduling of meetings, fees, tasks, and actions to be undertaken by the worker and the client. Whenever possible, the contract should also include the potential risks, as well as the benefits of service, and the alternatives that have been considered. When a written contract is used, a copy, signed by the worker and the client, should be filed in the record. When the contract is verbal, a brief statement of its major components should be documented, including, where applicable:

- who participated in decision making;
- what decisions were made;
- who has agreed to do what and when; and
- how the contract may be revised.

INTERIM NOTES

Once the plan of service is in place, interim notes describe and assess the client-need-situation and the service transaction at regular intervals. These notes may be brief or extensive, depending upon how much new information has surfaced, how much change has occurred, how frequently the client-need-situation is monitored, and how often information is entered into the record. In many agencies, interim notes are called progress notes, suggesting that an important criterion for selecting information for the record is that it demonstrates movement in the process of service and improvement in the client-need-situation. Historically, few other guidelines for the content of interim notes existed. In social work agencies where records were written primarily for use in supervision, interim notes often consisted of lengthy narrative reports that focused on the service process and the development of the worker-client relationship. Interim notes sometimes even included process recordings of interviews or group meetings. Practitioners who found it difficult to keep up with their recordkeeping tasks sometimes delayed recording for the record, but kept their own notes. As a result, some records of active cases included only opening summaries and lacked timely and meaningful updates to support practice and supervision.

In the 1970s, with increasing demands for accountability from funding sources, practitioners began focusing interim notes on service outcomes and changes in the client-need-situation. Some mental health agencies adopted Goal Attainment Scaling (Kiresuk & Sherman, 1968), while some medical and health-related agencies adopted the Problem-Oriented Record, using the SOAP (Subjective-Objective-Assessment-Plan) format for interim notes (Weed, 1968). (See chapter 4 for a discussion with examples of Goal Attainment Scaling and the Problem-Oriented Record.)

More recently, practitioners, agencies, and funders in all fields of practice have recognized the importance of documenting indicators of movement and change at regular intervals throughout the service process. This has given structure and meaning to interim notes. When records are regularly updated with important information on the process and progress of services, this information can be used in:

- monitoring and evaluating changes in the client-need-situation;
- monitoring and evaluating movement in the service process;
- recognizing milestones in implementing the service plan;
- determining whether and when to terminate services;
- demonstrating adherence to accepted practices;
- supervision, consultation, and peer review; and
- administrative decision making.

Interim notes should include some or all of the following information:

- updates and new information about the client-need-situation;
- indicators of movement;
- assessment of the status of the client-need-situation;
- descriptions of service activities;
- assessments of the purpose, goals, plan, process, and progress of service; and
- any changes in the purpose, goals, plan of service, and indicators of movement.

At regular intervals, interim notes should *update information about the client-need-situation. New information* may come to light; changes in the client-need-situation, due to service interventions or other sources, need to be documented. Interim notes may also correct or amend previous documentation, or substantiate or refute earlier assumptions. Interim notes should document any changes in or new information about the client-need-situation. They should also highlight new resources or barriers to service, planned or unanticipated consequences of services, and needs for additional or different services. Such updates serve as the basis for assessments that in turn may result in changes in the purpose, goals, or plan of service.

The following example, from an interim note, describes changes in the client's environment that may affect the client's goals and the feasibility of a preferred service plan:

> "In the interview 3/30, which included Mrs. Q, her daughter Ms. Q, and her son-in-law Mr. N, it became apparent that Mrs. Q's preference to move to her daughter's home may not be feasible at this time. Mr. N's layoff has been changed from temporary to indefinite. Ms. Q has taken a job and has placed her son Darren in day care. Mr. N will seek employment in another state."

Interim notes document *indicators of movement,* which are intended to demonstrate progress, lack of change, or deterioration in the client-need-situation. Such indicators may focus on the client-need-situation, documenting, for example, behaviors or thoughts, activities or actions, physical functions, or emotional states (Lueger et al., 2001). They may focus on the service process, monitoring the implementation of service plans. Sometimes indicators of movement are entered into the record on a *chart* or form to monitor specific indicators and show any changes. For example, a client's attendance at school or scores on a self-efficacy scale may be plotted on a graph. Sometimes the practitioner will simply describe changes and provide examples. For example, "Ms. L says she now understands how to set limits for Jacob; he is coming home on time and they are not fighting as much." Sometimes interim notes document unanticipated changes in the client-need-situation. For example, a teenager engaged in family therapy runs away from home. Sometimes interim notes describe barriers to change or changes in the client's commitment to service goals or plans. For example, the record may document that a client repeatedly fails to appear for employment interviews. Sometimes interim notes document improvement; at other times, they show temporary or long-term harm, deterioration, or relapse.

In the example that follows, a worker notes a client's developing insight:

> "After I interpreted her behavior as yet another example of her ambivalence about achievement and success, Ms. G said that she had been giving this idea a lot of thought recently. She could think of several situations at work that also showed that she was avoiding being 'too successful.' She had worked hard but had not sought 'showy assignments' that would have brought her work attention at the highest levels. Yet, she resented doing all the work and being treated as an assistant rather than an associate attorney."

Using the client's diary entries as a source of information, a worker documents a client's level of anxiety:

> "Martha's diary from 11/15/xx–11/29/xx showed four incidents of moderate anxiety and one incident of panic. She used relaxation techniques on all five occasions. Anxiety dissipated in 30 minutes.

Change: Number of incidents decreased 10 percent; no change in time elapsed after initiating relaxation.
Plan: Continue with relaxation training."

In an interim note, a worker documents a couple's responses to an index of marital satisfaction before and during the process of service. For example:

"Mr. and Mrs. L each completed the Index of Marital Satisfaction (Hudson, 1982) before service was initiated (9/19/xx) and again after six interviews (10/30/xx).
Scores were:

	9/19/xx	10/30/xx
Mrs. L	88	65
Mr. L	70	66"

There are no hard-and-fast rules about how frequently workers should update the record. Ideally, workers would update the record immediately after each service contact; however, in most agency settings, such an expectation would be unrealistic. Sometimes services are delivered over a very brief period of time, without an opportunity to update the record prior to termination. Sometimes the demands of practice make it impossible to update records regularly. However, practitioners and agencies would be well-advised to consider adopting the following guidelines:

- all emergencies and critical incidents should be fully documented within 24 hours;
- all significant changes in the client-need-situation and service transaction should be documented as soon as possible and certainly within three days;
- indicators of movement in goals and plans should be documented regularly (e.g., following every third service contact);
- records of active cases involving other providers and agencies should be updated weekly;
- interim notes should be documented regularly and certainly following every third service contact or at least once a month; and
- records should be updated prior to planned worker absences, case transfers, releases of information, and case reviews.

Interim notes often document an *assessment of the status of the client-need-situation* at a particular point in time. Here, the worker provides an appraisal of changes (or no change) in the client-need-situation based on direct observations, selected indicators of change, and other sources of information. The worker's purpose is to evaluate whether there has been movement toward achieving the purpose of service; whether goals or plans need to be revised; and whether the intended outcomes are likely to be achieved. The worker should document the information on which the assessment is based, as well as the criteria used in arriving at an appraisal.

> "3/21/xx: I received a message from the B Company Human Resource office that S did not show up for her interview Friday. This is her third missed appointment, and this time she did not phone to cancel. The B Company is now refusing to interview her. I have tried to reach S by phone, but she has not returned my calls.
> *Impression:* I have no information other than what I learned from the B Company HR office. It is unclear why S missed this appointment and is not responding to me. She may be avoiding things or there may be a crisis or something else may be happening that I'm unaware of."

Interim notes should always document *descriptions of service activities*. In the early years of the profession, social workers were advised against recording specific service activities in their records. Bristol (1936) called these "behold-me-busy" details because she considered them extraneous to the purpose for keeping records, which was to aid the worker in diagnostic thinking. Today, however, documentation of each activity with or on behalf of the client is an important component of accountability. For example, phone contacts with other agencies to check on the client's eligibility and the availability of services may be documented in the record. Even brief service activities should be included if they demonstrate accountability or explain service decisions, actions, and outcomes. Such documentation is useful in demonstrating the level of effort and the kind and quality of services the client receives. They may also be required by the worker's agency, necessary to claim reimbursement from funding sources, and critical in corroborating testimony in court.

Interim notes need not include a detailed report of all activities with and on behalf of the client; this practice would be far too time-consuming and costly. Rather, records should *chart all service contacts,* noting the date, setting, and participants involved, as well as the subjects discussed and decisions made. Whenever possible, this information should be recorded after each interview, session, phone call, or other encounter with the client, with members of the client's family or social network, and with other service providers. Of course, practitioners cannot always keep up with even routine recordkeeping tasks. Many agencies and practitioners use a chart, form, or computerized appointment software to simplify this task. Others rely on clerical staff to fulfill this and other basic recordkeeping tasks.

Reports of service activities may of course be supplemented with more extensive notes.

> "9/23/xx: Office interview with Mr. and Mrs. K. Final interview for marital counseling, initiated 4/17/xx. Reviewed changes that have taken place in their relationship with each other and with Mr. K's father. Planned for usual follow-up phone interview on 10/20/xx to assess situation and possible need for reopening."

> "3/18/xx: Met with Raven's teacher, Mrs. G. She indicates that Raven's classroom participation and overall performance have

improved somewhat during the past two weeks. She has noticed that other students, especially Garnet and Ethel, are trying to distract Raven. On my suggestion, Mrs. G will (1) separate Garnet and Ethel, (2) positively reinforce them for school-directed activities, and (3) have Raven lead reading group this week."

Today, records rarely include full descriptions of the service process or verbatim excerpts from meetings with clients. Rather, the record characterizes the approach (e.g., cognitive-behavioral intervention), method (e.g., systematic desensitization), or strategy (e.g., discussion of steps to be taken) used, without documenting in detail the actual process of service or interactions between the practitioner, client, and others. On occasion, however, a practitioner might choose to document a specific interaction in some detail to demonstrate:

- progress in implementing the service plan;
- movement through successive stages of a treatment process; and
- impact of services on the client-need-situation.

The following excerpt documents a stage in the process of group development that is used to demonstrate progress:

> "12/1/xx: During meeting #3 last week, Leslie called the group 'our group.' Later Sarah said that when one of the kids asked her where she had gone during math class, she said 'my group,' which in her opinion was better than saying 'my shrink.' Everyone laughed and looked at each other and at the worker.
> *Impression:* The group is beginning to develop an identity and some cohesion."

Interim notes also include the worker's *assessment of the process and progress of services.* This assessment may be based upon a number of factors, including the client's engagement in the service process, changes in the client-need-situation, and indicators of movement in implementing the service plan and toward achieving goals. The worker uses the assessment to address such questions as: Is the client-need-situation improving? Are services moving forward, and in a timely way? Are changes in the client-need-situation bringing about the need for a different approach or additional services? Are the existing purpose, goals, and plans still realistic and meaningful? Is the client-need-situation worsening or are there no changes, despite reasonable time and effort? Have new or additional problems arisen, or are there unanticipated consequences of service or other barriers to success?

Assessment of the process and progress of services should always include an *evaluation of the selected indicators* or "outcome" measures. However, it is sometimes difficult to assess the role that services play in bringing about change (or no change) in the client-need-situation. Certainly, practitioners should be aware that social work intervention is only one of a variety of influences on the client-need-situation that may be responsible for movement or the lack of change. Other factors in the client's environment and other service providers, for example, may be influencing services, goals, and outcomes (Kagle, 1982b). Whenever possible, practitioners should work with clients to identify factors that may be contributing to or undermining services. This information should be documented in the record, along with indicators of movement.

In the following example, Susan's school attendance was used as one measure of service effects. Her school performance had deteriorated, in part due to her frequent absences.

> "4/4: Susan's poor attendance in school in March (six absences) had been attributed to her continuing relationship with Chad. However, she revealed today that her mother returned to State Hospital early in March. Susan had also stayed home for a week in February with Larry (age 9) who had the flu."

If the record had not documented the extenuating circumstances that affected her attendance, these indicators might have been interpreted as a sign that services were ineffective or that Susan lacked motivation to attend school.

Assessments of the progress of service may indicate that the worker and client should make *changes in the purpose, goals, plan of service, or in the indictors* they are using to measure and evaluate movement. Any such decisions should be noted and highlighted in the record, along with the rationale for the changes. *Barriers to service delivery and goal achievement* should be noted, as should efforts to overcome such barriers. In addition, it is important to update the worker-client contract, if one exists, and leave notations elsewhere in the record referring the reader to the interim note for crucial new information and changes in the purpose, goals, plan of service, or in indicators of change.

SPECIAL MATERIALS

Social work records may include a variety of special materials, such as legal *documents*, agency *forms*, worker-client contracts, consents, documentation about releases and transfer of information, *reports and records from other agencies and practitioners*, or letters and messages from clients. Some of these special materials are prepared by the practitioner and are crucial to accountability.

Consents

Records include forms that document the client's (or others' acting on the client's behalf) authorization for actions to be taken by the agency and practitioner. These forms are often called "informed consents" or "authorizations."

For a consent to be "informed," it must meet the following standards:

- the client is competent to make judgments and enter into agreements. In the case of a minor child or adult with disabilities who is not competent or able to make such judgments, the form may be signed by a parent, legal guardian, or other authorized decision maker;
- the actions to be taken have been thoroughly explained;
- the client (or other decision maker) authorizes the agency and practitioner to take specified actions;

- the client (or other decision maker) has been informed as to how the consent may be revoked; and

- the client (or other decision maker) has been apprised about any consequences that may result from the decision to give or withhold consent.

Today, many agencies and practitioners initiate services only after the client has signed a consent agreeing to receive such services. Following medicine's example in seeking the patient's "consent to treat," social workers seek the client's "consent to initiate services" prior to beginning the exploratory process. This consent is different from a worker-client contract. While the contract follows the exploratory process and outlines specific goals, plans, and outcomes, consents to receive service document the client's or other decision maker's general understanding of what the agency offers, what is expected of them, and what the process is likely to entail.

Prior to seeking written consent to provide services, the agency and practitioner should inform the client about the:

- types of problems, needs, and clientele served;
- specific programs and services offered;
- extent and limits of confidentiality;
- costs, billing, and eligibility guidelines;
- agency's affiliations and the practitioner's qualifications;
- length and frequency of service contacts;
- making and canceling of appointments; and
- potential benefits and any risks of receiving services.

The practitioner should also provide any other information that may assist the client in deciding whether to enter into the service process. The client should be encouraged to ask questions and carefully consider the decision before signing the authorization. The record should document the procedure used in gaining the authorization; here a checklist or other form can be useful in ensuring that the proper steps are taken and documented. Of course, if the client or those acting on the client's behalf refuse to consent, services should not be initiated.

A similar process, with documentation, should accompany authorization to release information to outside agencies and practitioners. Here, too, informed consent means that the client is competent to make such decisions (or that a guardian or other decision maker is acting on the client's behalf), has been duly informed about the process and its potential effects, and authorizes the agency and practitioner to take specific actions. To consent to a release of information, the client must know:

- what information is to be released;
- to whom;
- how the information is to be used; and
- the potential benefits and risks of releasing or failing to release the information.

Today, agencies and practitioners should no longer seek "blanket consents," that is, all-purpose documents that permit the agency to release any information to outside parties at their discretion. Rather, they should seek individual consents for each release, with the goal of providing clients with sufficient information in each situation to make informed judgments. They should provide the client with detailed information about what would be released, often offering clients (or those acting on their behalf) direct access to the record. In rare instances where information is released without the prior consent of the client (e.g., in an emergency), the record should contain full documentation of the circumstances and the rationale for releasing information without client consent. Whenever possible, agency supervisors or other managers should participate in or sign off on the decision to release information without specific, prior authorization.

Accounting of Disclosures of Information

To comply with the HIPAA Privacy Rule, health care and other providers that are considered "covered entities" must document disclosures of protected health information (PHI) to outside individuals and organizations. Covered entities should be prepared to provide an accounting of those disclosures for a period of at least six years. Documentation should include:

- the date of disclosure;
- the names and addresses of the individuals or organizations that received the information;
- a copy or description of the information that was disclosed; and
- a copy of the request for disclosure or a statement of the reasons for the disclosure.

Although HIPAA does not explicitly require them to do so, agencies and practitioners would be well-advised to retain copies of consents for the release of such information as well as documentation about any waivers of consent. For a more thorough description and analysis of HIPAA, PHI, the Privacy Rule, and retention of records and related information, see chapters 8 and 9.

Critical Incidents and Emergencies

Urgent situations impacting the client and affecting services require full and immediate documentation. Some urgent situations are defined as critical incidents; that is, the client is directly involved in a life-threatening or potentially injurious situation.

Examples of critical incidents include:

- a client threatens or attacks another person;
- a client is threatened, attacked, or mistreated;
- a client threatens suicide; and
- a client reports that he was the victim or perpetrator of child abuse.

In contrast, some urgent situations are defined as emergencies, that is, the circumstances are serious and likely to have a significant impact on the client or the service plan, but do not pose an immediate threat to the client or others.

Examples of emergencies include:

- a client is arrested for shoplifting;
- a client is involved in an automobile accident;
- a day care provider loses her license; and
- a family is evicted from their home.

Whenever possible, the practitioner should review policies and procedures for handling such situations, then document decisions and actions taken, referring to the relevant standards. For example, social work practitioners in all states are required to report possible child abuse. If a possible incident surfaces, the record should document and provide the rationale for all decisions and actions taken in response, referring to state and agency expectations and requirements. Critical incidents and emergencies should always be fully and immediately documented in the record. For example, an agency may have a standard procedure for responding to clients' threats of suicide. The worker should respond immediately to the threat, undertake a full assessment, take all necessary actions, and document the incident in the record. Here again, the worker should provide a rationale for decisions and actions taken, with specific reference to the agency's standards. Unless agency procedures call for a different approach, practitioners would be well-advised to report critical incidents to their supervisor or another manager and obtain approval for decisions and actions to be taken.

Emergencies often require quick decisions and actions by the worker and client. These situations may also necessitate a change in service goals or a delay in implementing plans and achieving outcomes. For example, a client is arrested for shoplifting while he is in a half-way house following drug treatment. Here, the worker would document the situation and actions taken in response as well as any related changes in service goals and plans. A day care provider loses her license, thereby affecting availability of child care for a client who is in a job training program. The record would document the emergency, the decisions and actions taken to respond to the client's changed circumstances, and its potential effect on the client's ability to meet program expectations and goals.

Critical incident and emergency reports should include, at minimum, the following information:

- the date, time, setting, and participants involved;
- a complete description of what occurred, with diverging views attributed to their sources;
- an appraisal of the situation, with criteria used;
- decisions and actions to be taken, including alternatives;
- plans for follow-up and continuing review; and
- regular updates until the urgent situation is resolved.

For example:

> "12/22/xx, 8:00 AM: Mrs. R phoned. She said that Mr. R had been drinking all night, was 'acting crazy,' and was threatening her and their daughter Mary (age seven) with his shotgun. I told her that I would call Officer James, who had responded to her call on 12/16/xx, and would come with her or another officer to her home. We arrived at about 8:40 AM. She and Mary were waiting in the garage. I drove Mrs. R and Mary to the Women's Shelter, as I had done on 12/16/xx. Officer James entered the house and, I later learned, arrested Mr. R again. Rhonda F (a worker at the shelter) and I will talk with Mrs. R today (for the third time) about getting an order of protection. We will also discuss moving to the VV (domestic violence) shelter and other safety options."

> "10/13/xx. Ramika's foster mother, Mrs. G, has asked that all three children in her care be removed from her home by next week. Mr. G died last weekend, and she can no longer care for the children on her own. Mrs. G and I discussed the situation with Ramika and the other children today. Ramika was very upset; she has been in Mrs. G's care for three years, since she was nine. I arranged transfer to the N foster home on 10/16. This home is four blocks from the G home, and in the same school district. Mrs. G agreed to stay in touch with Ramika, and have her visit her at home. I will meet with Ramika weekly during the transition, and monitor the situation at the N home and at school."

Periodic Service Reviews

In cases that last more than a few weeks, records may document periodic reviews of the client-need-situation and service activities at specific intervals. Some agencies have procedures that require cases that have been active for a specified length of time to undergo administrative or peer review. For example, an agency providing at-home services for the elderly may require reviews every six months to ensure that services meet clients' changing health needs and social circumstances. Some reviews are guided by public policy. For example, all individualized education programs (IEPs) for children with disabilities are to be reviewed annually. Sometimes periodic service reviews are initiated by the practitioner or supervisor seeking new perspectives on interesting or problematic cases. Some reviews may be initiated by quality assurance programs, such as in a hospital social service department, where a client group or type of disability may be selected as the subject for a periodic peer review. These reviews often involve not just the social worker and supervisor managing the case. Other practitioners and professionals, administrators, outside consultants, and the client and the client's representatives may also take part.

In contrast with interim notes, which document the worker's ongoing observations and assessments of the case, periodic service reviews often document more formal reexaminations of service decisions and actions, and incorporate additional ideas and perspectives. Such reviews may focus on the assessment of the client-need-situation and the approach and plan for services. Those involved in the process may refer to the client's record, most notably the purpose, plan, and progress of services as reflected in interim notes. Service reviews are documented in the record for the purpose of accountability. In general, their content should include:

- the date, names of participants, and subjects addressed;
- a review of service activities and movement;
- recommendations for changes in the assessment of the client-need-situation;
- the alternative service options considered;
- recommendations for changes in the purpose, goal, plan, or measure of service outcome;
- the level of consensus among participants; and
- any other recommendations or plans.

For example,

Six-Month Foster Care Review, Team Meeting

"*Name:* Tanya N, eight years, four months; Rinaldo N, six years,
    six months
Date: 5/12/xx
Present: Mrs. R, foster mother; Miss P, Tanya's teacher
        Mr. T, central office; Mr. L, school liaison for Rinaldo
        Mrs. A, foster care supervisor; Mrs. N, the children's
        grandmother
        Ms. M, caseworker
Absent: Miss N, Tanya's and Rinaldo's mother. Miss N was notified by mail and phone of the scheduled meeting. At the time of the meeting, Ms. M called her. Miss N said that she could not attend the meeting because she was sick.
Meeting Notes: Worker's review of the case was presented. Mrs. R confirmed that Tanya's mother has visited Tanya and Rinaldo only once. When visits are scheduled, Mrs. R says that Miss N calls her to say that she has been sick, so she cannot come. Tanya is doing well in school. Rinaldo is withdrawn and falling behind grade level. Mrs. R says that Tanya is doing well at home but Rinaldo has started wetting the bed again. Mrs. N says that her daughter drops by her house only when she needs money for rent or when she has no food. She doesn't seem to be interested in 'getting it together' or getting her kids back. Mrs. N spoke at some length about how she'd like to take the kids in but is too old and sick.

Plan: Current plan is to encourage visiting; goal is to return home by end of year. Since Miss N has visited Tanya and Rinaldo only once in the last three months, worker will visit Miss N at home and look into her health, transportation, situation at home, substance use, and job status. Scheduled review at nine months (8/14/xx), to reconsider goal and plan. Rinaldo to be evaluated by school psychologist and MD within the next two weeks."

CLOSING SUMMARY

Records should include a closing summary, which documents the reasons for terminating services and the status of the case at termination. Closing summaries are most valuable when they also include:

- a brief description and analysis of the client-need-situation from opening to termination;
- a brief review of the purpose, process, goals, and activities;
- an in-depth analysis of the process and outcomes of service and its impact on the client-need-situation;
- any referrals or plan for additional services; and
- follow-up.

The closing summary is prepared after services are terminated. As a result, many workers fail to see the value in recording it, and delay or give the closing summary scant attention. Workers wonder why they should spend time recording a document that will just go into the closed case files. It is not surprising, then, that closing summaries are often perfunctory, incomplete, or absent. However, closing summaries can actually be valuable. They often include important information that does not appear elsewhere in the record. They are especially useful when the case is later reopened or when the client seeks services elsewhere and authorizes a release of information to another provider. Preparing the closing summary can be beneficial to the practitioner in evaluating the case and his or her own practice. Moreover, undertaking an analysis of the service process and its impact on the client-need-situation demonstrates the worker's and agency's accountability. The closing summary can also be useful when services have been long-term and the record lengthy. Here it can be used to abstract salient information from the body of the record, making information about the client-need-situation and the service transaction easily accessible for internal or external review.

Reasons for Terminating Services

Generally, the reasons for ending services are briefly documented in the closing summary. Services may be terminated by plan or may end as the result of independent client action, decisions made by others in the service environment, or unforeseen circumstances that affect the client, the worker, or the service transaction. Services may be terminated because the client has met goals and completed plans, demonstrated independence and coping, realized the return of physical function or emotional stability, or accomplished other personal or environmental milestones. They may end because the client no longer wishes to receive services or has completed or been discharged from the program. Services may end because the client moves, loses interest in the process, becomes angry or disillusioned with the practitioner, or no longer has the resources to continue.

> "Services were terminated on 4/8/xx, following eight sessions. Mr. G's insurance would not authorize additional sessions at this time and he refused offers of referral elsewhere."

> "Ms. T failed to keep her appointments on 7/1, 7/11, and 7/30. We have been unable to reach her by phone or mail."

> "Services were terminated on 9/15/xx, when S was discharged from inpatient services to the Rehabilitation Center in Madison."

Status of Case at Termination

The closing summary should include a brief statement describing the client-need-situation at termination.

> "Mr. P has separated from his wife. He describes himself at various times as relieved, angry, sad. He is living with his brother, and has started looking for an apartment. His work situation has stabilized; he has resolved conflicts with his supervisor and has an acceptable attendance record. He reports taking his depression medication, but continues to drink, heavily at times. He does not recognize his alcohol problem, and refuses to attend AA meetings."

Review of Client-Need-Situation from Opening to Closing

It is useful to include a brief review of the client-need-situation over time in the closing summary. This is especially important when the client-need-situation has undergone many changes during the process of service.

> "Mr. E was referred for services by his physician, Dr. N, who is treating him for colon cancer. Mrs. E, his wife of 42 years, died last year. They had no children, and his only living relative is a nephew who lives in another state. He has few social connections, is not affiliated with any church or service group. After some persuasion, Mr. E agreed to go to a nursing facility following surgery, so that he can receive care and learn to care for the colostomy. He then plans to return to his home."

Review of Service Purpose, Process, Goals, and Activities

A brief review of service decisions and actions can be very valuable, particularly when services have been lengthy or complicated.

> "Services were authorized for six sessions of counseling in conjunction with Mr. P's medical treatment for depression. We agreed to concentrate on three areas: difficulties in his marriage, prob-

lems at work, and drinking. I met weekly for counseling sessions with Mr. P; Mrs. P attended the third session. Mr. and Mrs. P then saw Rev. K-K (Mrs. P's minister) for marital counseling. At the time of termination, Mr. and Mrs. P had separated, and were no longer receiving marital counseling. Mr. P had made substantial progress in remedying problems at work, meeting with his supervisor and improving his attendance record. He continues to deny that he has a drinking problem, however, and refuses to attend AA meetings. Mrs. P was referred to Al-Anon."

"T called the crisis line on 1/12/xx, saying that she was 'at the end of her rope.' She came for an interview on 1/13 and was immediately accepted for individual, group, and drug therapy. She has attended one individual and one group session per week through 4/18, when individual sessions were terminated. She continued with group sessions until 6/22 when the group discontinued meeting for the summer."

"Individual therapy focused on identity issues, self-destructive and suicidal behavior, and making decisions about what she will do when she graduates. She attributes her depression to being 'dumped' by her girlfriend, but it appears to be more pervasive, linked to uncertainty about the future and failed relationships in the past. She was able to understand the relationship between her depression, her parents' divorce, her 'coming out,' and her ambivalence about relationships.

In group therapy, she developed new friendships inside the group, and learned to anticipate and manage events (like B coming by the apartment to pick up her things) that might make her anxious, angry, self-destructive, or depressed. The group also confronted her about bingeing and purging, alcohol dependency, and other self-destructive behavior."

Evaluation of the Outcomes and Impact of Services

Evaluating the outcomes of service and its impact on the client-need-situation is the most important component of the closing summary. Practitioners and clients who have carefully monitored movement toward achieving goals and realizing plans can review and analyze this as well as other information to assess whether and to what degree services have affected crucial issues in the client-need-situation.

"T has experienced a gradual lifting of depression, aided by individual, drug, and group therapy. This is reflected in her own statements, in her appearance, and on psychological tests. She has also dealt with ongoing issues of social isolation and identity. In the fall, she plans to use the employment center to help her find a job. She says that she feels much stronger now, but fears that things will 'fall apart' over the summer. Several serious issues remain, including social isolation, sexual identity, relationships with peers and family, the eating disorder, alcohol dependence, and suicidal ideation."

"Ms. E has attended 4 of 7 parent education classes, and did not miss a single supervised visit with Akello. She has taken out an order of protection against V, who may still be in the picture. Now that Akello is back at home, Ms. E has been cooperative with the early childhood development specialist and responsive to suggestions for improving nutrition and discipline. The situation looks stable, but I am concerned about V coming back when the case is closed."

Referrals or Other Planned Activities

Regardless of the means or reasons for terminating services, social workers have an ethical obligation not to abandon their clients (NASW, 1999). When services are terminated by plan, the practitioner should assist the client in ending the relationship, work with the client to sustain goals and plans, and ensure that the client knows how and where to seek additional services immediately or in the future. When services are terminated prematurely, practitioners should make special efforts to reach out to clients with this information. One way to assist the client in the process of termination is to plan follow-up contacts. Follow-up contacts are reassuring to the client, and may surface ongoing or new problems that arise after termination. Plans for referrals, follow-up contacts, and other activities on behalf of the client should be documented in the record.

"T and I will have weekly phone conversations over the summer. She has agreed to call me or the hotline if she begins having suicidal thoughts. She says she'd like to return to group in the fall (although I'm not sure we'll have enough people). If not, I will meet with her to find individual or group therapy."

"At our final meeting, I told Ms. E I was worried that V would come back once the agency closed the case. She said she'd call the police if he did. I told her she could call me or the agency. I doubt that she will call, though, because she's afraid of losing Akello again."

"I told Mr. P that we still had a lot of work to do, and was sorry that we would not be continuing. I hoped he would reconsider his decision to terminate following his insurance company's decision not to authorize additional sessions. I referred him to the Lynch Mental Health Center, and suggested again that he go to AA just to see what it is like. He continues to see his physician for treatment of depression, but no longer goes with Mrs. P to see Rev. K-K for marital counseling."

Follow-Up

Some practitioners and agencies routinely follow-up on closed cases via mail, e-mail, or phone calls. Often these follow-up contacts are conducted by agency personnel who have not been involved in service delivery; they are used to assess client satisfaction and agency and practitioner performance. Generally, these follow-up contacts are not documented in client records.

When undertaken by the practitioner or the client, follow-up contacts via phone calls or e-mail communications can be an important adjunct to the service process. They can support clients' continuing efforts to maintain and extend what they have achieved. They can also assist the practitioner in gauging the long-term impact of services. Moreover, during direct contacts between the practitioner and the client, practitioners may identify new or continuing problems or needs. They may find that service plans have unraveled, gains have diminished, or the client-need-situation has changed in unanticipated ways. Such contacts allow the practitioner to intervene before more serious problems surface. The practitioner can suggest reopening services or refer the client for assistance elsewhere.

Documentation of follow-up contacts between the client, practitioner, and agency are used in:

- demonstrating the practitioner's ethical commitment to clients;
- demonstrating the practitioner's and agency's accountability;
- evaluating the outcome of service plans and goals;
- evaluating the impact of services on the client-need-situation; and
- supporting continuity of service, should the client need additional services in the agency or elsewhere.

Follow-up reports should contain information about who initiated the contact, the current status of the client-need-situation, the status of plans or goals that were the focus of services, any recommendations for further service, and any action taken with or on behalf of the client.

Often, follow-up contacts are initiated by the practitioner:

> "Three-month follow-up, 6/15/xx: I called Mrs. R today, three months after Mrs. P's discharge from the hospital to her home. Mrs. R reported that she was unable to manage her mother at home, even with home health care. She moved Mrs. P to Apple Valley Convalescent Home last month."

Sometimes follow-up contacts are initiated by the client. Under these circumstances, the worker must assess whether the client wishes only a brief contact or is seeking an ongoing relationship or additional services.

> "4/25/xx: Ms. J agreed to call if she heard from L. She called to say that L had been released from jail, and had come to the house to see Maria. He said he would come back to see her any time he

wanted, and that Ms. J could not stop him. Ms. J is moving into the shelter this afternoon; will seek protective order. Case reopened."

WHAT SHOULD BE EXCLUDED FROM RECORDS

This chapter has suggested guidelines for selecting information for the record. The decision about what information to include should be guided by several criteria. First, information should be selected to demonstrate accountability and support practice. Second, in the interest of efficiency and to protect client privacy, information in the record should be limited to what is needed to meet the standards of accountability and support practice. Third, records that are "service-centered" document the bases, substance, and impact of services, and therefore fulfill the competing demands of accountability, supporting practice, efficiency, and privacy.

Some materials should not be included in social work records. Information that is interesting but not directly pertinent to the purpose of service should be omitted. Social work records are now available to a wide audience, potentially undermining client privacy. In addition, information in records cannot always be corrected, amended, or erased once they have been entered into computerized systems or databases. For these reasons, the practitioner's hunches, speculations, gut reactions, and unsupported hypotheses, as well as other information that is inconclusive and might be misconstrued, should be omitted. Only those assessments and appraisals in which the worker has some confidence, and which form the basis for practice decisions and actions, should be documented. Practitioners should also avoid judgmental language and derogatory characterizations of clients or others. Disparaging the client or others not only reflects poorly on the worker, it may undermine important professional relationships if the information becomes known to the client or is disseminated to other interested parties.

Process records, and other records that are created specifically to support workers' or students' professional development, should not be filed in the client's record. This information is more appropriately filed in personnel records or field instruction student records. Detailed information about the service process should also be omitted, because documenting it is inefficient and may unnecessarily undermine client privacy. Practitioners' personal notes, for example, things they jot down during sessions with clients and then use as memory aids when they record, should also be kept separate from the official agency record. If such notes are placed in the agency record, they become part of the client's permanent file, and are subject to access and disclosure. Practitioners should also be aware that even what they consider to be "personal notes," which they do not file in the official record, may still be subject to subpoena and used in court proceedings (Polowy & Gorenberg, 1997; Reamer, 2005). These subjects are considered in detail in chapter 9.

Chapters 3, 4, and 5 describe and provide examples of various record-keeping structures used by social workers in agency practice, private practice, and education for practice. These chapters also show how the structure influences the record's contents. The adoption of a particular form or format, then, can determine not just how information is presented, but also what information appears in the record.

CHAPTER 3

RECORDS USED IN SOCIAL WORK EDUCATION

This chapter describes, evaluates, and presents examples of three recording structures that may be used in educating students for social work practice. It concludes with an analysis of the current status of education for practice and recording, with suggestions for improvement.

The first and most frequently used approach to teaching practice through recordkeeping is the process record. This approach has a long history in social work, dating back to the beginning of the twentieth century. Social workers originally produced process recordings to document the social conditions under which their clients lived (Burgess, 1928). However, after Mary Richmond (1917) used process records in her study of social casework, process recording became an important method of recording and source of information about clients, practice, and practitioners. Today, process records are prepared and used principally to facilitate student learning in the field.

The second recordkeeping structure presented here is the Teaching/Learning (T/L) record, developed by Kagle in 1982, and published in the first edition of *Social Work Records* (Kagle, 1984b). Using narrative summary rather than process form, the T/L record incorporates far more description of the service transaction and of the process of decision making than does a typical agency record. The T/L record is intended to facilitate the development of interpersonal and cognitive practice skills along with summary recording skills.

The third recordkeeping structure presented in this chapter is Essential Recording, also developed by Kagle, and published in the second edition of *Social Work Records* (Kagle, 1996) and elsewhere (Kagle, 1991). Essential Recording is actually a combination of three or four recording structures used in sequence. In Essential Recording, students audiotape or videotape sessions with clients, providing student and supervisor with direct access to what happened in the service transaction. Using the tapes themselves or transcripts made from the tapes, students then prepare summaries of each session. Finally, students use their session summaries as a resource when they prepare narrative reports for the official agency record. This approach is called *Essential* Recording because it teaches the student to distill the *essence* of the client-need-situation and the service transaction for the record. Essential Recording aids the student in developing summary recording skills, and also helps the student produce records that are useful in supervision. Tapes, transcripts, session summaries, and narrative reports are all available for review and use in supervision. Thus, Essential Recording aids the student in developing cognitive and interpersonal practice skills as well as summary recording skills (Kagle, 1991).

As a general rule, records used to teach students practice and recording should not become part of the client's official record. Records used to teach practice and recording, like other records, are not given any special legal protections, and are therefore subject to subpoena. In the interest of client privacy, records prepared for educational purposes should not be retained by the agency or practitioner. They should be destroyed as soon as they have been reviewed and evaluated. During the brief period while they are in use, they should be kept in the social work student's or field instructor's files. If they were stored in the client's file, they would become part of the official record and would be subject to the same regulations as other components of the record.

Even if client privacy were not an overriding issue, records used in educating students about practice and recording are not suitable for use as agency records. There are several reasons for this. Records produced by students in the early stages of their professional development may include unintentional distortions of fact or premature judgments. They may omit or give only cursory attention to crucial information or alternative perspectives. Were such material to become part of the client's record, it might be damaging to the client, the student, the service relationship, or the organization. Misleading information could be disseminated within or outside the organization, to the client's detriment. Other professionals might use such information to make poor decisions and, unless the information is corrected, it could continue to affect practice decisions years later. Clients who read the record or who are informed of its contents could react negatively, losing faith in the worker, terminating services, or even taking action against the organization. These records might also undermine others' view of the student's competency and the social work program's level of professionalism. Even when records prepared primarily for educational purposes are accurate and fair, they generally focus on the student's actions and views rather than on information needed for accountability. As a result, important information about the client-need-situation and service goals, plans, and outcomes may be missing or difficult to find.

Process recordings and other records that focus primarily on the development of practice skills are quite different from the records social work students will be expected to produce as entry-level practitioners. Unfortunately, many agencies have found that their professionally educated staff have not been adequately prepared for this task. It is important, then, to ensure that social work students have experience preparing agency records, especially summary reports, during their field practicum. The field instructor or supervisor can help the student develop her or his recording skills and ensure that the student's recording meets agency standards by reviewing and providing feedback on drafts, signing off on all documentation before it becomes part of the client's record.

PROCESS RECORDING

A process record is an attempt by the practitioner to reconstruct, as accurately as possible, what transpired in an interview or meeting between worker and client. It usually takes the form of a script, and includes what the worker and client did and said. The process record has had an important place in the history of social work. First used in studying the client and the situation when an important purpose for practice was social investigation, the use of the process record has changed with the development of the profession. In earlier times, social workers documented everything they could remember about what their clients said and did, about what they themselves said and did, and about what they observed, believed, and surmised. By the time Hamilton (1936) wrote *Social Case Recording,* process recording was used not just for the purpose of social study but, more importantly, for "indicating the manner in which one person appears to relate himself to another person during the therapeutic experience" (p. 92). The focus of interest had broadened from the client-need-situation to the service transaction as well. Although the record that Hamilton described contained a great deal of information about the process of service, not all information about the process of service was recorded in process form. Workers no longer reproduced everything they could remember about the transaction. Rather, they selected specific information to process-record because of its importance in characterizing and individualizing the client, and then summarized the rest. Over time, the amount of information workers "processed" decreased and the amount they summarized increased. Today, process recording is seldom used in day-to-day practice. Records still contain information about the process of service, but it is likely to appear in summary rather than in process form.

The process record is still widely used in social work education. Students may process-record all or portions of their interviews or meetings with clients. Preparation, documentation, and review all contribute to the learning experience. Preparation for process recording requires that students concentrate on what clients say and how they behave throughout the encounter. Students must also remember their own statements, feelings, and behaviors, and how they responded to the client. Documentation itself causes the student to review the sequence of events and to reexperience the service transaction. Finally, reviewing the written record allows students to develop a better understanding of the client-need-situation, the service encounter, and their own performance.

The process record may be used in field instruction to develop students' assessment skills, self-awareness, knowledge of individual and group dynamics, and use of self in the service encounter. Indeed, a student's first experience in evaluating her or his own practice may be the act of creating, reviewing, and reflecting on the contents of a process record. The focus is twofold: understanding the client-need-situation and developing the student's knowledge and skills. The student creates a process record and, in some cases, a written analysis of what transpired. The field instructor then responds, in person or in writing.

Rather than relying on the process record alone, many students and field instructors now supplement process records with special formats for transcribing and responding to brief or extensive verbatim accounts of interactions with clients. Wilson (1980) recommended that process materials be transcribed in the center of the page, leaving wide margins to the left and right for the student's "gut reactions" and field instructor's comments. A number of authors have outlined additional recording structures for use in conjunction with process recording; their purpose is to encourage students to reflect on specific elements of the service process. These include, for example, analyzing their role in the interaction (Urbanowski & Dwyer, 1988) and identifying intervention skills used (Fox & Gutheil, 2000). Students working with groups would attend to group processes and developmental stages (Cohen & Garrett, 1995). Field instructors, too, could benefit from these and other formats that focus their attention on general or specific student learning objectives. For example, Neuman and Friedman (1997) suggest using a standard framework, such as Matarazzo's checklist, to review process recordings for focus, role, and communication errors. Some authors argue that process records can also be used to encourage a scientific approach to practice (Fox & Gutheil, 2000).

Process recording is far too time-consuming to be cost-effective for practitioners in agency-based or private practice. It is most often used in students' field work, where more time may be available. Even when time is available, process recording is very labor intensive, for the student and the field instructor, and sometimes for clerical staff, and may not be a good use of resources. There are other major limitations of process recording as well. Process records are not accurate accounts. As Timms (1972, appendix) demonstrated, a process record is not a verbatim report but a selective reconstruction of the service encounter. Thus, if a student and field instructor wished to study the actual service process, they would gain a more accurate picture of what took place if they used audiotapes or videotapes. Taping reproduces the interview and allows the student to observe him- or herself. Although taping may seem invasive and may initially make the student and client self-conscious, it can be introduced naturally into most service encounters as a means of improving the quality of service. Moreover, process recording does not prepare students with the summary recording skills they will use in practice. In fact, practitioners trained in process recording often have difficulty making the transition to summary recording, and may need considerable supervisory support. Therefore, whenever possible, a student's experience in the field should not be limited to the use of process recording, but should include some practice preparing summaries and other reports. Exhibits 3.1 and 3.2 present excerpts from student process records.

**Exhibit 3.1   Excerpt from a Student Process Record:
Mental Health Crisis Line**

		Worker Comments
Worker:	Crisis Line; Mary speaking.	
Client:	Hello. *[pause]* Is this the place . . . you call for help if you are in trouble?	
Worker:	Yes it is. Can I help you?	
Client:	Well, I don't know. *[pause]*	*I was really nervous.*
Worker:	We try to help everyone who calls. Nothing that's bothering you is too big or too small.	*I sound like I'm in sales, not social work.*
Client:	You sound kind of young. Are you?	*This upset me—did I handle it right?*
Worker:	Yes, I am. Does that matter?	
Client:	I guess not. *[pause]* I do have a problem . . . and I really don't know where else to turn. *[pause]*	*Jumped in too fast.*
Worker:	That is what we are here for.	
Client:	Yeah.	
Worker:	Sometimes it's hard to start. Just tell me what you are feeling right now.	*This is about the best thing I did.*
Client:	Well . . . I am feeling lost . . . tired . . . alone.	
Worker:	Yes?	
Client:	You see, I really have no one any more.	*I could have asked her about herself.*
Worker:	You seem to feel very lonely right now.	
Client:	Yeah. *[pause]* I have been crying a lot tonight. Just watching TV and crying. I was watching this really sad show, and I started feeling like there is nothing to live for.	
Worker:	You started to cry when you were watching a sad show.	
Client:	Yeah. It was about a family that had all kinds of trouble but stuck together. The father lost his job. Then the mother got cancer. The father took care of the kids while the mother was in the hospital. She was real bitter but then she realized how lucky she was . . . and they all lived happily ever after.	

(continued)

Worker: Has anything like that happened to you?	*Pretty good.*
Client: No. That's why I was crying. Because they all loved each other . . . and I'm alone.	
Worker: You're alone and lonely. Are there any other problems you're having right now?	*I really don't seem to want to hear how lonely she is!*
Client: A lot of other problems. Like my job. And like my health. I feel sick all the time.	
Worker: Could you tell me some of your symptoms?	*Am I trying to be a doctor?*
Client: I feel tired all the time. Can't get out of bed. I've been late to work, missing work.	
Worker: So feeling sick and staying home is affecting your job. But you called because you thought we could help you with something. Can you tell me a little bit more about what made you decide to call?	*I am willing to talk about her job, her sickness, but not her loneliness.*
Client: It's how lonely I feel. I thought that if I just had someone to talk to I wouldn't feel so lonely right now.	*She brings up her loneliness again, but I change the subject again.*
Worker: And we've talked a little, but I really don't know very much about you.	
Client: There's not very much to tell. I'm divorced, 45 years old. I work at N *[department store].* My kids are grown; my folks are dead. And I come home at night to an empty house.	
Worker: Sometimes talking to someone else helps.	
Client: Yes, it does. Talking to you has made me feel less lonely.	*She is indicating some interest.*
Worker: And we can talk a little more. But I wonder if you have ever thought about talking about your problems with a counselor?	
Client: Well, when I was getting a divorce, I saw a counselor. But the marriage was already a lost cause.	
Worker: Uh-huh.	
Client: Yeah. I have thought about going to a counselor, and I thought about it before I called tonight.	
Worker: Have you thought about getting in touch with that counselor again?	
Client: It was in another city.	

Worker:	I could refer you to a counseling agency here.	
Client:	You could?	
Worker:	Yes. In fact, if you give me your name and phone number, I could have an intake worker from the agency call you and make an appointment.	*But I am trying too hard.*
Client:	I don't know.	
Worker:	No obligation, of course. You could talk about anything: your job, your health, your loneliness.	*Selling again!*
Client:	Uh-huh. Well, I'm not sure.	
Worker:	Or I could give you the name of the agency, and you could call them.	*I was scared that I'd lose her—and felt anxious through the rest of the interview.*
Client:	I suppose I could give you my name and you could have them call. I wouldn't want them to call me at work, though.	
Worker:	No. You could tell me when they should contact you at home.	
Client:	Well, I guess that would be okay. So long as no one at work knew. Is this going to cost a lot of money?	
Worker:	Well, I can't tell you exactly how much, but the agency has different programs and different fees for different clients. And they have a sliding scale.	*Unclear.*
Client:	What does that mean?	
Worker:	The fee is set by how much you can afford to pay.	
Client:	That sounds okay.	
Worker:	Then I'll take your name and number. And when you want to have the agency call. *[takes information]* I'm glad you are willing to consider counseling.	*Is she committed or am I?*
Client:	Just thinking about it.	
Worker:	I know.	
Client:	Well, thanks. It helped. Goodbye.	
Worker:	Goodbye, Mrs. T.	

Exhibit 3.2   Excerpt from a Student Process Record:
Developmental Disabilities, Parents' Group

Meeting Number 11

Date: 11/11

Members present: Mrs. B, Mr. and Mrs. W, Mr. and Mrs. Z, Mrs. F, Mrs. C

Goals for the meeting: Discuss use of community resources and the need for
additional resources to meet the needs of families caring for children with
developmental disabilities.

I opened the meeting by describing our planned agenda. We would discuss
what kinds of community services each family uses in caring for their develop-
mentally disabled children and also what kinds of needs they had that could be
met by additional services. What did they use and what did they need? Mrs. W
said that she was sorry more of the parents were not at the meeting, since this was
a very important subject. Mr. W nodded; he said that whenever the meeting was
planned around a "serious matter" rather than a party or a sports activity, most of
the parents did not show up. (The agenda for the meeting had been proposed by
the Ws.) Mrs. Z and Mrs. C nodded in agreement, and Mrs. C said that the regular members (those attending tonight) are the only ones who seem to see the group
as more than a place to go in the evening. The discussion of the "others" (that is,
those parents who are not part of this core group) continued for several minutes.

I said that I had sent a letter to each parent, to inform them of the meeting
and the planned agenda. I wondered if anyone had any suggestions about how
to encourage other parents to attend meetings. Mrs. W said that all she could
suggest was to have meetings where there was a party or a baseball game rather
than meetings about important things. Mrs. B said that she could understand
why some of the "others" came if it was a social event . . . the meeting was
"fun" and gave them something to do in the evening. Not everyone enjoys sitting around and talking about their kids. (They come to the meeting to get away
from them.) Mr. W said that he thought the other parents should take some
responsibility and should see this group as a way of making life better for the
kids, rather than just as a social club. The group then discussed the purpose of
the group—social club or helping the kids. Mrs. B said that different people had
different reasons for coming to the meetings; she asked if that was all right. The
Ws continued the theme of "responsibility, not fun."

Mr. W said, as he had said many times before, that he thought the group
should be like the Jaycees, with formal meetings, elected officers, and so forth.
Mrs. B, looking very disgusted, said that his attitude might be a reason why parents didn't come to the discussion meetings. Mr. W responded by citing their
lack of responsibility for the kids.

I said that what we had been discussing was very important, but that it was
also important to get to the agenda for the meeting. Could we discuss participation and the purpose of the group again at the next meeting and move on to community resources? There was general agreement that we should move on to the
agenda, but disagreement on how to handle the issues of attendance and purpose.

I said that the meeting next month was a holiday party, but that the January
meeting had not yet been planned. Since the January meeting would mark the
beginning of the second year of the group, could we use that meeting to talk

about the past year and about plans for the future? This would give everyone an opportunity to discuss the purpose of the group as well as the agendas for future meetings. There was some discussion of this suggestion. The Ws thought the suggestion was good, but that the other parents either would not show up or would suggest parties and games. Mrs. B thought we should take a vote on the January agenda, which passed unanimously.

The meeting was more than half over by the time we got to the issue of resources. Mrs. F, who had been restive through the earlier discussion, asked if we could just move on to the resources that were needed rather than beginning with what resources were being used. Without waiting for approval from the group (meaning approval from Mr. and Mrs. W), she went on to say that what she really needed was a bodyguard for her son, a housekeeper for herself, a taxi service to and from the doctor, and a gun to rob a bank so she could pay for all of the things she needed. Everyone laughed, but she said this wasn't a joke. Her son, Manuel, now 12 and quite large for his age, was getting into fights in the neighborhood while walking home from the bus. She used to meet him at the bus, but this year she had let him walk home alone. He is old enough, and the teacher thought it would be good for him. But he is getting into fights because the kids call him names, and he "goes crazy." He needs to learn how to take care of himself, but the neighborhood kids won't leave him alone. She went on to describe many problems that she was facing at this time.

Mrs. Z said that she also had many problems, not big ones that required a new program, but many small ones that added up.

I suggested that we make a list of all the small and large problems each family was facing, and that maybe we could come up with some common themes. This might help us in trying to find some solutions. Over Mrs. W's opposition, the group spent the rest of the meeting listing problems. These will be discussed at a future meeting. I also made an appointment to meet with Mrs. F about her problems with Manuel.

Summary

Primary Function: Social work education.

Current Usage: Field instruction.

Organizing Rationale: The worker records as completely as possible all or selected portions of the service encounter. The record includes client statements and actions as well as worker statements, actions, and feelings. The record may resemble the script of a play or it may be organized into paragraphs, using "I said" and "(client's name) said." It is useful to have the record transcribed, leaving a wide margin for comments by the worker and the supervisor.

Strengths: The practitioner learns to remember the service transaction in detail. The record is a useful learning tool.

Limitations: It is time-consuming and costly.

It does not teach recording skills needed for agency practice.

It is selective and does not replicate the actual worker-client interaction.

It risks client privacy.

The Teaching/Learning (T/L) Record

The Teaching/Learning Record was developed by Kagle in 1982 to meet the special learning needs of social work students in field agencies, and to respond to the limitations of process recording in preparing students for agency-based recordkeeping. The T/L record is intended to assist in the teaching and learning of cognitive and interpersonal practice skills and of narrative summary recording skills. The student prepares an extensive record of the service transaction, one that incorporates far more information about the process of service than is included in most agency records. The record can then serve as the basis for the development of practice skills. In preparing and reviewing the record, the student has the opportunity to describe and assess the client-need-situation, the service transaction, and his or her own practice skills. At the same time, the record provides the field instructor with a "window" into the service process and into the student's professional development. This information allows the field instructor to collaborate with the student in making decisions about service and to assess and facilitate the student's progress in knowledge and skill development.

Although the T/L record, shown in exhibit 3.3, is more extensive than the records kept in most social service agencies, it is prepared in the summary style most agencies use in records and reports. As a result, students have the opportunity to practice the recording skills they will use as practitioners. The acquisition of these writing skills is critical to professional development; yet, although social workers are expected to possess these skills, their development is often neglected. Today, many practitioners find that writing is their most difficult task. Therefore, developing summary recording skills with the intensive supervision offered in the field can help to prepare students with the recording and writing skills they will need in a variety of practice roles. Exhibit 3.4 presents excerpts from a T/L record.

Summary

Primary Function: Social work education.

Current Usage: Field instruction; field seminar.

Organizing Rationale: The student records in narrative summary style following the outline provided (left column). Some teaching/learning issues, relevant for discussion in field supervision or in the field seminar, are also included (right column).

Strength: The student records sufficient information about the process to facilitate the teaching and learning of interpersonal and cognitive practice skills. The student uses the narrative summary style used in many agency records and reports.

Limitations: Time-consuming and costly. It is also selective and does not actually reproduce the service transaction. To study process, the student and instructor should use videotapes or audiotapes.

Exhibit 3.3   The Teaching/Learning Record

Content of the Record	Teaching/Learning Issues

Initiating Service

A. Reason for service request, referral, or offer. Describe the circumstances as well as the people and organizations that brought the client and worker together.

How do the methods of case finding influence the client and the worker?

B. Description of relevant client-situation factors. Describe the client. Be sure to include important:

- Behaviors
- Feelings
- Values, preferences
- Strengths
- Unmet needs

Who is the client? What is a social history? What should it include?

   The family and natural social network: Identify and describe those in the client's interpersonal environment who are interested parties. What are their expectations of the client, of service? Identify people or groups who are potential resources or barriers (e.g., work, neighbors).

How do we identify how others feel? Is culture or ethnicity a factor in this case?

   The physical environment: Identify and describe any aspect of the environment that acts as a resource or barrier (e.g., distance from public transportation).

Does the physical environment have a bearing on this case?

   Formal social organizations: Identify and describe current and past relationships with social organizations (for example, school, public aid) that bear upon the current situation. Identify agency or public policies that may influence the client-situation.

Can organizations be a barrier and a resource?

C. Describe the process of data collection, including where and from whom the information was obtained. Characterize each interview by answering the following questions in summary form:

- How did the interview begin? Was the purpose of the interview made explicit? Who did most of the talking?

How did you feel before, during, and after the interview? What were your assumptions about the client? How did you test them out? How did you show warmth? empathy? genuineness? What did the client get from the interview? What information is lacking, and how can you find it out?

(continued)

Content of the Record	Teaching/Learning Issues
• What techniques were used to encourage the source to talk?	
• What techniques were used to show interest, acceptance, and so forth?	
• What emotions did the source show?	
• What information did the worker share? What decisions or plans for the future were made? How did the interview end?	
• What were the strengths and weaknesses of the interview?	
D. Assess the current client-situation by answering the following questions in summary form:	How do we know what is important? How do we know what is not important? How does the setting influence the focus? How do you organize a summary?
• What are the client's most salient needs? problems? strengths? preferences?	
• What are the relevant existing resources in the natural social and physical environment?	
• What are the relevant existing barriers?	
• What are the relevant current relationships with social organizations?	
E. Explore the range of interventions, services, and resources. List:	How do you find needed resources? What do you need to know about them (e.g., eligibility)?
• Problems and needs	
• Relevant interventions, services, and resources	

Establishing Goals (and Contract)

A. Describe the process of formulating and planning goals by answering the following questions in summary form:	How does this phase of the process differ from data collection? How do worker and client values influence goals and plans? How does agency policy influence goals and plans? How important is client motivation? Will referrals be followed up? What are the benefits?
• How did the interview begin?	
• Was the purpose of the interview made explicit? How was the range of possible goals and services presented?	
• What were the client's views and preferences? How were the worker's and the agency's views presented? What goals were selected?	

- To what extent is the client committed to the goals (give examples of statements and behaviors)?
- What plans were made?
- What interventions, services, and resources are involved?
- What are the client's responsibilities? How were these responsibilities explained?

What action will be taken? Were responsibilities appropriately distributed?

- What are the worker's responsibilities?
- How did the interview end?
- What were the strengths and weaknesses of the interview?

B. Briefly describe the contract. Describe and give a rationale for any decisions made with or on behalf of the client.

What is a contract?

C. Describe any barriers to implementing plans or reaching goals. How can barriers be minimized?

Interim Notes

A. Interviews with clients:

1. Describe the interview by answering the questions under Initiating Service, part C, in summary form.

How has the relationship changed through time?

2. Describe worker and client activities since the last report.

3. Describe any changes in the client-situation or other people or environments that demonstrate:

Compare this phase with earlier phases of the process. What factors in the client-situation or the service environment are influencing goals and plans?

   - Movement toward goals
   - Barriers
   - New problems and/or needs

4. Describe and give a rationale for any decisions made with or on behalf of the client.

5. Briefly describe any changes in goals or plans.

B. Interviews with other resource persons:

1. Identify the resource person and the setting of the interview.

2. Describe the purpose of the interview.

What is privacy? Confidentiality? How do these values influence our contacts with clients and others? Are other professionals or organizations influencing service?

(continued)

Content of the Record	Teaching/Learning Issues
3. Describe the content of the interview by answering the following questions in summary form: • What information was learned? • What information was shared (include the signed release of information in file)? 4. What was accomplished regarding goals and plans?	
Terminating or Transferring Service A. Briefly review the process of service by answering the following questions in summary form: • What was the client-situation at the time service was initiated? • What were the service goals and plans? What interventions, services, and resources were involved? • What did service accomplish? • What is the current client-situation?	Why review the service process? What were the intended or unintended benefits of service? Compare this phase with other phases in the process.
B. Describe the reasons for termination or transfer.	How did you feel during the last interview?

Exhibit 3.4 Excerpts from a Teaching/Learning Record: Shelter for Runaway Youth, Casework Services

Reason for Service Request: Nancy was picked up by the police in D, 40 miles from here. She had hitchhiked there and was walking along the highway, trying to get another ride at about 12:30 AM on Saturday, when the state highway patrol spotted her. She said that she did not want to go home, so she was brought back to the shelter. Her mother was notified at about 7:30 AM that she was in residence here. Mrs. R did not know that Nancy was gone.

Description of the Client-Situation: Nancy R is a physically mature 14-year-old ninth-grade student. Nancy lives with her mother, two younger brothers, and her mother's boyfriend in a small house near the highway. Nancy was truant from school three days last week. Her grades were average (Cs) until this year, when she has been absent from classes frequently. She now is failing most of her classes.

Nancy is very attractive and pays a great deal of attention to her appearance (wears lots of makeup, fusses with her hair). She seems very bored and uninterested when she talks with me about school or her family situation. When she is with the other kids in the shelter, she is talkative and involved. When I ask her about her feelings, plans, and so forth, she says she doesn't know. When asked to describe school, she says it is boring and like a prison. When asked to describe her family, she says that everything was fine until Bill (her mother's boyfriend) moved in. He orders her around, orders everyone around. She says that she will not go back to her mother's house unless Bill goes; when asked where she would like to go, she says that she wants to stay at the shelter.

Mrs. R appears to be a very tired woman. She said that Nancy has been fighting with her "stepfather." Bill says that Nancy needs discipline, so he has been disciplining her. Nancy never used to help around the house or keep regular hours. Bill makes her help out and be in by a certain hour. Nancy does not like this; last week Nancy and Bill had a screaming fight that turned into a hitting fight. After the fight, Nancy left the house. Mrs. R thought that she had gone to stay with Lana, which is where she had stayed other times. That was why Mrs. R did not know that Nancy was missing when she was picked up in D; she thought that Nancy was at Lana's. Mrs. R works the evening shift as a nurse's aid at S Hospital. Nancy used to baby sit the younger children while Mrs. R was at work. Now Bill, who works days, is home while Mrs. R works, and most of the fights between Bill and Nancy seem to happen then. Mrs. R says that Bill is sorry he hit Nancy, but he says that she tore his shirt and that made him real mad. Mrs. R wants Nancy to come home but says that she will have to get along with Bill better.

Nancy's school counselor said that Nancy's school behavior was not really a problem until this year. Many students seem to have a "bad year" during junior high or high school, a year when their grades go down. The counselor did not notice anything unusual until a few weeks ago, when Nancy began to skip classes. She was called in to the counselor's office and told that a special report on her attendance would be sent to the counselor each day. Since that time, Nancy has been attending classes, although she has been absent from school six days in the past month.

No other agencies are active with the family. The police filed a report, which means that if Nancy runs away again the case will have to go before the juvenile court. She can stay in the shelter for one week only; at the end of the week, other plans must be made. . . .

Interview with Nancy (Day 4): I had left a note on her door asking Nancy to come to my office after she returned from school. (This was her first day back at school.) My purpose for the interview was to discuss with Nancy the family interview that was planned for that evening.

We began by talking about what had happened when she went back to school. She said that all the kids seemed to know that she had run away and was staying at the shelter. She described at length many encounters she had had with kids at school that day. In general, it appears that she is getting a great deal of attention from other students about her "adventure." She said that she told Lana (her best friend) that she had a "shrink" (me!) and that she might not have to go home.

This is when I introduced the subject of the family interview. She seemed surprised about it, although I had spoken to her about it several times before. I explained again about the time limits, and that some arrangements would have to be made by the weekend (three more days). I explained that her mother would take the evening off to be home for the interview. She asked if Bill would

(continued)

be there. (I did not handle this part well.) I told her that I thought that it would be important to have him there, since he was living with her family. Nancy said that she would not go if he were there, that he was not her father. I then went into a long explanation about how he was willing to work on the problem and about how her mother felt it was important that she and Bill work things out.

Weaknesses: I realize now that I did most of the talking in this interview. Nancy really had no chance to tell her side of the story. Nancy went to the family interview without realizing that I would be there to support her in expressing her feelings. It would not surprise me if she views me as just another person who is trying to get her to do things that she does not want to do, when my real purpose is to support her and to be her advocate. In looking back over what occurred in the interview, it seems that what was important to her about school (her friends' reactions) was not what was important to me (the family interview, her schoolwork). Also, her attitude gets to me.

Strengths: Not many. I am in touch with how exasperating Nancy can be. I know that she gets prestige from being a runaway. The time factor that I find so important does not seem to be important at all to her. . . .

Client Needs and Problems	Services, Resources, and Interventions
1. Living arrangement	Return to mother's home
	Extended family (?)
	Foster home
	Group home
2. Relationship with family	Counseling agency
3. School problems	School social worker
	Counseling agency
	After-school program
4. Running away	Counseling agency
	Police
	Juvenile court

Family Interview (Day 4): Purpose of the interview: to establish a contract. Nancy and I arrived at Mrs. R's house about 15 minutes early. After saying hello to her mother (who was in a bathrobe) and her brothers, Nancy went off to her room and her mother went to get dressed. I sat in the living room with Bill, who was watching TV. He did not talk to me for the half hour I sat there.

The house is clean but small and threadbare. The boys share a room, and Mrs. R and Bill share a room on the main floor. Nancy has a room in the basement. The house is in a neat, working-class neighborhood.

Finally, the interview began. Mrs. R and Nancy sat on the couch. I sat opposite on a chair. Bill sat in front of the TV, which remained on. I began by explaining the need to make some plans by the end of the week. I described the possibilities: coming home (with counseling), foster care, or a group home. Surprisingly, Mrs. R did most of the talking. She said that she had been thinking a lot. She wanted Nancy to come home. Nancy would have to follow some rules but nothing too hard. Nancy, who was very subdued, asked what rules. Mrs. R talked about curfew, cleaning up around the house, and babysitting. Nancy said that that would be okay. She expected to do some work. But what about Bill?

Bill had been watching TV up to this point. He said that he did not want any more trouble with Nancy. He had talked it over with Mrs. R. To him, Nancy had it easy. But this was Mrs. R's house, and she wanted to pamper Nancy. That was her business. He said several times that he did not want any trouble.

We all agreed that Nancy would return to the shelter for the night; I would bring her home after school the next day. Before we left, I restated the contract, that Nancy would agree to perform some chores and follow the rules we would agree upon; that Bill would allow Mrs. R to be the disciplinarian; and that each would call me if there were any difficulties. In addition, all three would be involved in counseling at the family agency, beginning next month.

Strengths: Nancy and Mrs. R seemed to be able to talk together. Nancy was reassured that her mother really cared for her. Mrs. R is a much stronger person than I first thought. She is able to solve problems and make decisions. We did not go too far into the relationship between Nancy and Bill; this was part of the plan, since they agreed to go for counseling, where this relationship would be handled in-depth.

Weaknesses: Should have been more specific about what would happen when Nancy returned home. Depended too much on Mrs. R's ability to keep things going. What will happen when she is at work and Bill and Nancy are at home together? Should have made child abuse report right away. I filed a report on 3/9/xx, immediately following meeting with field supervisor, G. Edwards.

Assessment: At this point, Nancy needs to know that she still has a place in the family. Mrs. R showed a great deal of strength in her role as mother. But will she be able to discipline Nancy? It seems that this crisis, which began with the fight between Nancy and Bill and included Nancy's running away, had some positive effects. Mrs. R has taken some action. Bill seems to be taken aback by the anger he showed toward Nancy. It is hard to know whether any real change will take place; Bill and Nancy each want the other to change.

As far as Nancy's school is concerned, the school counselor is aware of the family situation and is keeping up with Nancy's school attendance. I will consult with her regularly. Nancy is not engaged in her education; a plan should be developed to involve her in classroom work and other activities in the school.

ESSENTIAL RECORDING

Social work students have taped their sessions with clients for more than half a century (cf. Itzin, 1960). Audiotapes and videotapes of classroom exercises help students model and monitor elementary interviewing skills (Ivey, 1987); they are also used in teaching, learning, and supervising advanced clinical practice, notably family therapy. Audiotapes and videotapes offer practitioners, supervisors, and educators an opportunity to observe practice "in action." Reviewing tapes helps the student practitioner develop a deeper understanding of self and of clients, and gives supervisors direct access to what has transpired in the worker-client transaction. Tapes are a powerful and dynamic tool for use in the development of cognitive and interpersonal practice skills and practitioner self-awareness.

Tapes can also be used to facilitate the development of recordkeeping skills. Good records are not just clear, concise, and well-written; they also focus on the most salient information about the client-need-situation and the service transaction. Kagle (1991) developed Essential Recording to assist students in learning how to "distill the essence of the case" from what takes place in sessions with clients, and how to prepare well-written and meaningful narrative reports. In Essential Recording, students tape sessions with clients, review the tapes, and prepare summaries of each session for use in supervision. Through the Essential Recording process, students learn to observe their clients carefully, to reflect on their own and their clients' communication, and to write summaries based on careful and thorough analysis of the content and process of service.

Essential Recording has many advantages over process recording. Through the Essential Recording process, students learn vital summary recording skills and have the opportunity to observe themselves and their clients on tape. Tapes can even be used in the service process, allowing clients to become more aware of their own behavior. Of course, some clients decline to be taped, and others are uncomfortable at first. Some practitioners are concerned that the tape recorder may affect the service process since both the worker and the client respond to its presence. However, routine taping is usually accepted by the client if it is accepted by the worker. Moreover, over time both the worker and the client come to forget or ignore the machine. In contrast, process records are based on what students remember about their interactions with clients. Even the most skilled practitioner may have difficulty recalling the details of complicated and emotionally painful communications. In addition, a student's process recording may fail to document or misinterpret important information as well as misunderstand or fail to recognize critical verbal and nonverbal interchanges. Process records also do not encourage the development of summary recording skills.

Essential Recording includes five to six steps.

1. The student seeks and is granted permission from the client to tape sessions.

2. The student tapes sessions with the client.

3. The student transcribes the tape into a verbatim record. (This step may be omitted.)

4. The student prepares a session summary for each session, using either an unstructured or a semistructured format (see exhibits 3.6 and 3.7).

5. The student and the supervisor review and discuss the tape or verbatim record and session summary from the perspectives of practice and recording.

6. The student prepares narrative reports for the official client record, using the customary agency format.

In Essential Recording, students begin by recording a session with a client. After listening to the tape (and in some cases preparing a verbatim transcript for use in supervision), the student prepares a session summary in narrative style. The student can then use the tape, transcript, and session summary in supervisory conferences and in preparing narrative reports for the client's record. The social history, opening summary, interim notes, closing summary, and other narrative reports prepared in conformity with agency guidelines become a part of the client's record, but session summaries, tapes, and verbatim transcripts do not. These educational records, like process recordings, are part of the student's rather than the client's record; the client's name and other identifying information should be obscured.

Essential Recording offers supervisors the opportunity to listen to the tapes directly and to review tapes, transcripts of sessions, and session summaries with their students. Supervisory meetings are enriched by this wealth of materials. Moreover, after students have completed each step of this process, they are better prepared to write in the official client record. By that time, they have reviewed tapes, written session summaries, and discussed these materials in supervision. As a result, they should be more knowledgeable about the case and more skillful in its documentation.

Essential Recording may not be feasible for use in every case. However, students can learn a great deal about practice and recording by using Essential Recording in just one case or for a few sessions with an individual client, group, or family. Educational programs or faculty who choose to adopt Essential Recording may need to persuade field agencies and field instructors that Essential Recording will not interfere with services to clients. They may be concerned about client resistance, confidentiality, and cost. Agencies need to know how clients will be asked to participate in the taping process. The student should present taping as a means of offering quality services, but not as a requirement for receiving services. The student should tell clients who will review the tapes and how they will be used. The student should ask the client to sign a release form agreeing to be taped and indicating that he or she, or the group, or the family, understands how the tapes will be used. In addition, agencies need guidelines for the confidential handling of tapes. In general, tapes should be used only in student supervision and should be erased as soon as is feasible. Unless specifically authorized by the client, the tapes should not be used for any other purpose. To protect against unwarranted use, tapes should be stored securely. Finally, agencies may not have the necessary equipment for recording interviews or sessions, and few will be able to transcribe the tapes. The student or the academic program may need to provide recording equipment, tapes, and transcription.

Exhibit 3.5 is the transcript of a tape of the first session between a student practitioner and a family referred for counseling by a school social worker. Exhibits 3.6 and 3.7 are session summaries of this interview. Exhibit 3.6 is an unstructured, open-ended narrative; exhibit 3.7 presents similar information using a semistructured form.

Exhibit 3.5 Example of Essential Recording: Family Service Agency, In-Home Counseling Program

Transcript of Audiotape: Session Number One, 3/30/xx

Worker: Okay. I am a student at the School of Social Work at the University and you are all a family that has been assigned to me. You were referred by . . .

Mrs. G: Angela Martin.

Worker: Exactly. Exactly. She said that you might be able to use services and the reason that I have a tape recorder is because since I am a student, I am supervised and that's for everybody's best interest. Okay? I want to make sure that I can provide the best services for you and my supervisor listens to these tapes before I come to see you again next week and offers suggestions.

Mrs. G: Oh, okay.

Worker: I guess it would be helpful if you gave us an idea of what's going on with you and your family now.

Mrs. G: Okay, well, the reason why I was talking to Angela and I was telling her that me and May, we lost count of, you know, we got kind of a generation gap. And I remember when she was little we could talk, and now that she's older and goin' different places and things, we can't. I don't seem to be able to talk to her like I used to. And I feel I'm losin' control of somethin', you know. And so I just wanted to know, maybe there's someone that could be neutral and could listen to us talk or something and maybe they could find out what the problem is. That you know, it's not that I'm pickin' at her or anything. I want her to understand that I love her, that's why I'm doin' this, you know—to try to keep the relationship between me and her to where when we get older she can always come back to her mother.

Worker: How do you see it, May?

Mrs. G: Well, go ahead. That's what it's about. Tell how you feel.

May: They're always pickin' at people.

Worker: Picking at people?

May: *(Crying)* Like if I go somewhere and she tells me a certain time to get back and I forget that certain time she's always hollerin' at me. She says, "Your brother don't act like that."

Mrs. G: Mm hmm. Anything else, May? Okay, so she's right about that. Only one thing is her brother is older than her, and he don't go as much as she does. You know, May is 12 years old, and he is 14 and will be 15 in July.

Worker: Donald is 14?

Mrs. G: Yes.

Worker: And, May, you're 12?

Mrs. G: Uh huh. Okay, I don't mind her goin' but, you know, I would like it if she come back, or if she's goin' somewhere else, to let me know if she wants to go somewhere else. Several times I had let her go somewhere, and I sent over to where she's gonna be, and she's not there. Then I want to know why, you know, why she didn't come back and let me know anything about where she's gonna be at. So, yes, I do yell at her, and maybe that's where she thinks I'm wrong, but then I don't feel that I'm too far wrong because I don't spank them, you know, cause I could get a little out of control by that, so maybe I do yell a little too much at her.

Worker: Donald, what do you see going on in your family?

Donald: Not much.

Worker: Not much? May, you said that there's a lot of picking on you. Is that what you said?

May: See, if I have my feet on the wall, my mother yells at me to get my feet off the wall.

Mrs. G: Because you wipe your feet on the wall.

May: If I mess with the TV, they yell at me. I get in trouble, like nobody else. I'm gettin' tired of it. I just don't like nobody pickin' at me too much. *(Begins to cry)*

Mrs. G: Okay, well, she do have a stepfather which is Clarence's father—we aren't married—so maybe that's why she feel that he's pickin'. You know, 'cause he's her stepfather. But as far as her feet bein' on the wall and everything, she's the only one that does it. She's the only one that does it.

Worker: So, you feel as if all of this attention, that the picking, is on you. Is that what you're saying? And that's what makes you feel bad, is that right? So if there weren't all that picking you wouldn't feel bad. Is that it? I'm trying to understand what you're saying.

May: Yes, if they wouldn't pick on me I'd be okay, but they pick on me too much.

Worker: Tara, you're 10? How is it when your Mom gets mad at May? How do you see it?

Tara: As I see it, it's not really hollerin'. She's just trying to tell her right from wrong.

Worker: May, how long do you think people have been picking on you? Is it a long time or is it recent?

May: Sorta long. It started when I was 10.

Mrs. G: Yes. When she started in the double digits, 10, 11, 12 years old. Because, at first I thought it was the girls that she would be around, but then she stopped hanging around them, okay. The problem at that time changed. It didn't stop, it just changed from one thing to another. And then, after that, like right now I can talk to her a little bit more than I could a couple of months ago. So I think it was the crowd she was hanging around.

Worker: Oh, so things have gotten better.

Mrs. G: A little better, yes. I tell you, her only problem is she is under her step-father.

Worker: You say it's gotten better because May stopped being with some of her friends?

Mrs. G: Yeah.

Worker: But what have you tried? Have you tried anything specific in your dealings with May, or has May tried?

(continued)

Mrs. G: No, I mostly tried to talk to her. Because Tara is my daughter and I'm quite sure she is watching some of the things May is doing and seein' if I'm letting her get by with this and get by with that, so I'm trying to get them separate and talk to them. Like, I done told May. Okay, she wanted a boyfriend. I said fine, you know, he come by and talk to me and I get to meet him or something. Don't sneak around. You know, and so she says she'd try to do that, but I haven't met anybody but I've heard her say that she like this boy, you know, but I still haven't met him. But, I trust her because when she was younger, from birth up until 10 years old, I raised her. I'm hopin' that my values that I gave her at that younger age she can kind of look back on those, although she might think that I'm being mean to her. When she leaves I don't keep track of her like I used to. I'm just hopin' that when she comes back she comes back like she leaves. Safe and without being harmed.

Worker: So, your concern is really out of love. May, do you know what time you're supposed to be home, is that clear to you? Or is it not clear?

May: Yeah, but sometimes I'll be at my friend's house and she'll want to go by the park. So I'll be at the park. Say we leave about 5:00 or 5:30, and I'm supposed to be home at 5:00 and I'm still at the park at night and when she goes home I go over to her house, right? And say she goes home at 6:00 and say I gotta go. And I come home and I get yelled at.

Worker: Because—

May: 'Cause I didn't go into the house to see what time it is, my friend's house to see what time it is.

Mrs. G: There's nothing wrong with the girls. The one she's hanging around right now. I like the girl. She's a very nice girl. You know, I don't know too much about her family background, but as for her, she seems like a really nice child.

Worker: I wonder if the rest of you feel like your mother and May are doing most of the talking. Since it's our first meeting as an introduction of the family, could each of you kind of sketch out, draw, what you all think the family is? Stick people are fine. It doesn't just have to be family members. It can also be things that are real important to you, like, May, it sounds like you have a real close friend that is real important to you. Or maybe, Donald, you have a friend who's real important. And I'd like you to draw it. Maybe you can draw the people inside or outside your house. This is going to tell us something. Okay. And I want you to be as creative as possible.

May: I don't draw too good.

Worker: Oh, I don't really care about that. Just draw something that shows who is in this family, who are the important people, and what this family is like.

Mrs. G: Now just draw a picture like the lady says.

Worker: While everyone is drawing, maybe you could tell me something about the children and about you and about Walter. Does Walter live here?

Mrs. G: Yes, he lives here. Another thing about this is, I'm getting a divorce, going through a divorce. And that's probably why May feels, you know, a little hard tension problems. Like I have an order of protection against him, but he's still here. It's because—I don't know. I want out of the situation, but just the same I feel, you know, he has an aunty here, and some cousins here, but he really don't have nowhere to go. So—

Worker: You have an order of protection against him? But he's still . . .

Mrs. G: He's still here.

Worker: That's hard.

Mrs. G: Mm hmm. So that's probably some of the reason why May feels the way she feels, you know, because when she says someone pickin' on her, she's not just talkin' about me, she's mostly talkin' about him.

Worker: Is Walter the father of Byron and Clarence?

Mrs. G: Yes, Byron and Clarence.

Worker: And the rest of the kids?

Mrs. G: Well, Walter be their stepfather.

Worker: And their father?

Mrs. G: They don't have no real father. Walter is their stepfather and he's the only one they know. And May don't get along with him.

Worker: What about the rest of the kids?

Mrs. G: Well, Byron and Clarence are still small. They don't give Walter no trouble. Donald is away a lot. And Tara's easy. It's mostly him and May that get into it. So we're supposed to be drawing houses? A family unit?

Worker: Yeah. The house and all the people you think are part of your family and your important friends.

Mrs. G: I have a lot of people I can really turn to, but you know people don't listen like they used to. Like I've got a sister—I'm from a family of 10. I've got five brothers and four girls, 10 of us all together. Okay, so out of the 10 it's just me and her, we're real close, you know, so I can turn to her and talk to her and she'll listen, you know. There's nothing she can say or do, 'cause I'm going to do what I want to do anyway. And then there's my girlfriend, you know, she has a lot of problems and stuff, too, maybe that's why I kind of feel I can talk to her. And my mom is here.

Worker: Your mom is here and your sister's here.

Mrs. G: Uh huh. I have two sisters and two brothers here. But, like I said, my sister don't mind—she's the only sister that I can really talk to and she's younger than I am and she's the only one that I can really talk to and know that she'll listen. And then my mother, she's very outgoing herself. I don't feel a close relationship between me and her.

Worker: Was that always the case?

Mrs. G: Always. I felt it from a child.

Worker: It sounds like you're concerned about having a close relationship with May. That's something we can talk more about next time. I want to set up a time for our next appointment. But first I want to look at each of your drawings. . . .

(The interview continued for another 10 minutes. The worker discussed each picture with the artist. She asked that Walter be present at the next family session and set a time when he could attend.)

Exhibit 3.6   Unstructured Session Summary

Interview Date: 3/30/xx
Worker: Linda T, MSW student
Session Number One

Mrs. Queenie G and all of her five children attended the session. Mr. Walter G, who Mrs. G says she is divorcing but who still lives in the house, was not present. I have asked that he attend the next session, scheduled for 4/5/xx.

The family structure is unclear. The genogram of the family, based on information collected so far, appears below.

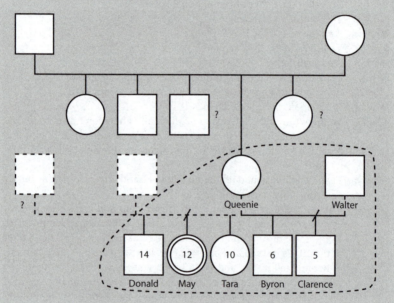

Mrs. G, who sought help from the school social worker about her relationship with May, a special education student, did most of the talking in the interview. May also talked. According to Mrs. G, May does not follow rules. She does not come home when she is supposed to, and she does not call when she is going to be late. According to May, who cried during the early part of the interview, everyone in the family picks on her. She does not feel that she should be blamed when she forgets to come home on time. It does seem that she is singled out as the one who causes trouble. Mrs. G says that things have gotten better during the past two months, since May is no longer hanging around with the friends who Mrs. G considered a bad influence. Mrs. G seems to worry that May will get in trouble when she is out with her friends. But Mrs. G also says that a lot of May's problem is with Mr. G, May's stepfather.

Unfortunately, I did not learn much about this, or about him or the other children's father. Mrs. G did say that she has an order of protection against Mr. G but that he still lives in the house because, according to Mrs. G, he has no other place to go. At one point, Mrs. G said she was not married to Mr. G; at another point she said she was getting a divorce from him. Mrs. G indicated that there is tension in the house, but I did not learn what actually happens. There is a lot that still needs to be explored, including: current and past family violence; the relationship between May and the other children, Mr. G, and Mrs. G; and any other problems that members of the family have at work or in school, at home, and so on.

The interview could have been improved if all members of the family had been encouraged to talk. Also, the picture drawing was a good idea, but I did not know what to do with it. Finally, I asked a lot of stacked questions (two or three in a row) and seemed to get off track several times.

Exhibit 3.7   Semistructured Session Summary

Date: 3/30/xx   Worker: Linda T, MSW student
Session: One   Case: G family, #88028

1. Briefly describe what happened during the session.

Mrs. G and her five children attended. Mrs. G and May, a special education student, described conflicts regarding May's behavior. For example, May does not always come home when she is supposed to. Mrs. G wants her to call; she worries about May when May is late or out with friends. May feels that she is being unfairly blamed and "picked on."

Mr. G was not at the session. Mr. and Mrs. G are "divorcing," although their relationship is unclear. Mr. G is the father of Byron (six) and Clarence (five) but not of Donald (fourteen), May (twelve), and Tara (ten). Mrs. G has an order of protection against Mr. G, but he is living in the home.

2. List the problems, needs, and issues that surfaced.

Conflict exists between Mr. G and May, between Mrs. G and May, between Mr. and Mrs. G.

Mrs. G thinks things have improved since May has acquired new friends; she sees the problem now as May being "under" her stepfather.

May feels picked on. She is the identified patient (IP) in this family. Mrs. G is very worried about May's behavior, her friends, and so on. Her special place in the family (as the oldest girl and as a special ed student) makes her vulnerable.

Mr. G may be abusive.

3. What techniques or interventions were used?

We explored Mrs. G's and May's view of the problem, but other family members were not drawn in enough.

Each member drew a picture of the family. I discussed each picture but did not know where to go with it.

I explored Mrs. G's family network as a possible support.

I tried to find out about the family history but was not successful.

4. Suggest areas for future exploration or intervention.

- Relationship between Mr. G and other members of family
- Question of abuse, violence
- Involve all family members
- Problems at school, in the neighborhood

Summary

Primary Function: Social work education.

Current Usage: Field instruction.

Organizing Rationale: This approach combines existing recordkeeping structures in a process in which students produce and review a series of products with the goal of distilling the essence of the case and then presenting
this information in well-written narrative reports. Students produce tapes
and session summaries prior to preparing the customary agency record.

Strengths: Essential Recording teaches students to describe and analyze the
case using the narrative style they will be expected to use as practitioners.
The process focuses the student's and supervisor's attention on what
actually happens in the service transaction, facilitating the development
of cognitive and interpersonal practice as well as recordkeeping skills.

Limitations: The process is time-consuming and may not be suitable in some
agencies or with some clients. This limitation may be overcome by using
Essential Recording with only one or two of the student's cases. Videotape
equipment may be prohibitively expensive, but audiotaping equipment is
inexpensive. Tapes may be vulnerable to breaches in confidentiality.

IMPROVING EDUCATION FOR RECORDKEEPING

Records of the transactions between social work students and their clients are an important vehicle for teaching and learning about practice. When
students prepare and review their records, they recall what occurred in their
sessions with clients and they reflect upon what it meant. The recording process, then, helps students to develop their perceptual and conceptual skills.
Records aid in supervision, focusing discussion on critical aspects of the client-need-situation and the service relationship, and facilitating the development of students' understanding of their clients and themselves.

Students' records can also be used in teaching and learning recordkeeping concepts and skills. Ideally, education for recording should be founded
upon four precepts. First, education for recording should take place throughout the educational process: in the classroom, in the field, and in entry-level
practice. Second, education for recording should move from generic to specific, that is, from general concepts learned in the classroom to their specific
application in fieldwork and in entry-level practice. Third, skill development
should proceed along a continuum. Skills acquired at an early stage should
not be supplanted by other approaches to recording, but should become the
foundation for more advanced skills. Finally, education for practice and for
recording should be linked and continuous; recording should not be introduced as a necessary evil of agency practice but as an integral part of practice
throughout the student's learning experience. To this end, students should be
exposed to records and recordkeeping concepts in all their practice courses.

Reality stands in sharp contrast to this ideal. What has been notably absent from the experience of most current and recent students has been:

- the classroom (or generic) component of the classroom-field-practice sequence;
- a well-conceived continuum of skill acquisition and development; and
- early and continuous integration of recording with practice.

The most significant of these deficiencies is that many students are not learning about records and recordkeeping in the classroom. The primary responsibility for teaching social work students about records and record-keeping has fallen to the field agencies. Agencies assume this responsibility not by choice but by default when their students have not been taught about recording in the classroom. Although field instructors expect to teach specific recording policies, practices, and procedures, they assume that students have been introduced to recording concepts, knowledge, and skills. The field experience is already too crowded to give sufficient attention to recording theory. Moreover, this content is better taught in advance of, or concurrent with, the field experience in the broader context of the classroom.

Deferring to the field has not only overcrowded that component of social work education, it also has made education for recording inconsistent. Because the field experience is necessarily dependent upon the field supervisor and the field agency, a student's experience with recordkeeping reflects that supervisor's and that agency's approach to documentation. Some supervisors give careful attention to records and to recording; others do not. And different agencies record differently. Thus, an individual student's experience with recording is limited by her or his agency's and supervisor's approach. One student's experience is often very different from another's. As a result, social work education for recordkeeping is varied and uneven.

Inadequate classroom preparation also sets the stage for a breakdown in the continuum of skill acquisition and development. Students who have not learned recording theory and concepts in the classroom have no framework for understanding and placing in context the specific practices and procedures they learn in the field. Each new policy, format, and procedure may appear to be a discrete task, unrelated to the ongoing development of their practice knowledge and skills. In addition, if students have not been introduced to recording concepts in the practice curriculum, they may fail to recognize and understand the connection between practice and its documentation. Students who learn about recording for the first time in the field tend to identify the task as a bureaucratic function rather than as a component of practice.

In addition to the discontinuities that arise as a result of lack of preparation in the classroom, new graduates may find that the skills they developed as students are different from those they will need as practitioners. There are many differences in purpose, content, and style between students' records and practitioners' records. For example, students who have spent much of their time in field work preparing process records may not have had adequate instruction and experience preparing forms, summary reports, and other agency records. Indeed, new practitioners are often surprised and dismayed by the attention directed toward their records. Many feel unprepared in knowledge, experience, and skill. They also may not have realized how much of their day-to-day practice would be devoted to recordkeeping.

Any agenda to improve education for recording, then, must begin with the return of the social work record and recording concepts to a prominent place in social work education. The curriculum plan in exhibit 3.8 is intended to pave the way for that return. Students are introduced to generic concepts in the classroom and to specific concepts in the field. Moreover, the plan includes not just core content that is relevant both to undergraduate and graduate students, but also specialized content appropriate for graduate-level students in clinical and managerial programs.

The second item on the agenda for improving education for recording is to select an approach that integrates practice with recording skills and proceeds along a continuum. Skills students learn in the classroom and the field should prepare them for entry-level practice. This means that students should be taught practice using their records and taught to record based upon their practice experiences. The records they prepare while they are students should help them develop their interpersonal practice skills and their ability to prepare the narrative summary reports they will write as practitioners.

Unfortunately, the approaches adopted by many programs today (using process recording, agency records, or a combination of the two) do not usually fulfill these goals. On the one hand, students may spend an inordinate amount of time developing process recording skills that are useless or even a hindrance later. Moreover, because process records do not reflect what actually occurs during an interview or session (Timms, 1972), they have only limited value in teaching practice skills. On the other hand, agency records usually do not include sufficient information about the process of service to facilitate teaching practice skills, and may not give students sufficient experience preparing narrative summary reports.

If process recording is used, it should be used sparingly; in addition, more time should be spent on developing narrative summary skills. Given the limitations of the traditional approaches, educators may wish to experiment with other approaches that fulfill the goals outlined here. Earlier in this chapter, two such approaches were presented. The Teaching/Learning Record is a narrative record that combines elements of content that are included in a typical agency record along with additional information about student-client interaction and the student's thinking process. Essential Recording uses a process that begins with audiotapes or videotapes and ends with narrative summary reports.

A final item on the agenda to improve education for recording is the early and continuous integration of practice and its documentation. This goal requires that records be used as a means of teaching practice and that recording be taught as a part of practice. There are a variety of techniques through

Exhibit 3.8   Curriculum Plan for Teaching and Learning about Recording

Generic Content (Classroom)	Specific Content (Field)
Core Content	
Purpose of Recording	
Service documentation	Agency's uses of records
Case continuity	
Interprofessional communication	
Evaluation	
Supervision	
Agency management or funding	
Types of Records	
Educational records	Records kept by agency
Clinical records	Recording for teaching and learning
Management records	social work practice
Reports, letters	Agency's procedures for protecting
Privacy principles	client privacy
Recording Approaches	
Elements of content	Agency guidelines on content and style
Structures	Agency forms and outlines
Recording process and procedure	Agency procedures, aids for writing records (Dictaphone, computer)
Specialized Content	
Recording by modality (e.g., family therapy records)	Practice in making such records
Recording by field of practice (e.g., records used in mental health)	Analysis of records used in agency
Accountability systems	Analysis of agency's accountability system

which this goal may be accomplished. In direct practice courses, students might read records in preparation for discussion of practice principles, or students might write records following the role plays they perform. In courses in supervision, accountability, and administration, students might compare the utility and efficiency of different recordkeeping styles and formats; they might design forms or develop procedures and guidelines to meet particular agency requirements. All of these changes in education for recording are predicated upon the willingness of social work educators to reintroduce recording concepts and skills into the practice curriculum. Many educators are reluctant to do so because they regard recordkeeping as an agency-based function that is extraneous to practice. It may fall to the field instructors and to their students to persuade them of the importance of returning the record to the classroom.

CHAPTER 4

THE STRUCTURE OF RECORDS I
NARRATIVE AND OTHER CLINICAL RECORDS

There are a variety of recording structures that are used to guide the selection and organization of information in social work records. Record-keeping structures vary along several dimensions, which are useful in understanding and evaluating their advantages and disadvantages. Recordkeeping structures differ in *standardization;* that is, they vary in the degree to which content and organization are left to the discretion of the practitioner or are predetermined by form or format. Standardized forms and formats increase the likelihood that required information will be documented as well as increase the accessibility of that information. They tend to typify clients, services, and workers, and to routinize recordkeeping. In contrast, formats that are less standardized and more open permit practitioners to individualize clients and services, reflecting the worker's perspective about the salient issues in the case. However, such records can be idiosyncratic and may fail to include important information in a form that is accessible to the user.

Recording structures also differ in *scope;* that is, some apply to the entire record, while others are used only for a specific element of content, such as the interim note. They differ in *selectivity;* that is, they vary in the degree to which they encourage documentation of a breadth of information about the client-need-situation and the service transaction, or limit content to particular observations, assessments, decisions, or actions. They also differ in *style;* that is, they vary in the mode of expression used. Some structures are used to organize comprehensive narrative reports, others call for brief summaries of specific information, and still others are composed primarily of fill-in-the-blanks or checklists.

Finally, recordkeeping structures differ in *rationale;* that is, they vary in the underlying principles that give focus and unity to the record and meaning to the recordkeeping process. Some recording structures are based on functional principles. Information is recorded for a purpose and organized to serve that purpose, for example, to support interprofessional communication. Other structures are based upon conceptual principles. A theory of human behavior or the assumptions of a practice approach undergird the selection and organization of information for the record. Unfortunately, in some agencies, the rationale for selecting and organizing information in the record is not clear. Forms and formats, each with its own purpose and rationale, have been added to the record over time, undermining the overall rationale and organization of the record.

Recordkeeping structures are often selected because they:

- minimize costs by limiting time spent in composing, transcribing, storing, retrieving, or using the record;
- meet external accountability requirements and standards of practice;
- meet internal information needs, facilitating decision making, case continuity, supervision, interprofessional communication, business functions, or agency management;
- are congruent with recordkeeping practices in other professions or agencies in the field of practice; and
- are suited to the range of personnel in the agency who document information in and use the record.

Prior to the 1960s, social work records tended to be open ended and individualistic. Practitioners developed a personal approach to recording, which reflected their approach to practice. Typically, their professional development began with process recording in field work. They then moved on to narrative recording, which was the prevailing model of recordkeeping in agency practice. Agency records were usually organized chronologically and by topic; with the exception of identifying information, the record's content was not standardized. Practitioners trained in process recording often included detailed accounts of the service process in their narratives. The 1960s brought about many changes in recordkeeping, including an increased emphasis on external accountability and the emergence of more structured approaches to practice. Agencies began developing and adopting forms and formats that encouraged greater standardization of content and structure across clients and practitioners. Agencies differed in the degree to which they standardized content and structure, but few continued to rely heavily on unstructured narratives. There was considerable experimentation with new forms and formats, reflecting the special documentation needs of diverse settings, service modalities, and client populations. New approaches to recordkeeping were developed, often in response to a particular approach to practice, such as behaviorism. New formats were adopted, sometimes based on the practices of another discipline, like medicine. In the 1990s, agencies began the transition from paper forms and formats to computerized records. This increased the standardization of records, giving agencies greater control over the content and organization of records.

In practice today, most agencies use a combination of structures, ranging from standardized forms to narrative reports. Some practitioners still prepare their records by hand or via dictation, but many prepare their records directly on computers. Agencies are strapped for funds, so practitioners must produce records as efficiently as possible. Practitioners must not only be familiar with a variety of recordkeeping structures and approaches. They also need to develop skills in writing clear, succinct, meaningful, and well-organized narratives that capture the essence of the client-need-situation and the process and progress of services. This chapter and chapter 5 review a number of recordkeeping structures that are prototypes of those used in social agencies and other social work environments today. Rather than combining structures, as they would be in practice, chapters 4 and 5 present various recording structures one by one, using a common framework for comparison. First, the form or format is described, analyzed, and outlined. Then each structure is evaluated on the basis of six dimensions: primary function, secondary functions, current usage, organizing rationale, strengths, and limitations. Finally, examples of the use of each form or format are presented.

The formats included in this chapter follow certain conventions of structure, organization, and content. At the same time, each is open and flexible enough to meet the documentation needs of a variety of organizations, programs, practice approaches, and practitioners. Such flexibility is both a strength and a potential limitation. These formats permit workers considerable latitude in deciding what information to include in the record, and they allow workers to present that information in their own style and from their own perspective. Because they allow workers to document the specific characteristics of the case, they are especially useful in maintaining case continuity, communicating with other practitioners, monitoring service delivery, and facilitating consultation. However, unless agencies establish minimum standards and guidelines regarding what and how information is to be documented, records may include too much or too little information. They also may be too idiosyncratic to permit comparisons among cases or to facilitate administrative review.

NARRATIVE REPORTS

Narrative recording permits practitioners to describe and assess the client-need-situation and the service transaction in their own words, emphasizing issues they consider most important. Narrative reports remain crucial to the recording process, and are included in computerized as well as "paper" records. Today, social agencies usually use structured formats for organizing the content of narrative reports. The practitioner's role is to select, organize, and document information to reflect what is significant about the:

- nature of the client-need-situation;
- purpose of service;
- decisions and actions affecting services;
- process of service; and
- impact of services on the client-need-situation.

The narrative report is the most individualizing and idiosyncratic style of recording. A narrative can reflect the special nature of the client-need-situation and of the service transaction; it is therefore especially appropriate in documenting clinical practice with individuals, families, and groups. It certainly reflects the practitioner's knowledge of human behavior, theory and practice of social work, selection and provision of services, service evaluation, and recording. However, a narrative record may also be incomplete and oversimplified or excessively long and meandering. In addition, the quality of the record may depend more on the worker's ability to write and the availability of time for recording than on the quality of the service provided.

The adoption of structured formats for focusing and organizing the content of narrative reports has remedied many of the limitations of this approach to recording. Structured formats can control the size of the record, making information more accessible and retrievable, and limit intrusions on client privacy. Shortening the number and length of narrative reports in a record can also help reduce the time and, therefore, the costs of preparing the record. It may also help reduce the practitioner's recordkeeping backlog, making records more timely, accurate, and useful. Of course, if narrative reports are simply replaced by a large number of forms to complete, there is little net gain.

Agencies can maximize the assets and minimize the limitations of narrative recording in a number of ways. They may use narratives only for complex, individualized services and structured forms for short-term or routine services. They may limit narrative recording to certain elements of content, such as the social history, assessment, and significant decisions and actions affecting services, and use forms, lists, or outlines for tracking service activities and outcomes, for example. They may establish explicit guidelines or develop forms that prompt practitioners as to what information should be included in the narrative and what information is to be excluded. For example, to improve efficiency and accessibility, content should not be included in narrative reports if it is documented elsewhere or in another form. Exhibits 4.1 and 4.2 are examples of narrative records.

Summary

Primary Function: Individualized service documentation.

Secondary Functions: Clinical supervision.

Current Usage: All fields and modalities of practice.

Organizing Rationale: Information is organized (1) temporally and (2) by subject matter.

Strengths: Because the record is not standardized, it is inclusive and can truly represent the special characteristics of the client-need-situation and the service transaction. Thus, the record is especially responsive to individualized service approaches.

Limitations: It is time-consuming and costly. Information is often difficult to retrieve. The quality of the record depends on the recorder's ability to select information appropriately, organize information clearly, find time to record regularly, and write cogently.

Exhibit 4.1   Example of a Narrative Record: Chemical Dependency Treatment Program

Family Assessment
Outpatient Unit
Patient name: Charles M (41)
Interviews: 5/7/xx, Anne M (40)
                       5/8 and 5/9, Charles M, Anne M, Chip M (16), Caroline M (14)
Report dictated: 5/12; transcribed 5/14

Presenting Problem: Charles M was referred for service by his employer, T Corporation, where Mr. M is employed as a regional sales manager. Mr. M has been employed by T Corporation for eight years, moving up in the ranks to his present position four years ago. His position requires that he travel extensively; he is usually out of town two weeks out of the month, meeting clients and supervising local representatives. Mr. M began drinking heavily during these trips, first with clients and subsequently by himself or with other companions. According to the company, Mr. M's job performance and his reputation with clients and within the company have deteriorated during the past year. Mr. M recognizes that his position with T depends on his successful completion of the treatment program. He believes, however, that his drinking is not the primary problem. He feels that company politics are involved in both his referral to the program and his problems within the company.

Family Background: There is a history of heavy drinking in Charles M's family of origin. Both mother and father drank regularly; his father drank to excess. Mr. M remembers his father coming home drunk on Friday nights when he was a teenager. His father died at age 45 in a car accident. His mother is "bitter" and "bossy." Mr. M seldom sees his mother, who lives in another state. He does, however, maintain contact with his four (older) siblings, two of whom have had "drinking problems." His eldest brother has been a member of AA for 10 years; a sister, who was recently divorced, is currently attending AA meetings.

Mr. M says that there is nothing "special" in his background. He completed high school and two years of college. After four years in the service, he began his career in sales. He and Mrs. M met at college. She completed college after Mr. M dropped out. They were married, over Mrs. M's family's objections, after Mr. M was discharged from the Air Force. Mrs. M's father never accepted her marriage, considering Mr. M a "low life." There was a reconciliation between Mrs. M and her parents at the time that Chip was born, and she has grown closer to her mother since her father died five years ago. Mr. M, however, has no contact with Mrs. M's family. He does not attend family functions; rather, Mrs. M and the children attend without him.

Current Family Functioning: Although Mr. M's job is now "at risk," he draws his full salary during his treatment here. The Ms own their own home, which is in an upper-income section of the community. Both Chip and Caroline attend the local high school, have above-average grades, and participate in extracurricular activities. Mrs. M describes herself as a housewife: she has a group of friends with whom she plays bridge, tennis, and so forth.

(continued)

The M family does not spend much time together. Both Chip and Caroline stay at school late and are engaged in sports and other activities on the weekend. Often, even when Mr. M is at home, each member of the family eats dinner at a different time.

Mr. and Mrs. M have been personally and sexually distant for several years. Mrs. M became aware of Mr. M's extramarital affairs shortly after Caroline was born. She threatened to leave but was convinced by Mr. M that he would give up these liaisons; he told her that he did not love these other women. She believes that this is true, that his need for other women is a "weakness," as is his alcoholism. Mrs. M says that she has thought of leaving her husband several times but never has been able to do so.

A pattern has developed over the years: Mr. M "slips up" and reveals a liaison. Mrs. M threatens to leave. Mr. M begs her to stay, promising to give up other women (which he does for a time). Eventually, the pattern repeats itself. She does not want her family or social friends to know about Mr. M's "drinking and carousing." Her mother would say that she had been warned; her friends would be sympathetic but would turn away from her. She has tried to maintain the image that hers is a "perfect family."

Assessment: This family's relationship, in the assessment interviews and in their day-to-day life together, is characterized by emotional estrangement and superficial communication. Mr. and Mrs. M's relationship, which is at the core of this family, is remarkably distant. At the same time, Mrs. M can be viewed as an enabling spouse, since her personal withdrawal from Mr. M, while maintaining a "social image," has allowed him to continue to drink and to deny the impact it has on himself and his family.

In observing the family together, one immediately senses the need of each member of the family to maintain denial of Mr. M's drinking by not really talking to each other and by involving themselves in activities and relationships outside the family. Each family member has more frequent and more significant communication with peers than with any other member of the family. At the same time, the commitment to the family secret is very strong. Both Chip and Caroline glanced repeatedly at Mr. and Mrs. M when speaking, to seek reassurance that what they had said had not revealed too much.

Recommendations:

1. Marital counseling for Mr. and Mrs. M, to begin immediately. Their relationship has been strained for many years as an outgrowth of Mr. M's drinking and extramarital liaisons. These difficulties result from, but also sustain, Mr. M's drinking behavior. They are at the core of the estrangement of the family.

2. Teen group for Chip and Caroline, next session, 5/14. Each could benefit from support and sharing of experience with peers. The group will also model the behaviors appropriate for family counseling sessions.

3. Family counseling, to be initiated two weeks after marital and group counseling have started. By that time, Mr. M's individual and group therapy, Mr. and Mrs. M's marital counseling, and the teen group will have broken through some of the denial, allowing the family to open up to family therapy.

Family Therapy Session Number Three, 6/6

Planned Interventions: The plan for this session was to discuss what changes each member saw taking place in himself or herself; what changes each saw taking place in others; what changes were taking place in the family itself; and what changes were not taking place. The worker planned to intervene by suggesting that certain changes could not take place because these changes would mean giving up things that the family could not relinquish. The worker planned to explain using this example: Dad could not give up drinking if it was important to other members of the family that he continue to drink.

Interview: Chip and Caroline were very active early in the session. Each saw change in his or her relations with parents. Chip felt that he could now bring friends home, that he could tell anyone in his family anything that was bothering him. Caroline thought her parents were changing; before, they had seemed to hate each other, and she often worried that they would divorce. Now she was not worried any more. Mrs. M said that she felt the kids were happier, relieved of a burden. Mr. M said that he never thought the kids had any troubles, and he now saw that was not true.

The example of maintaining alcoholic behavior led to an important revelation: Caroline said, "Like if Mom wanted Dad to keep drinking so that she could keep drinking too." At first, both Caroline and Mrs. M denied that this was in fact occurring. Some probing led Mrs. M to talk about her own drinking behavior. It appears that she is alcohol dependent, something known to Chip and Caroline, although Mr. M appeared not to be aware of his wife's secret drinking. She drinks at home in the evenings when Mr. M is away, sometimes falling asleep in a chair. The children find her there in the morning when they get up to go to school. Mr. M's drinking was less evident to Chip and Caroline, because of his pattern of drinking away from home and away from the family. They had been quite aware of Mrs. M's drinking behavior, but they had never discussed it with each other or with Mrs. M before this meeting.

Future Plans: Mrs. M acknowledges her need for treatment as alcohol dependent. She will be admitted to the program as a patient as soon as an opening occurs (one to two weeks). Until that time, she will continue to participate in family and marital counseling sessions. She will attend an AA meeting with Mr. M on Monday.

Exhibit 4.2   Example of a Brief Narrative Report: Hospital Social Work Department

Social Work Report

Referral: Joey Smith was referred to social work upon admission, 9/24/xx. He was admitted through the emergency room (ER), where police had brought him. Joey had burns on his legs and buttocks, as well as bruises on his arms and legs. Mr. Smith (his father) told the ER nurse that he had bathed Joey after Joey had made a mess in his pants. After the bath, he noticed the burns and called for help. Mr. Smith said that Joey's bruises must have come from a fall off the

(continued)

swings at the park earlier in the day. Mr. Smith said that Joey is very clumsy and always falls and bumps into things.

Background: Joey is three years, five months old, although he appears no more than two. He is small, frail, and quite fearful of strangers. He does not smile or respond verbally, although he complies with what the ward personnel ask him to do. Joey is the youngest of Mrs. Smith's six children; the other children range in age from five to 14. All the older children attend school; three are in a special education program.

In interviews with the Smiths, Mr. Smith did most of the talking, while Mrs. Smith said little, nodding or shaking her head when asked a question. Mr. Smith is looking for work but has not been employed steadily for two years. He is sometimes able to find a day's work but usually is at home. He and Mrs. Smith have known each other all their lives—they are kin—but have been married only four years. Mr. Smith describes Joey as "slow, like his mother"; he knows that Joey is slow because he is not potty-trained, doesn't talk, and is clumsy. Joey has never been evaluated by a doctor or by a teacher.

Service Information: The physician filed an abuse report on 9/24, stating that Joey's burns were from scalding bath water and that the bruises indicate Joey's attempts to resist and pull himself from the tub. Dr. P and I immediately informed the parents of the abuse report; she explained that all suspicious injuries must be reported. The Smiths threatened to remove Joey from the hospital but were persuaded that he should stay. I asked them to bring their other five children to the hospital for checkups the following day (9/25). All were evaluated, and, although some of the children had health problems that needed treatment, none showed signs of abuse.

We have coordinated services with the Child Welfare Department, which investigated and found evidence of abuse. Although the Smiths have been encouraged to visit Joey daily, they have visited only briefly once or twice a week during Joey's two-week hospitalization. Upon discharge, Joey will return home, under department supervision. On 10/21 he is to be evaluated for the Early Childhood Education Program.

E.H., Social Worker
10/15/xx

THE PROBLEM-ORIENTED RECORD

The Problem-Oriented Record (POR) is a format that is widely used in health and mental health settings. Weed (1968) intended that this format be adopted by all disciplines in all health organizations, but he was primarily concerned with its use by physicians-in-training in health settings. The format reflects these origins and requires some adaptation if it is to be used in mental health settings or by social work practitioners in any setting. Weed divided the POR into four major sections: data base, problem list, initial plans, and progress notes.

DATA BASE

Collected during intake or upon admission by various members of the health team, the data base includes:

- the patient's chief complaint;
- a patient profile (description of an average day);
- social information;
- present illnesses;
- past history and review of systems;
- findings of a physical examination; and
- laboratory reports.

PROBLEM LIST

Working together or independently, service providers list and number all problems defined during the process of data collection. The problem list acts as an index to the record and is an accountability document. As new problems are defined, they are numbered and added to the list. As problems are resolved, redefined, or no longer the focus of service, their change in status is noted. At discharge, the problem list forms the basis for reviewing service provision.

INITIAL PLANS

Working together or independently, service providers draw up plans to respond to each of the problems listed. The plans are numbered and labeled to correspond to the relevant problem. Each plan is updated as necessary in the progress notes. Weed suggested that a plan might include further collection of information, additional treatment, and education of the patient.

PROGRESS NOTES

After plans have been drawn up and are being implemented, progress and change are noted by the relevant problem number and labeled in:

1. Narrative notes: These notes (often referred to as SOAP notes) update information in the data base and revise the initial plans. They may include:

   S—Subjective information, such as the patient's and family's description of the problem

   O—Objective information, such as the practitioner's observations of the patient

   A—Assessments

   Rx—Treatment or care given

   P—Plans

   A particular entry need not include all categories of information. If, for example, only new subjective information and changes in previous plans are to be added to the record, the interim note would include only S (subjective information) and P (plans).

2. Flow charts: These notes, which collect specific information about the patient over time, are intended to act as intensive studies of the client's current and changing status. A flow chart may be used to document overall health status or specific signs that indicate response to treatment.

3. Discharge summary: The provider of service reviews each problem and each service response.

Several changes are necessary to adapt the POR format for use by all disciplines in mental health settings. First, the data base should be expanded to include:

- relevant and current personal, social, and environmental factors;
- a detailed personal and social history;
- a history of previous mental health services;
- a mental status examination; and
- findings of psychological tests.

Second, the problem list should include:

- mental health (*DSM*) diagnoses, where relevant, and
- problems in daily living, especially:
  - self-care and self-management and
  - relationships with family, peers, community, and in the work environment.

If the POR is to document social work services fully and fairly, in health, mental health, or other settings, it needs to be expanded and refocused. Although the POR is sufficiently open ended and flexible to accommodate social service issues and activities, its focus may oversimplify and distort:

- the breadth of social work concern by emphasizing problems rather than needs, resources, and strengths;
- the complexity of relevant phenomena by emphasizing the person rather than the person-need-situation;
- systemic influences by emphasizing individual dysfunction over social and ecological factors; and
- the special nature of social work activities by emphasizing case management while deemphasizing therapeutic intervention.

These limitations can be ameliorated to some extent if social workers expand and adapt the POR format to incorporate the full range of relevant psychosocial information, social service issues, and social work activities. Thus, the data base should go beyond a focus on the person and the problem to include:

- relevant interpersonal, social, institutional, and physical environmental influences;

- client strengths, resources, and abilities; and
- available resources in the client's personal environment.

If feasible, the problem list should be relabeled "issues," "needs," or "goals." The list should include not just problems conceived in personal terms but also needs (e.g., "maintain relationship with children despite placement in care facility") and goals (e.g., "return to limited employment") stated in transactional terms. Plans, too, should include social service activities that respond to the expanded list of relevant service issues. Therapeutic and organizational intervention should not be omitted but should take their place alongside case-management activities.

Finally, the progress note format might be modified. Many social work practitioners have recognized that the organization of progress notes into the SOAP format omits important social service information and also seems to discredit information provided by the patient and family by labeling it subjective. They may wish to adopt an SOAIGP format to update information in the record. Note that content has been relabeled and that new classes of information have been added:

S—Supplementary data base information provided by patient and family
O—Observations by worker and other service providers
A—Activities with and on behalf of the client
I—Impressions and assessments
G—Goals
P—Plans

Tebb (1991) proposed that social work adopt a more client-centered approach to recordkeeping. In her view, the POR assumes that the practitioner "gathers objective and subjective information, then makes an assessment and devises a treatment plan." The practitioner is also responsible for implementing the plan and "determining when a problem has been resolved" (p. 428). As an alternative to the SOAP format, she proposed the CREW format, which is intended to encourage a more collaborative approach to practice. The CREW format focuses the narrative on "the situation and how the client and worker mutually view the situation" (p. 430):

C—Contributors. What factors contribute to the need for change?
R—Restraints. What constitutes the restraints or barriers to change?
E—Enablers. What factors seem to be enabling or contributing to change?
W—Ways. How can change be fostered?

The CREW format highlights the change process, and is congruent with the principles of Service-Centered recordkeeping, as described in chapter 2. However, because of its limited focus, it does not meet the full documentation requirements for accountability. Furthermore, the CREW format would not be an acceptable substitute for the SOAP format in many health and mental health agencies. Nonetheless, it provides a meaningful and useful addition to the POR and to other formats for recordkeeping. Exhibits 4.3 and 4.4 provide excerpts from Problem-Oriented Records.

**Exhibit 4.3   Excerpts from a Problem-Oriented Record:
Hospital Social Work Department**

Data Base

Social Information: Mr. T, a 69-year-old widower who lives alone, was admitted on 4/4 with congestive heart failure. He has been hospitalized three times in the past year in similar condition. Mr. T was referred for social service consultation on 4/7; he and his daughter, Mrs. V, were interviewed on 4/9.

Mr. T is a retired plumber who has lived alone for the past two years, following his wife's death. His home, which he owns and where he has lived for 39 years, is in a deteriorated inner-city neighborhood. He remembers walking to the local store for milk, but there are no longer any stores close by. His daily activities are limited to caring for the house, preparing meals, and watching TV. He prepares the "TV dinners" his daughter brings to him once a week. Both Mrs. V and Mr. T have noticed that Mr. T is getting to be forgetful. They think that is why he ends up in the hospital. He may overeat or forget to eat at all some days. He probably takes his medication irregularly.

Mr. T refuses to leave his house, saying that he is too sick and tired. He resists going to visit his daughter and her family and seldom leaves the house except to go to the doctor's office or to the hospital. Mrs. V says that she has tried to get him to take his medicine, to comply with his diet, and to exercise, but that she has her own job and family responsibilities. Also, her father does not cooperate with her, and it is easier not to fight with him but to bring him what he wants (fried foods and sweets).

Both Mr. T and Mrs. V said they want Mr. T to stay in his home. Mr. T seems sufficiently concerned about not being able to return home, so he is likely to comply with the medical regimen if proper supports are provided.

Unified Problem List:

Number	Problem	Active	Inactive/Resolved
1	Congestive heart failure	4/4	
2	Lack of compliance with diet	4/4	
3	Abuse of medications	4/7	
4	Forgetfulness	4/7	4/12
5	Depression	4/12	

Initial Plans:

4/9: T.T., Social Service

No. 2—Lack of compliance with diet

- Explore and assess current psychosocial situation to determine cause of problem.

- Reinforce nutrition education.

- Work with patient and daughter toward improved nutrition support.

- Explore community support network. Example: Meals on Wheels.

No. 4—Forgetfulness

- Participate in assessment of mental status.

- Collect further information for personal and social history.

- Assess effect of mental status on no. 2 and no. 3.

Progress Notes:

4/12: T.T., Social Service

No. 5—Depression

    A—Assessment: Forgetfulness appears to be related to emotional reaction to death of wife and retirement from work role.

    P—Counsel Mr. T regarding grief and loss. Assess potential for increasing physical and social activities during and after hospitalization.

4/17: T.T., Social Service

No. 2—Lack of compliance with diet

    S—Mr. T is beginning to express his recognition that he needs to change his diet when he goes home. He says that he used to live for fried chicken but now he knows that he might have died from it.

    O—In contrast with earlier hospitalization, when he had to be cajoled into accepting a new diet, Mr. T is cooperating fully. He is now taking an active part rather than a passive, noncompliant stance. Staff is responding positively to his decreased demands and "manipulations."

    A—As depression begins to lift, Mr. T seems able to accept the need to give up old habits. With further support and education, he is more likely to maintain improvements at home.

    P—Involve daughter in planning and implementing change in diet support upon return home.

Exhibit 4.4 Excerpts from a Problem-Oriented Record: Community Mental Health Center, Long-Term Care

Background: (Summarized from Charts of Previous Admissions)

Mr. R is a 32-year-old patient with the following history:

    Ages 16–18: Three admissions to inpatient psych unit, local hospital. Psychotic episodes.

    Ages 18–29: Repeated admissions to B State Hospital for periods of four weeks to 18 months. Diagnosis: schizophrenia, paranoid type.

Between hospitalizations, Mr. R would return to this community, where he lived with his sister and her five children. He attended group meetings and doctor appointments at the center irregularly. Psychiatrist noted that his compliance with prescribed antipsychotic medication was as irregular as his participation in the center's programs. He was aggressive or withdrawn in relationships with staff and other patients. Within a few months of his discharge to the community, he would leave his sister's home (possibly leaving town) and not return to her home or to the center for long periods of time (months). Eventually he would return to B State and repeat the described pattern.

    Three years ago, Mr. R left again. This was the longest absence without contact either with his sister or with B State. Five months ago, he was picked up by police in T (400 miles from here); he requested that he be returned to B State. He came "home" to his sister's house this week.

(continued)

Discharge summary from B State indicates that he entered the hospital in severe distress. He was agitated, combative, and actively delusionary. He demonstrated ideas of reference and persecution. After drug therapy (Thorazine) was instituted, psychotic symptoms were reduced.

Case Reopened: 8/18/xx Mental status examination by Dr. K on 8/22. Meeting on 8/23, attended by Mr. R and his sister (Miss R), produced the following problem list:

1. Takes antipsychotic medication irregularly

2. Paranoid ideation (suspiciousness)

3. Poor self-care

4. Combative in relationships with other patients

5. Conflict with sister

6. Prevent "running away"

Conflict with Sister: 9/1/xx

S—Mr. R's sister, Miss R, says that she would not mind having her brother staying with her if he would do some things for her (care for the house, run errands) and give her his money (disability). She feels that he is "lazy, not crazy."

A—Mr. R and his sister have a relationship that meets each other's needs during periods when he is able to meet her demands. During previous periods when Mr. R stayed with his sister, a pattern recurred. Immediately after he was discharged, Miss R was glad to have him around to help her and to keep her company. As his willingness (or ability) to fulfill her needs decreased, she would put increased demands on him. He would then flee the situation.

P—To "short-circuit" the previous pattern of conflict followed by flight, teach Mr. R and Miss R to negotiate responsibilities in the home, and involve Miss R in a family group. This will offer her support and increase her knowledge about schizophrenia.

K.N., MSW
Caseworker

Summary

Primary Function: Accountability.

Secondary Functions: Interdisciplinary communication and physician education.

Current Usage: Health and mental health organizations.

Organizing Rationale: Medical model; structured around presenting problems, which may include, but are not restricted to, disease labels.

Strengths: Facilitates accountability; the practitioner or the health team is responsible for responding to the problems listed. Facilitates peer review, medical education, and interdisciplinary collaboration.

Limitations: It is time-consuming and therefore costly. It must be adapted to incorporate salient social work issues and interventions. It does not address (1) whether listed problems were significant or appropriately labeled, or (2) whether significant problems were overlooked.

MONITORING MOVEMENT

There are a number of recordkeeping forms and formats that may be used to document indicators of movement toward achieving the identified goals of service. These formats are used to record information, for example, about the behaviors, actions, attitudes, or relationships that are the focus of social work intervention over time. They display information in a meaningful and accessible way, assisting practitioners, clients, and others in making decisions about the direction and effects of service. These formats may also be used to record data for single case research. However, the intricacies of design, implementation, and interpretation of findings in such research are beyond the scope of this chapter (see, e.g., Bloom & Fischer, 1982; Jayaratne & Levy, 1979; Nugent, 2000).

The process of monitoring movement begins as soon as the purposes of service are established, goals are set, and indicators selected. Once decisions have been made as to what information is to be documented, when and how frequently it is to be recorded, and who is to do the recording, documentation is relatively straightforward. For example, a group worker notes the number of times an especially shy client speaks during each group meeting. Another practitioner notes the number of requests for pain medication made each day by patients participating in a pain-control program. An agency notes the number of new cases of child abuse reported each day in the month before and after a community education program is initiated. A client fills out a written questionnaire prior to interviews. Each member of a family keeps a log describing family conflicts, and what happened before and afterwards. A client keeps a diary and rates him- or herself on "How angry was I today?" using a scale of one to 10. In some cases, documentation begins before intervention is initiated. For example, a teacher's assistant observes and documents what occurs in a classroom at brief intervals during the day. The information, which is collected before, during, and following social work intervention, can be used to evaluate the impact of services on the actions of a child with behavior problems and those of other children and teachers in the classroom.

Several general principles apply, regardless of the approach to the collection and recording of information. First, there should be consistency in what indicators are documented, who does the documentation, and when and how often information is collected and recorded. Using forms or formats for recording information can encourage consistency. Forms and formats assist the recorder not just in organizing the information, but also in recalling what information needs to be collected and recorded. This is especially helpful when time has elapsed or when a different practitioner assumes responsibility for delivering services or documenting indicators of movement.

In addition, at minimum, forms and formats used to document indicators of movement over time should include the following information:

- instructions for the use of the form (who, when, where, what);
- information about indicators (description, source);
- when, how often, and by whom information is collected; and
- special factors in person or situation that may influence the collection of information or the indicator itself.

Finally, whenever possible, more than one indicator and source of information should be used to monitor movement. In complex client-need-situations, using a variety of indicators helps surface small changes, unexpected responses, and varying perspectives. Combining self-report indicators (e.g., the client's responses to a quality of life scale with others' observations of the client's participation in a rehabilitation program) offers a better picture of the client's responses to services than would any single indictor used alone. In general, documentation of different indicators should not be combined. For the purposes of clarity and reliability, each indicator should be documented separately, using its own form or format.

The most challenging component of monitoring movement is evaluating progress and impact. Has the client-need-situation improved, stayed the same, or deteriorated? How much improvement is sufficient? How much time should elapse before deciding whether the service plan is working and goals are likely to be achieved? What criteria should be used to decide whether services should be continued, changed, or terminated? Sometimes decisions are made in consultation between the worker and the client. For example, a family may agree to continue receiving services, based on improvement in a child's school behavior, despite little change in other areas. Sometimes standards are provided by the measures themselves. For example, some indices of depression, quality of life, and self-esteem provide norms for evaluation. Sometimes decisions are linked to prior agreements with the client or third parties, such as that services will be limited to a specified number of sessions. Sometimes decisions are determined by agency or program policy. For example, a client may be terminated from an inpatient treatment program for breaking rules against substance use. However, when decisions are primarily based on a visual analysis of indicators of movement, they are not always clear-cut. Some indicators may show a clear trend in one direction, but others may show considerable variability. Sometimes the client-need-situation changes unexpectedly or the service process moves in a new direction. The selected indicators may not accurately reflect the purpose or goals of service, or adequately represent the change that has occurred (Kagle, 1982b; Thomas, 1978). Practitioners, clients, and others involved in decision making must also rely on additional information about the client-need-situation, the client's preferences and resources, the availability of services, and the views of key actors in evaluating the process and impact of services.

Several examples of records that monitor movement in social work services follow. Exhibit 4.5 presents a progress log; exhibit 4.6 presents a behavior report. Exhibit 4.7 presents a time chart from a supported work program. Exhibits 4.8, 4.9, and 4.10 present examples of time-series graphs.

Summary

Primary Function: Documentation of service effects over time.

Secondary Functions: Ongoing assessment of the client-need-situation; practice research.

Current Usage: Widespread in cognitive-behavioral intervention; limited but increasing use in all fields of practice.

Organizing Rationale: Information is presented graphically to show any changes in indicators over time.

Strengths: The recordkeeping formats are very usable and useful. Specifies content and procedures for recordkeeping. May be used as an interim note format and combined with other approaches to documentation. Identifying indicators and collecting information over time focuses the worker and the client on defining and achieving goals.

Limitations: Using indicators may intrude on the service process, focusing it too narrowly on influencing indicators. Indicators may not adequately reflect the complexity of the change process or surface what takes place in complex client-need-situations.

Exhibit 4.5   Monitoring Movement: Family Therapy

Progress Log
Family: R
Members: Mr. R (38)   Mrs. R (38)
             John R (16)   Claudia R (14)
             Mrs. R, senior (77)
Modality: Family therapy
Goal or Task: Redefine IP's (John's) problem in family terms
Measure: Number of occurrences of "John is or has problem" or "Family has problem"
By: Worker from tapes, every second session

Session	Measure	Change	Comments
1	8/0		Most of the statements were made by Mrs. R.
3	4/0	+	Mrs. R continues to make most of the negative statements. Claudia is both uncomfortable and pleased that John is the focus. Mr. R speaks little.
5	4/2	+	Mr. R made two statements acknowledging family issues. Mrs. R's statements are less overt but perhaps more cutting.
7	2/2	+	Mrs. R has decreased the number of negative statements made about John in the interview. However, the two negative statements voiced were made by her. She is not giving up but is less overt. Mr. R again acknowledged family difficulties.

Exhibit 4.6 Monitoring Movement: Behavioral Intervention in a Public School

Behavior Report
Name: Bobby L
Age: Seven
Grade: One
Class: Self-contained
Referred by: Mr. Peterson, for "disruptive, undisciplined behavior in class"

Measurement Plan: Observe Bobby's behavior for two five-minute periods daily, selected at random. Record (1) whether Bobby is complying with expected behavior during observation period and (2) antecedents and consequences of compliance or noncompliance.
Recorder: N.R.

Date	Observation Initiated	Antecedents	Compliance Y	N	Consequences
11/1	9:10 AM	Lots of talking in class, told to settle down, all do except three boys		X	Mr. P reprimands B only
	11:30 AM	N/A		X	Time-out
11/2	11:05 AM	Music teacher begins song	X		—
	2:20 PM	Playground activities		X	Removed from game
11/3	8:55 AM	Reading begins		X	—
	2:10 PM	Getting ready for play		X	Detained before going out
11/6	9:10 AM	Reading	X		—
11/7	11:00 AM	Music teacher absent, free time, sits alone	X		—

Exhibit 4.7   Monitoring Movement: Work Program for Individuals Experiencing Chronic and Persistent Mental Illness

Name: *Lark*				Month: *September*	
Day	Present	Pieces	Appearance	Remarks	By
Mon.	yes	10	poor	fight with Lucille	M.G.
Tues.	yes	21	fair	stayed to herself	R.R.
Wed.	yes	18	poor	said she was getting sick	M.G.
Thurs.	no			called in sick	M.G.
Fri.	no				
Mon.	no				
Tues.	yes	10	poor	withdrawn, talking to self	M.G.
Wed.	yes	8	poor	called social worker will have appt. tomorrow	M.G.
Thurs.	no			social work appt.	

Exhibit 4.8   Example of a Time-Series Record Showing a Self-Anchored Scale: Mental Health Clinic

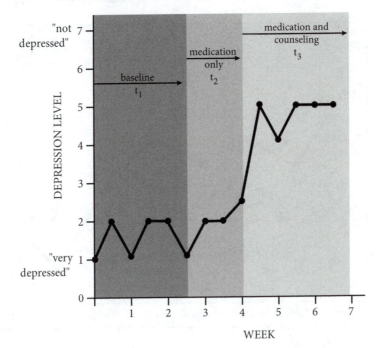

Exhibit 4.9 Example of a Time-Series Record with a Multiple Baseline: Using "Time-Out" to Decrease a Child's Tantrums

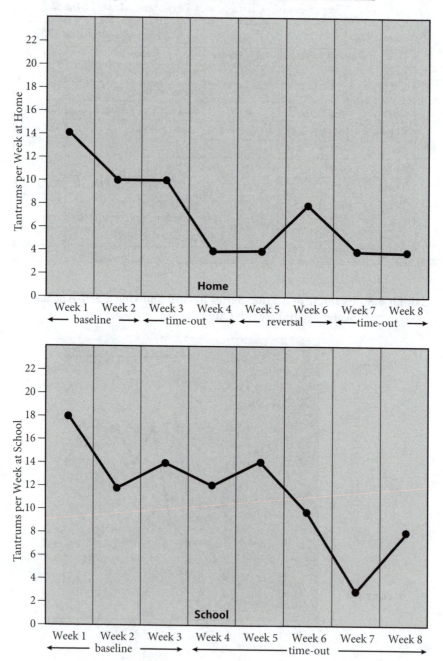

Exhibit 4.10   Example of a Time-Series Record: Measuring the Effects of a Child Welfare Community Education Plan

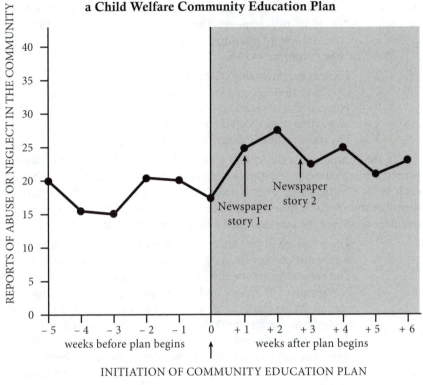

INITIATION OF COMMUNITY EDUCATION PLAN

GOAL ATTAINMENT SCALING

Goal Attainment Scaling (GAS) is a special method for documenting and evaluating movement and outcomes; it is used primarily in mental health and other agencies that serve children and adults with mental health or behavior disorders. Documentation focuses on three elements: (1) specifying goals, (2) identifying measures that represent movement toward attaining those goals, and, most important, (3) monitoring and evaluating movement toward goal attainment. GAS was first developed by Kiresuk and his colleagues (1968, 1979) and has been applied to social work practice (Bloom & Fischer, 1982; Corcoran & Gingerich, 1992). Its purpose was to quantify the evaluation of mental health service programs. Today GAS is also used to monitor individualized services to clients, who are sometimes referred to as consumers or recipients of service.

The first step in GAS is to specify a goal of service. In the example below, the worker and the recipient of service decided that their goal was to improve the relationship between the recipient of service and her parents. The second step is to choose a method for documenting movement toward attaining this goal. In this example, the worker and recipient of services decided to use as their measure the number of arguments per day between the recipient and her parents, as recorded by the recipient. The third step is to develop a GAS for evaluating movement toward attaining the goal.

There are five points on a GAS:

–2 = The most unfavorable outcome thought likely
–1 = Less than the expected level of success
  0 = The expected level of success
+1 = More than the expected level of success
+2 = The most favorable outcome thought likely

In the example in exhibit 4.11, the worker and the recipient of service prepared a verbal description of the client-need-situation at the outcome for each point on the scale. This is called a "self-anchored" scale, because it describes the special nature of the recipient's situation. Here, the worker and recipient described the best and least favorable possible outcomes:

–2 = The recipient of service and her parents increase the number of arguments per day from the baseline level (three) to five or more. The parents withdraw their financial support.
–1 = The recipient of service and her parents continue the number of arguments per day recorded during baseline (three). The parents continue to threaten withdrawal of their financial support.
  0 = The recipient of service and her parents decrease the number of arguments per day from the number during baseline (three) to two. The parents continue to support the recipient of service financially.
+1 = The recipient of service and her parents decrease the number of arguments per day from the number during baseline (three) to two or fewer. The parents continue to support the recipient of service financially; they no longer threaten to withdraw financial support.
+2 = The recipient of service and her parents argue infrequently (no more than once per day). The parents continue to support the recipient of service financially; some long-term plans for her support are being discussed by the client and her family.

The above example focused on a single goal. Most often, however, services are intended to accomplish not one but several goals. When this occurs, a separate scale is developed and used to evaluate movement toward each service goal. When goals are not equally important, each goal is individually weighted so that more important goals are given greater numerical value.

GAS is most often used in programs that serve groups of recipients with common goals and intended outcomes. Progress for each recipient is monitored individually using the same scale. Scores may then be compared over time, across recipients, and among programs. However, it is very important to recognize what the numerical value on a GAS scale actually represents, so that it is not misinterpreted. First, the score on a GAS scale does not reveal anything about the recipient's level of functioning. Rather, it quantifies the

**Exhibit 4.11   Example of a Goal Attainment Scale:
Community Mental Health Center**

Client: Leslie R
Program: Outpatient Counseling

Date Prepared: 2/18/xx
Worker: S. Khinda, BSW

Measure	Goal One (Value = 3): Improve Relationship with Parents	Goal Two (Value = 5): Decrease Depression	Goal Three (Value = 5): Decrease Substance Use
–2	Five + fights per day Parents withdraw money	Cries several times daily; stays in bed; poor self-care; feels useless	Uses drugs or alcohol daily Stays high
–1	Three fights per day Parents threaten to withdraw money	Cries; sleeps late, but arises; self-care some days; some hope	Uses drugs or alcohol three + times per week
0	Two fights per day Parents give money, no threats	Seldom cries; usually up by 9:00; regular self-care; hopeful	Uses drugs/ alcohol < one time per week
+1	< Two fights per day No threat to withdraw money	Expresses sadness infrequently; up by 9:00; good appearance; initiates activity	Uses drugs/ alcohol < one time per two weeks
+2	< One fight per day Planning for long-term money	Expresses positive feelings, little sadness; up by 9:00; pride in appearance; making decisions	Abstains

actual goal attainment against expectations. Second, GAS scores are linked to initial expectations of outcomes. A recipient of service who achieves a +2 GAS score, for example, may not have achieved optimal functioning, but rather is functioning at the optimal *expected* level. Third, lower expectations will produce higher scores than high expectations. In the above example, it would be much more difficult to achieve a +2 score if the expectation was for one argument per week rather than per day. Finally, it is very difficult to compare GAS scores on different scales where goals, measures, expectations, and scaling differ.

It is important to remember that GAS scores cannot explain the reason for negative or positive outcomes. A low GAS score may be caused by a variety of factors, among them inappropriate selection of goals, unrealistically high expectations, poor indicators, deficient measurement, uncontrollable events in the recipient's environment, or inadequate services. Similarly, a high GAS score may result from a positive service experience or from other factors. If scores are to be used to assess the effectiveness of service, then, much more information about the client-need-situation and the service environment must be documented.

Summary

Primary Function: Accountability.

Secondary Function: Monitor service effects over time; research.

Current Usage: Mental health.

Organizing Rationale: Individualized goals and measures of their achievement form the basis for a scale that quantifies the level of goal attainment in terms of expected goal attainment.

Strengths: Focuses worker and client on outcomes that are attainable. Makes explicit the method of evaluating progress.

Limitations: The GAS cannot measure whether the goal was appropriate or significant. Nor can it determine whether services were efficient, effective, or responsible for the outcomes achieved.

CHAPTER 5

THE STRUCTURE OF RECORDS II
FORMS

Social work agencies use a variety of open-ended and fixed-choice forms in their records. Some forms are actually outlines for narrative reports, placing no boundaries on the amount of information to be documented. Most, however, provide limited space on the screen or paper for brief narratives, short answers, or check marks. Additional information may be documented elsewhere, but most forms are constructed to encourage concise, direct, and concrete responses.

Forms are used to collect specific information that is used to meet accountability requirements. They make information accessible to the user, and allow comparisons among clients, services, programs, processes, and outcomes. While narrative reports are intended to document information that individualizes the client-need-situation and services, forms are intended to characterize and classify them. Forms help to ensure that important information is recorded. They standardize recordkeeping and can have a similar effect on decision making and service delivery. That is, practitioners learn what is to be documented and may conform their data collection, and even their practice decisions and actions, to meet those expectations.

Forms can also make recordkeeping more efficient by focusing documentation on certain information and by decreasing the need for narrative reports. Over time, however, the addition of new forms to the record can have the opposite effect. The efficiencies that result from the use of forms may be lost when practitioners are expected to complete more and more of them. Indeed, one study found that a new recordkeeping system consumed more of the practitioner's time, resulting in a reduction of time available for service delivery (Edwards & Reid, 1989). The need to do a great deal of paperwork, particularly filling out forms, is linked to the high demand for accountability in publicly and privately funded organizations. It may also be the result of inadequate access to or inefficient use of computers in some agencies.

CREATING FORMS

Creating paper or computerized forms involves two steps: planning and designing. Those who are involved in planning for a new or updated form should consider:

- the relationship of the form to the entire recordkeeping system;
- the purpose or function of the form;
- the information to be included on the form;
- ease of information entry, use, and retrieval; and
- how to limit the content of the form for efficient use.

As a preparatory step, some agencies may benefit from an analysis of all of their forms and narrative records to identify redundancies and gaps in information collection. An index of the information currently collected on all agency forms and in narrative reports can assist planners in deciding which forms might be eliminated, combined, or redesigned and what might be added. Although this step is not always necessary, it is important to begin the planning process by clarifying the relationship between the form being planned and other forms and formats in the agency's recordkeeping system. This allows for clear specification of what information is to be entered, when it is to be recorded, and how the information will be used.

Once the agency has defined the purpose or function of a form, it is useful to make a list of all the information that could conceivably be included on it. Expanding the range of possibilities early in the planning process increases the likelihood that the form will be complete. The next step is to limit the content to information that is necessary for decision making at some level of the organization. The goal, as in other recordkeeping decisions, is to balance accountability with efficiency.

In developing new or updating existing forms, agencies should recognize that good form organization and design encourages complete and accurate documentation. Good form organization means that information is easy to enter and can be documented in the order in which it is received.

Good form design means that:

- instructions are placed at the top rather than at the bottom of the page or screen;
- there is sufficient space for entering the requested information;
- there is a clear spatial relationship between labels or queries and the space provided for responses;
- checklists are meaningful and comprehensive;
- categories within checklists are revised when they are no longer meaningful or when too many responses fall into the "other" (not specified) category;

- queries are clear and can be answered briefly and succinctly;
- information is sequenced so that it can be entered in a logical order;
- related information is grouped together on the form or screen;
- key information is described before it is summarized or coded;
- labels are small and borders are narrow to maximize the space available for responses and minimize the size and length of the form;
- when more than one form is used to collect related information, the same language and design elements are used;
- on forms that are to be typed,
  - vertical lines are placed at natural single- or double-space intervals,
  - vertical lines begin and end on the same horizontal space, and
  - whenever possible, all stops (for tabulations) are placed on the same horizontal space;
- on forms that are to be completed by hand, box design is used whenever possible:

Poor: Date of Birth _____

Better: | Date of Birth

or

(Date of Birth)

- in checklists that are to be completed by hand, parentheses (rather than lines) are used and are placed close to the appropriate caption. Of course, enough space is provided between the caption and the parenthesis so that check marks or blackouts are properly placed and are legible.

Poor: Sex: Male __ Female __
       Marital Status: Married __ Never Mar __ Sep __ Div __ Wid __

Better: Sex: ( ) Male   ( ) Female   Marital Status: ( ) Married
                           ( ) Never Married
                           ( ) Separated
                           ( ) Divorced
                           ( ) Widowed

Today, widely available form templates have made designing paper and computerized forms relatively easy. Templates that are offered by Microsoft Office™ and other computer software vendors, or downloaded from the Internet, can be used in the design of paper or computerized forms. Agencies with computerized record systems may adopt software programs that allow practitioners or clerical workers to complete forms online. Some computer software includes such analytic functions as automatic calculations and summaries.

EXAMPLES OF FORMS

The forms that follow represent some of the many forms that are used in social work agencies, departments, and programs. They illustrate commonly used forms in manual as well as automated recordkeeping systems. Of course, this set of examples is in no way exhaustive. There are simply too many different forms in use to make it possible to show them all. In fact, some organizations in which social workers are employed use more than 300 different forms in their recordkeeping systems. When differences among organizations are considered, then, the actual number of different forms being used by social workers is probably in the thousands.

Due to changing regulations and legislation at the state and federal levels, it is difficult to describe the requisite information for certain requirements. For example, form 15 is HIPAA-compliant as of 2007. Because state law may have specific requirements for disclosure, agencies and practitioners need to be sure that the forms they adopt contain the information necessary to be in compliance. These types of forms should be modified as necessary for field of practice and updated as laws and rules change.

Summary

Primary Function: Systematic information collection.

Secondary Functions: Simplifying and routinizing recordkeeping.

Current Usage: Universal.

Organizing Rationale: Each form is organized around specified purposes. Documentation usually requires only brief narratives, short answers, or check marks.

Strengths: A well-organized form can simplify recording. Information can easily be accessed to support accountability, service continuity, and decision making. Specified information is likely to be documented.

Limitations: Characterizes but may not individualize clients, services, and providers. May undermine professional decisions and actions by standardizing documentation and service delivery.

Form 1

FACE SHEET < adult, individual >

Side 1: Personal Data

Print or type. Mark as many as apply.

(case number)

(service)

(date opened/reopened)

Client Name		
(last)	(first)	(middle)

Address		
(number)	(street)	
(city)	(county/state)	(zip) (census track)

Sex	Birth	Phone
M ( )	Date _____ _____ _____	(day) _____ _____
F ( )	(month) (day) (year)	(area)

Religion	Ethnicity	Primary Language	Marital Status	Veteran Status
( ) Cath.	( ) Afric. Am.	( ) English	( ) Never married	( ) None
( ) Prot.	( ) Asian Am.	( ) Spanish	( ) Married	( ) Veteran
( ) Jew	( ) Nat. Am.	( ) Polish	( ) Separated	( ) Child of
( ) None	( ) White	( ) Chinese	( ) Divorced	( ) Parent of
( ) Other	( ) Other	_____	( ) Widowed	( ) Spouse of
_____	_____	(specify dialect)		( ) Widow(er) of
(specify)	(specify)	( ) Other		
		_____		
		(specify)		

Lives		Family Income (Annual)	Source of Income
( ) Alone	( ) Nursing home	( ) Less than $10,000	( ) Wage/salary/investments
( ) Parent(s)	( ) Foster home	( ) $10–20,000	( ) Soc. Security/pension
( ) Spouse	( ) Institution	( ) $20–30,000	( ) SSI
( ) Child(ren)	( ) Community group home	( ) $30–40,000	( ) TANF
( ) Other relative(s)		( ) $40,000 +	( ) County
( ) Non-relative(s)			( ) Other
			_____
			(specify)

Education (highest level)	Occupation	Employment Status
( ) Preschool	( ) Student	( ) Unemployed
( ) Special education	( ) Homemaker	( ) Retired
( ) K–8	( ) Professional/ managerial	( ) Employed—part time
( ) 9–11	( ) Clerical/sales	( ) Employed—temporary
( ) High school	( ) Skilled/tech.	( ) Employed—full time
( ) Some college	( ) Unskilled	( ) Self-employed
( ) College degree		
( ) Postgraduate	Disabled	Seeking Change
	( ) Yes ( ) No	( ) Yes ( ) No

Form 1 *(continued)*

FACE SHEET < adult, individual >	*DSM* Diagnoses

FACE SHEET < adult, individual >

Side 2: Service Data < mental health >

Print or type. Mark as many as apply.

DSM Diagnoses

1. _____
2. _____
3. _____
4. _____

Source of Referral/Request

( ) Self   ( ) Attorney   ( ) School
( ) Personal network   ( ) Court   ( ) Employer
( ) Physician   ( ) Police   ( ) Clergy
( ) Psychologist   ( ) Social worker ( ) Other
( ) Outreach
                    _____   _____
                    (specify agency)   (specify)

Contact with Referral Source

( ) Yes, they initiated
( ) Yes, we initiated
( ) No

Reason for Referral/Request

( ) Depression/suicidal   ( ) Developmental disability
( ) Anxiety/stress   ( ) Mental retardation
( ) CMI/thought disorder   ( ) Education problems
( ) Antisocial behavior   ( ) Employment problems
( ) Substance use/abuse   ( ) Physical disease/disability
( ) Psychotic episode   ( ) Financial difficulties
( ) Situational crisis   ( ) Interpersonal difficulties
( ) Information/referral   ( ) Other _____
( ) Medication   (specify)

Services Planned

( ) Information/referral   ( ) Individual counseling
( ) Assessment   ( ) Family counseling
( ) Medication   ( ) Couple counseling
( ) Education   ( ) Group counseling
( ) Inpatient/milieu   ( ) Crisis intervention
( ) Day care—sustaining care   ( ) Residential placement
( ) Detox/substance program   ( ) Early childhood stimulation
( ) Sheltered workshop   ( ) Employment placement
( ) Other _____
        (specify)

Service Review	Plan Approval	
_____ (case opened/reopened)	_____ (signature, recipient)	_____ (date)
_____ (dates of previous service)	_____ (signature, guardian)	_____ (date)
_____ (previous primary provider)	_____ (signature, primary provider)	_____ (date)

Form 2

FACE SHEET < family >

Side 1: Personal Data

Print or type.

| (case number) |
| (service) |
| (date opened/reopened) |

Name (responsible adult)

| (last) | (first) | (middle) |

Address

| (number) | (street) |

| (city) | (state) | (zip) |

| Home Phone | Business Phone (adult no. 1) | Business Phone (adult no. 2) |

Family Members Adults	Sex	Birthdate	Resides	Occupation	Education Level
1					
2					
3					
4					
Children					
1					
2					
3					
4					
5					
6					

| Family Income | Debts | Insurance/Aid |

| Religion | Ethnicity | Language |

Family Characteristics (reconstituted, foster children, and so forth)

Form 2 *(continued)*

FACE SHEET < family >

[(case number)]

Side 2: Service Data < Child/family >

(case number)

Print or type.

[(surname)]

(surname)

Source of Referral/Request	If Referred, Reason for Referral
_____	_____
_____	_____

Family's Definition of Problem/Need (include differing views)
_____
_____
_____
_____

Worker's Initial Assessment of Family
_____
_____
_____
_____

Contract
Service Goals: _____
_____
_____

Service Plans: _____
_____
_____

Worker's Assessment of Client Commitment: _____
_____
_____

Service Checklist

____	____
(date) (master file)	(date) (foster file)
(date) (privacy form)	(date) (adoption file)
(date) (release-of-information form)	(date) (problem pregnancy file)

Form 3

SOCIAL HISTORY FORM

Aging

_____   _____
(client name)   (birth date)

Information gathered from:

Source(s)   Date(s) _____

_____

_____

_____

1. Description (physical appearance, behavior, affect, speech, and so forth)

2. Health History (significant illnesses, disabilities)

3. Current Health Status (mobility, self-care, medications, and so forth)

4. Family History (early life, marriage, children, and so forth)

5. Current Family Situation

6. Work History and Status

7. Community and Organization Activities (current and past)

8. Special Talents and Abilities

9. Special Needs or Problems

_____   _____
(form completed by)   (date completed)

Form 4

Session Summary—Individual or Couple
Case:
Date: Worker:
Session Number: Session Length (in minutes):
Who was present?
1. Briefly describe what happened during the session.
2. List all the new problems, needs, or issues that surfaced.
3. What interventions were used?
4. What new recommendations, referrals, or plans were made?
5. What is the status of the case?

Form 5

Session Summary—Family	Side 1

Case:

Date: Worker:

Session Number: Session Length (in minutes):

Who was present?

---

1. Briefly describe what happened during the session.

---

2. List all the new problems, needs, or issues that surfaced.

---

3. What interventions were used?

---

4. What new recommendations, referrals, or plans were made?

---

5. What is the status of the case?

Form 5 *(continued)*

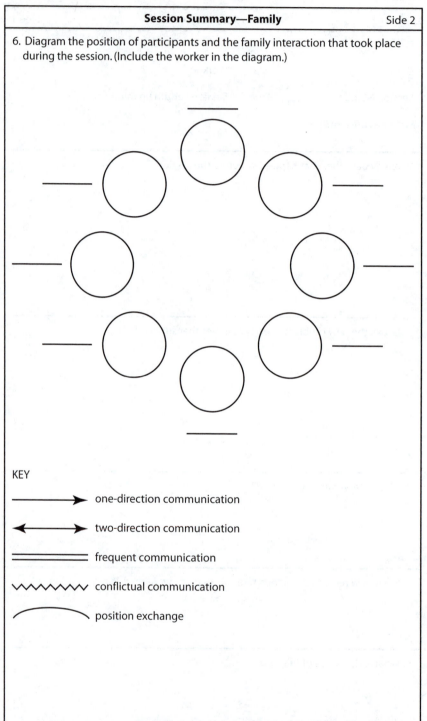

| Session Summary—Family | Side 2 |

6. Diagram the position of participants and the family interaction that took place during the session. (Include the worker in the diagram.)

KEY

——————▶ one-direction communication

◀——————▶ two-direction communication

══════════ frequent communication

〰〰〰〰〰 conflictual communication

⌒ position exchange

Form 6

Session Summary—Group	Side 1

Case:

Date: **Worker:**

Session Number: **Session Length (in minutes):**

Who was present?

1. Briefly describe what happened during the session.

2. What interventions were used?

3. What new individual problems, needs, or issues surfaced?

4. What plans were made for future group activity?

Form 6 *(continued)*

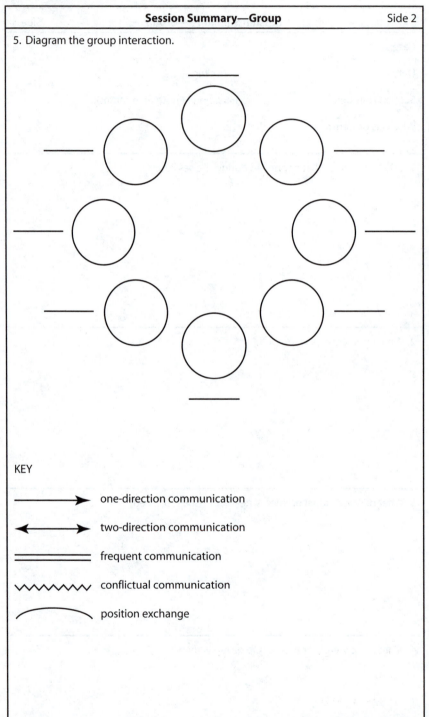

Session Summary—Group   Side 2

5. Diagram the group interaction.

KEY

⟶ one-direction communication

⟵⟶ two-direction communication

⟹ frequent communication

⌇⌇⌇ conflictual communication

⌒ position exchange

Form 7

SERVICE FLOW CHART	Client Name
	Identification

Referral Source < if other than client >	Reason for Referral

___ / ___ / ___ ___ / ___ / ___	Client's Description of Presenting Problem
(date opened) (last date opened)	

Assessed Problems/Needs

No. 1 _____	No. 2 _____	No. 3 _____
(date identified)	(date identified)	(date identified)
(referred to)	(referred to)	(referred to)
(date referred)	(date referred)	(date referred)
Agency Activity ( ) Client refused ( ) Service denied/ unavailable ( ) Service contract	Agency Activity ( ) Client refused ( ) Service denied/ unavailable ( ) Service contract	Agency Activity ( ) Client refused ( ) Service denied/ unavailable ( ) Service contract

Form 7 *(continued)*

Service Plan		List Each Service > 15 minutes					
		Month	Day	Code	Month	Day	Code

Service Plan

Code

a ( ) Information referral only
b ( ) Individual counseling
c ( ) Marital/family counseling

Code

d ( ) Group work
e ( ) _____
f ( ) _____
g ( ) _____

List Each Service > 15 minutes

Month	Day	Code	Month	Day	Code

Staffings/Reviews

_____ / _____ / _____   _____
(date)   (description)

_____ / _____ / _____   _____
(date)   (description)

Documentation
Completed

__/__ Intake summary   __/__ Interim note

__/__ Social history   __/__ Interim note

__/__ Goals/plans   __/__ Interim note

__/__ Contract   __/__ Closing summary

__/__ Release of info   __/__ Follow-up

_____ / _____ / _____   _____
(date closed)   (reason for closing)

	1	2	3
Resolved/improved	( )	( )	( )
No change	( )	( )	( )
Unresolved/ deteriorated	( )	( )	( )
No information	( )	( )	( )

List additional information on reverse side.

Worker of Record (add name when case is assigned)

_____   _____
(worker)   (date)

_____   _____
(worker)   (date)

_____   _____
(worker)   (date)

_____   _____
(worker)   (date)

_____   _____
(worker)   (date)

Form 8

CLOSING SUMMARY < health >

[(chart number)]

Print or type.
Mark all applicable responses.

(worker)

Client Name		Date Admitted ___ ___ ___

Date S.S. Opening ___ ___ ___

Date S.S. Closing ___ ___ ___

Birth Date   Sex
                  ( ) M
                  ( ) F
___ ___ ___
(month) (day) (year)

Primary Diagnosis (medical)

_____

Secondary Diagnoses (medical)

_____
_____
_____

Health Status at Discharge
( ) No impairment
( ) Temporary impairment
( ) Permanent impairment—good prognosis
( ) Permanent impairment—poor prognosis
( ) Deceased

Physician

_____

Service Area(s)

_____
_____
_____
_____

Continuing Care
( ) None
( ) Medication/prosthesis
( ) Home health
( ) Other home supports
( ) ECF / nursing home
( ) Hospice
( ) Rehabilitation
( ) Other _____
          (specify)

Referred by _____   Number of interviews / consultations
( ) 1   ( ) 2–5   ( ) 6–9   ( ) 10+

Primary Problem / Need
(social service)

_____

Secondary Problems / Needs
(social service)

_____
_____
_____

Status at Closing

( ) Resolved/ ( ) No change ( ) Deterio- ( ) N/A*
improved   rated

( ) +   ( ) 0   ( ) –   ( ) N/A
( ) +   ( ) 0   ( ) –   ( ) N/A
( ) +   ( ) 0   ( ) –   ( ) N/A

* Not addressed

Services
( ) Information / referral   ( ) Individual counseling
( ) Transportation   ( ) Group work
( ) Continuity of care   ( ) Couple, family counseling
( ) Assessment   ( ) Education
( ) Advocacy   ( ) Other _____
                                      (specify)

Form 9

DAILY CALENDAR < direct service >

Instructions: Using an X, enter activities for each 15-minute period. At the end of the day, tally columns.

| Worker | | Office | | Assignment | | | Date ____ / ____ / ____ | | | | |
| | | | | | | | (month) (day) (year) | | | | |

Time	Client Services						Support Services				
	Client Name (Status)	Interview/ Meeting	Consultation		Records/ Reports	Supervision/ Education	Meetings			Research	Admin-istration
			Internal	Outside			Social Work	Organization	Community		
__ hr 00–15 15–30 30–45 45–00											
__ hr 00–15 15–30 30–45 45–00											
__ hr 00–15 15–30 30–45 45–00											
__ hr 00–15 15–30 30–45 45–00											

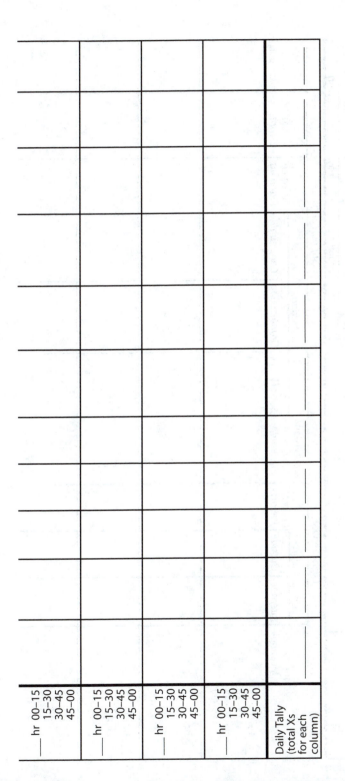

__ hr 00–15 15–30 30–45 45–00										
__ hr 00–15 15–30 30–45 45–00										
__ hr 00–15 15–30 30–45 45–00										
__ hr 00–15 15–30 30–45 45–00										
Daily Tally (total Xs for each column)										

Form 10

DAILY CALENDAR < administration >

Instructions: Using an X, enter activities for each 15-minute period. At the end of the day, tally columns.

| Worker | Office | Assignment | Date _____ / _____ / _____ |
| | | | (month)   (day)   (year) |

Time	Client Services					Support Services					
	Interview/ Meeting	Consultation		Records/ Reports	Supervision/ Education (Name)	Meetings			Research Planning	Oversight/ Grants	Other Admin- istration
		Internal	Outside			Social Work	Organization	Community			
___ hr 00–15 15–30 30–45 45–00											
___ hr 00–15 15–30 30–45 45–00											
___ hr 00–15 15–30 30–45 45–00											
___ hr 00–15 15–30 30–45 45–00											

				Daily Tally (total Xs for each column)
hr 00–15 15–30 30–45 45–00	hr 00–15 15–30 30–45 45–00	hr 00–15 15–30 30–45 45–00	hr 00–15 15–30 30–45 45–00	

Form 11

SERVICE LOG < case >					INSTRUCTIONS: Log each activity with or on behalf of the client.

(client name)

(worker name)

Date	Time		Activity	With	Brief Description of the Purpose / Content
	From	To			

Form 12

SERVICE LOG < group >			INSTRUCTIONS: Log each activity with or on behalf of the group.

(group name)

Date	Activity		Participants	Purpose / Content
	Group Meeting	Other		

Form 13

Service Agreement

INSTRUCTIONS: This form is to be completed by worker and client by the end of the third interview. One copy is to be retained by the agency and placed in the client's record. One copy is to be retained by each client.

We have agreed to the following:

1. Purpose(s) or Goal(s) of Service: _____

_____

_____

2. Plan of Service: _____

_____

_____

3. _____ agrees to undertake the following responsibilities:
   (client name)

_____

_____

_____

4. On behalf of the agency, _____ agrees to undertake the following
   responsibilities: (worker name)

_____

_____

_____

This Agreement covers the period from _____ to _____
                                              (date)   (date)

Signed _____   _____
        (client)   (worker)

       _____   _____

Form 14

Authorization for the Release of Information

INSTRUCTIONS: This form is to be prepared in triplicate. These copies are to be distributed:
1. To the client or the client's guardian
2. To the party that releases information
3. To the party that receives information

I, _____ , hereby give consent
    (full name)

to _____
    (name of party to release information)

of _____
    (address of party to release information)

to release the following information: _____

_____
    (description of information to be released)

to _____
    (name of party to receive information)

of _____
    (address of party to receive information)

for _____

_____
    (description of how information will be used)

My signature means that:
1. I have read this authorization or have had this authorization read to me. I understand and agree to its contents.
2. I have been informed that no other information may be released without my written consent.
3. I have been informed that I may revoke this authorization by written statment at any time and that this authorization will be automatically revoked on _____
                                                             (date)

Signed:

_____   _____
(client)   (date)

_____   _____
(guardian)   (date)

_____   _____
(witness)   (date)

Form 15

Authorization for the Release of Health Information

I, _____, request that
(insert full name of patient/client)

_____ release the health information
(name of person or organization or provider)

as specified on this form to _____.
(name or category of person)

I have checked each type of information for which I authorize disclosure (patient/client should check each item to be released).

( ) Admission information   ( ) Psychological evaluation
( ) Assessment   ( ) Psychosocial evaluation
( ) Diagnosis   ( ) Treatment plan
( ) Discharge summary   ( ) Progress notes
( ) Nursing/medical information   ( ) Mental health information
( ) Toxicological reports/drug screens   ( ) Substance abuse information
( ) Demographic information   ( ) HIV/AIDS information
( ) Lab reports   ( ) Other _____
( ) X-rays or radiological images   ( ) Other _____
( ) Dietary logs   ( ) Other _____

The purpose of this disclosure is to _____.
(determine eligibility for services, coordinate treatment, referral, or other)

This authorization is valid until _____ or until _____.
(insert calendar date)   (insert event)

I understand that I can revoke this authorization at any time, in writing, by sending a written

notification to _____.
(insert the name and address of person or organization or provider)

I also understand that any revocation of this authorization does not affect any action that has already been taken in reliance on the authorization.

I understand that signing this authorization is voluntary on my part and that I am not required to sign it to be eligible for treatment, payment, benefits, or enrollment.

However, I also understand that if I do not sign this authorization, the following consequences may result:

_____

_____

_____

Form 15 *(continued)*

Authorization for the Release of Health Information (continued)

I understand that information disclosed under this authorization might be redisclosed by the recipient of the information and no longer subject to the protections of federal law.

I understand that I will be given a copy of this authorization.

_____   _____
Signature of patient/client or personal representative   Date

_____
Print name

_____
Print address

If you are signing this authorization as a personal representative, identify your authority to act on behalf of the client:

_____
(Parent, guardian, power of attorney, health care surrogate, other)

_____
(Signature of person who verified the identity and legal authority of the representative)

_____
Print name

_____
Print address

Chapter 6

Practice Issues

Chapters 6 and 7 use a question-and-answer format to address many of the recordkeeping issues facing social workers and their agencies today. This chapter includes questions about quality, the benefits of recording for the practitioner, client recordkeeping, recordkeeping in private practice, and recordkeeping under managed care. Chapter 7 discusses the administrative uses of records, addressing questions about reducing costs, security, computers, and using records in research.

The Quality of Records

How can the quality of records in our agency be improved?

The quality of a record depends on the quality of thought and action that go into service delivery. Ultimately, records can be no better than the practice they document. However, the quality of social work records also depends on the way information is selected and presented. In many agencies, the quality of records in no way represents the quality of services.

Good practice is a prerequisite of good recording, but good practitioners do not always prepare good records. Sometimes practitioners do not have sufficient time or, for other reasons, do not keep up with their recordkeeping. Sometimes practitioners have not been adequately prepared by education or experience for the task. Sometimes expectations are unclear. Certainly, social workers have not always agreed on what constitutes good recording.

One issue on which social workers sometimes disagree is the focus of the record. Should records be complete or selective, objective or subjective, descriptive or analytic? Should records concentrate on the client-need-situation, the service transaction, or the worker's diagnostic thinking? Should records be used retrospectively to document what has occurred, or prospectively to plan for the future? In large part, this debate reflects differences about the very nature of practice and the function of the record. Social workers have differed not just about the basic purposes of the record but about what information the record should contain. Those with different theoretical backgrounds have argued for different approaches to recordkeeping. Those who believed that the record was primarily a means for teaching the process of service delivery took a different approach than those who viewed it as an administrative document.

The Service-Centered Record developed in this book seeks to resolve this debate by redefining the nature of recording, refocusing the record's content and linking structure to use, while encouraging variations based on field of practice, funding arrangements, theoretical perspective, service approach, personnel, and clientele. The Service-Centered approach is built on the assumption that the four competing goals of recordkeeping (accountability, supporting and improving practice, efficiency, and client privacy) can be reconciled if records are focused on the purpose, process, and impact of service.

In the context of this approach, a good record:

- focuses on service delivery;
- contains information about the client-need-situation and available resources that form the basis for assessment, intervention, and evaluation;
- contains information about decisions and actions at each phase of service, including its purpose, goals, plans, processes, progress, and outcomes;
- carefully documents and labels the worker's appraisal, as well as the descriptions, observations, sources, and criteria on which it is based;
- is structured so that information can be documented, retrieved, and used efficiently; and
- is used not just in accountability but to support practice (see also the 15 Principles of Good Records in chapter 1).

Furthermore, good records are concise, specific, relevant, clear, logical, timely, meaningful, useful, and grounded in fact, professional ethics, and established theory and research. Good records are well-organized and well-written. A good record documents the views of professionals and other interested parties without neglecting the client's perspective. In contrast, poor records are unfocused, vague, biased, speculative, imprecise, and inaccessible to the potential user. Poor records often contain too much or too little information, and may be disorganized or poorly written. Poor records may result from practice deficiency, inaccurate assessment, faulty judgment, unethical behavior, inappropriate intervention, disrespect for the client, or unfamiliarity with best practices and accepted standards of care.

Improving records may require action at four levels:

1. Practitioner skills
2. Agency guidelines
3. Supportive resources
4. Organizational atmosphere

IMPROVING PRACTITIONER SKILLS

Even the most skilled practitioners can often improve their records if they prepare systematically for recording and work to develop their writing skills.

Systematic preparation for recording takes place before, during, and after each encounter with or on behalf of a client. Before such encounters, especially early in the service relationship, the worker should prepare to seek the information necessary for the record. Reviewing agency forms, outlines, and guidelines can help the worker keep in mind what information is needed.

During or shortly after each encounter the worker should make brief notes about what was learned and what transpired during the service transaction. Key words and phrases are often sufficient to help the worker remember essential information. The habit of brief note-taking can be effective in helping the practitioner prepare accurate and specific records, especially when record-keeping takes place more than a day or two after the service encounter. Experienced workers find that note-taking helps them retain complex observations and re-create in detail the sequence of events in complicated cases. Students and new workers find that notes form the foundation for building skills in observation and assessment as well as recordkeeping. In general, note-taking strengthens the content of the record and aids in the recording process.

Narrative records can be improved if workers briefly outline each entry prior to dictating, writing, or entering information into the record. Working from their notes and from agency guidelines, workers can organize each entry chronologically or topically. The use of headings such as "Background Information," "Assessment," or "Phone Interview with Dr. Slake, October 17" helps to structure the content for the user.

Records also can be improved by eliminating some recurrent writing problems that appear in all fields of practice and at all levels of practice skill. In fact, these writing problems seem to be passed along from one generation of practitioners to the next with the old records that are used to introduce students and practitioners to the profession, the agency, and their clientele. These common writing problems include: technical errors, overuse of the passive voice, poor diction, and oversimplification.

Technical errors are the easiest problems in writing to solve. In most cases, mistakes in spelling, grammar, and punctuation can be minimized if workers proofread their records and reports. With the use of word processing technology, spelling and grammatical errors are highlighted and easily corrected, as are run-on sentences, repetitions, and wordy phrases. In a few cases, workers have not acquired the necessary communication skills. They may find that their writing will improve if they read a textbook or attend a class on writing. Technical errors are probably not as important as other writing errors since they do not ordinarily undermine meaning; the reader can usually figure out what the worker intended to say. Yet, they are important enough to warrant some concern. Recurrent technical errors can undermine the reader's perception of the worker's competence and professionalism.

Poor: "Mrs. B's physical needs, not to mention nutrition, are poor. It is not being attended to adequately."

Better: *"Impressions:* Mrs. B's physical needs, particularly her nutrition, have not received adequate attention."

Poor: "Mr. T and Mrs. T and John and Linda and even their grandmother have repeatedly told me again and again how much they wanna have Joseph return home in despite of the troubles that they were encountered during his last visit home which was on 4/4."

Better: "Although Joseph's last visit home on 4/4 resulted in a trip to the ER after his grandmother slipped in the kitchen, his parents, brother John, sister Linda, and grandmother have each told me that they look forward to his next visit."

Some practitioners *overuse the passive voice* in their records. Using the passive voice produces awkward sentences, and creates ambiguity because the writer fails to identify the subject or actor involved. Some practitioners were taught not to use "I" in formal writing, and use the passive voice when describing their own activities or views. Although some use of the passive voice may be warranted, its overuse leads to an impression of inaction or concealed motives. Overuse of the passive voice can make a practitioner appear passive or unwilling to take responsibility for her or his role in decisions and actions.

To locate the passive voice in records, look for:

- sentences in which the actor is not identified; and
- use of the verb "to be" as a helping verb ("was raised," "was felt").

Poor: "Concern was raised that. . . ."

Better: "The worker expressed concern that. . . ."

Poor: "It was felt that. . . ."

Better: "The medical team decided that. . . ."

Problems in *diction,* that is, the use of language, can also undermine the quality of social work records. Carefully selecting words to describe and evaluate the client-need-situation and the service transaction can improve the accuracy, specificity, clarity, and meaning of the record. Here again, word processing software can assist practitioners in ensuring that they are using language correctly and choosing just the right word. In addition, practitioners should proofread their records and reports to eliminate meaningless terms, pejorative (judgmental) language, and overwriting.

Poor: "All attempts to mobilize and utilize Mr. K's environmental network were met with resistance. Mrs. K was basically hostile to all pursuance. She was not respondent to my efforts at supportiveness."

Better: "Mrs. K did not respond to several phone calls and an appointment letter. She became angry when a nurse asked her to contact me about Mr. K's discharge.
Impressions: It is clear that Mrs. K is aware of, but does not wish to respond to, my efforts to offer support. It is not yet clear, however, whether she is resisting Mr. K's discharge or social work services."

Poor: "Ms. R is very masculine in her demeanor. I often have to hold myself back from offering to buy her a dress!"

Better: [Omit]

Oversimplification is the most troublesome writing problem, and may also be a sign of problems in practice. Workers who fail to document the complexity of the client-need-situation, issues involved in service delivery, or varying perspectives of interested parties may also neglect these issues in assessment, intervention, and evaluation. Workers who stereotype the client in the record may also fail to individualize the client in practice. For example, a record that includes only a teacher's assessment of a pupil as "disruptive" is an inadequate description of the child's behavior. It also fails to include the child's and family's perspective and the worker's observations of the student in the classroom environment, and is therefore oversimplified and biased. A worker who would base a plan of service on this oversimplified view of the client-need-situation is apt to make inappropriate decisions in the delivery of services.

Practitioners sometimes oversimplify their assessments by failing to clearly identify and separate observations from appraisals of the client-need-situation. This problem, which has been discussed at some length in chapter 2, can be difficult to recognize. For example, "the client appeared to be depressed" may seem to describe but actually assesses the client. In contrast, "the client wept often during the interview; she talked about losing her appetite and her interest in others since her mother's death" is an observation. Practitioners can correct this error by making sure that assessments are systematic, that is, that they include observations, sources of information, criteria used, and the worker's appraisal. Because social work decisions and actions are based on both observations and conclusions, each needs to be carefully documented, and labeled, in the record. Practitioners can sometimes identify oversimplification by searching for diagnostic terms in descriptive passages. Whenever such information appears in the record, it should be clearly labeled as an assessment, diagnosis, working hypothesis, or judgment and be accompanied by the observations on which it is based.

To locate oversimplification in records, look for:

- overuse of personal labels ("The client *is* disruptive");

- conclusions without supporting observations and criteria; and

- singular or authoritarian views of the client-need-situation, especially those that blame or negatively label the client.

Poor: "Mrs. S is passive-aggressive, withholding, manipulative, and narcissistic."

Better: "Mrs. S sat with her arms crossed and refused to speak for more than five minutes. Other members of the family tried to draw her out. Finally, Mr. S said that this is how she gets her own way. He explained that Mrs. S often stops talking and waits for others to guess what is bothering her.

Impressions: Mrs. S is coping with the stress of her illness and hospitalization using a typical pattern. This pattern, of which Mr. S is aware, appears to be accepted by the family but has not worked here where the staff views her as manipulative and narcissistic."

Narrative reports can often be improved by ensuring that the complexity of the client-need-situation is explored, and the bases for the worker's appraisal are fully documented. Too often, in their efforts to be brief and specific, workers present a single viewpoint or draw conclusions without showing how their decisions were reached. The above example was improved by adding description and presenting the source of the negative views of Mrs. S's behavior. The "better" entry provides not just improved accountability. It suggests new directions for practice, including the need to work with Mrs. S, the family, and hospital staff to ensure that her actions do not undermine her treatment and care.

Improving practitioners' practice and recording skills alone, however, can seldom produce good records for an agency. Such skills can only be put to use in an agency that promotes quality recording with clear, reasonable, and adequate guidelines; sufficient resources; and a supportive atmosphere. With these goals in mind, many agencies may need to reevaluate and revise their recordkeeping policies, procedures, and practices.

IMPROVING AGENCY GUIDELINES

With limited resources for social work services and increased demands for documentation, agencies and departments seeking to improve their records may need to develop or revise existing recording guidelines. The argument for establishing clear and explicit guidelines for the content, structure, and procedures for recording is persuasive: agencies must use their most precious resource, professional time, prudently. It is wasteful for practitioners to spend too much time recording too much, too little, or too late. Guidelines can simplify the recording process, since many of the choices about what and how to record are made explicit in advance.

The opposing argument, that such guidelines undermine professional autonomy, is less persuasive. Recording guidelines do not, in themselves, diminish a practitioner's autonomy or responsibility for practice. However, guidelines that focus on administrative concerns while failing to consider the realities of practice or practitioners' views can be a serious problem (Edwards

& Reid, 1989). Although such guidelines may be intended to improve recording, they often have the opposite effect. They can lead to practitioner resistance and to an increasing disparity between practice and the record. That is, practitioners may fail to comply with administrative requirements or keep two sets of records, one to meet agency demands and another to support their practice.

Guidelines developed with the full participation of those who are responsible for service delivery and its documentation can actually improve recording. Practitioners can work to ensure that guidelines are reasonable and congruent with practice, while meeting administrative expectations. Such guidelines should specify the content, form, and procedures for recordkeeping. Rather than attempting to systematize all recordkeeping, guidelines should establish minimum standards and leave specific decisions to the worker. In general, guidelines should make clear:

- what types of records to keep, and what is their purpose and use;

- what information to document in all cases, and what information to document only in special circumstances;

- what forms or formats to use, and under what circumstances to use them; and

- when specific elements of content are to be documented, and how frequently records are to be updated.

IMPROVING RESOURCES

The conflicting goals of accountability and efficiency can be met only if an agency allocates sufficient resources to the tasks of preparing, transcribing, storing, and retrieving records. First and foremost, workers need enough time to prepare records. Many agencies assume that workers will find time to record in periods between interviews and meetings, or during scheduled recordkeeping periods. However, the time available for recording has eroded. Sixty-five percent of the social work managers responding to the Records II survey (conducted in the late 1980s) indicated that there was not enough time available for recordkeeping, and 58 percent indicated that recordkeeping took too much time (Kagle, 1993).

Over the succeeding decades the situation has gotten worse. Standards of accountability have increased the demand for documentation, often without an increase in allocation of time or resources for the task. What little time is available for recordkeeping must sometimes be used to respond to client needs or to fulfill other duties. In addition, time-saving equipment and support personnel may not be available. With limited resources, many agencies have chosen not to purchase or update computers and other equipment, and have cut back or eliminated clerical staff. Many practitioners do not have direct access to computers or terminals. Some have purchased their own computers for preparing documents and reports. Others may be handwriting or typing their records. Few practitioners today are experienced in dictating their records, and fewer still have access to clerical staff for transcription. Well-intentioned efforts to cut back on other costs to preserve professional staff may have inadvertently undermined recordkeeping and increased practitioners' burden. No wonder records are not up-to-date.

Even with limited funds available, agencies can reduce the backlog of recordkeeping by redirecting resources to the task. Among the options they may wish to consider are:

- developing forms for documentation of routine or short-term services;
- studying recordkeeping practices to determine actual and optimal use of professional time;
- purchasing or upgrading computer hardware and software and other time-saving devices;
- adding or redeploying support personnel; and
- increasing practitioners' access to computers and other time-saving devices.

IMPROVING THE ORGANIZATION'S ATMOSPHERE

If records are to improve, the culture of the organization may also need to change. Managers often fail to encourage practitioners, inhibiting rather than promoting accurate and timely recording. For example, when the record is the primary source of information about the worker's performance, and when that information is commonly used as a means of finding and correcting weaknesses, recording may suffer. The worker finds himself or herself in a no-win situation: what is written in the record is used to demonstrate the worker's weaknesses in practice, and what is not in the record is used to demonstrate his or her weaknesses in meeting administrative responsibilities. In response, the worker may avoid, delay, or stint on recordkeeping. If this problem is to be corrected, the focus and atmosphere of supervision must often be altered. Whenever feasible, evaluative supervision should draw on a variety of sources of information about the worker's performance, not solely on the worker's records. The record's content should form the basis for discussion of substantive practice issues rather than criticisms of the practitioner's recordkeeping and work habits. The atmosphere surrounding any discussion of recording should be supportive rather than accusatory, reinforcing strengths and efforts at improvement rather than looking for weaknesses and lapses in performance.

Practitioners, too, contribute to the agency's atmosphere. Those who have not been adequately prepared, have had bad experiences in supervision, or are overwhelmed by the task can convey their frustration and dissatisfaction to others. Students and beginning practitioners are often surprised to find their coworkers beleaguered, angry, scornful, and even defiant about recordkeeping. Of course, practitioners will never love paperwork or consider it their favorite part of the job. However, improving records often means that managers and direct service workers need to work collaboratively to understand and alleviate the sources of workers' frustration and dissatisfaction. Many of the issues have already been addressed here. They include workload, resources, guidelines, preparation, and supervision.

The role of the record in practice also contributes to the agency atmosphere. If recordkeeping is perceived as an administrative rather than a practice activity, it will not receive the full commitment of direct-service workers. In many social work organizations, practitioners view recordkeeping as a meaningless responsibility imposed on them by managers. They put off recordkeeping not just because other tasks demand their attention but because they do not consider recordkeeping an important practice-related activity. If agencies are to overcome what is sometimes called worker resistance, they must reconsider the role of the record in the day-to-day life of the practitioner. Recordkeeping achieves full legitimacy among direct-service workers only if the record is useful to them in their practice. The content of the record should focus on information that is crucial to practice decisions and actions, most notably assessment, monitoring intervention, continuity of services, and evaluation of processes and outcomes. The process of recordkeeping should fit seamlessly into the day-to-day activities of the practitioner.

BENEFITS OF THE RECORDING PROCESS

I have been told that the process of recording is helpful to practice and the practitioner. I find it tedious work. How can it be helpful?

Although recording can be helpful, many practitioners are suspicious of efforts to convince them of it. They have been told that, like a bitter pill, recording is really good for them. However, when they have "taken their medicine" and completed the task, the benefits of their efforts have not always been evident. Their experience leads them to question the notion that recording is genuinely helpful.

In fact, the recording process can be very beneficial to the practitioner and, ultimately, to the client and organization. During the process of documenting what has occurred, the worker recalls and reconsiders the content and context of the service transaction. This review allows the worker to confirm or revise assumptions and reassess the purpose, goals, and plan of service. Simply put, writing aids thinking. It allows the worker to think back, think ahead, and think again.

The act of recording clarifies thought in a number of ways. Recording involves *selection*. The worker sorts through the array of information about the client-situation and the service transaction with the goal of documenting what is most important. Thus, recording focuses the worker's attention on the most salient features of the case. Recording also involves *organization*. Information is arranged topically and in sequence. Thus, writing aids the worker in logical thinking and in perceiving temporal, spatial, and causal relationships. Recording requires *substantiation* of fact, decision, and action.

As a result, gaps in information and distortions in interpretation often become clear. Recording involves *analysis,* separating the whole into parts, as well as *synthesis,* making connections between observations and inferences. As a result, the worker may generate new options and alternative ways of conceptualizing relationships. Recording may involve *classification.* In so doing, the worker typifies the client-need-situation and compares it with others in the light of theory, values, empirical evidence, and accepted practices. This process can aid the worker in linking a particular case to the body of professional knowledge and ethics. Finally, recording involves *judgment* and therefore can facilitate critical thinking. As a component of the recording process, the worker develops and tests hypotheses and evaluates action and impact. The worker may examine relationships between knowledge and supposition, attitudes and actions, and intention and implementation. The worker examines indicators of movement in light of the purpose, goals, and intended outcomes of service to assess the direction and impact of services. By means of this process, the practitioner not only may come to understand the client-need-situation and the service transaction in new ways, but may also gain self-awareness and professional skill.

The record mirrors practice and, through the process of recordkeeping, the worker reflects upon practice. Writing takes place away from the practice it documents, thereby offering the worker a new perspective on the client-need-situation and the service process. Recording at its best can help the worker to reconsider what has taken place, reevaluate the process and impact of services, reexamine plans for the future, and give form and substance to inchoate impressions and ideas. Admittedly, recording is an aid; it is no substitute for the thinking and planning that must take place with the client and within the service transaction. Nonetheless, recording can be a means for improving services if it is not too far removed from the practice it documents. If recording is to enrich practice, the content of the record must focus on crucial practice issues, and the recording process must be closely connected in time to the services being documented. Records should be written shortly after service events and continuously monitor the client-need-situation. Recordkeeping should not be delayed until long after service decisions have been made and implemented, and changes in the client-need-situation have ensued.

RECORDS THAT CLIENTS PREPARE

I've seen some reports of client recordkeeping. How does this work?

Clients can often benefit from writing down their thoughts and actions. Called *client memoranda* here to differentiate them from the *client records* workers prepare, these writings can be an important source of information about the client-need-situation and, at the same time, contribute to the service process. Clients who keep diaries or logs have the opportunity to reflect on their own feelings, thoughts, behaviors, and decisions. When they share their memoranda with the practitioner, they open new and meaningful areas for discussion. Client memoranda can be used in conjunction with any practice approach and can be adapted to meet the needs of diverse clients with a full range of abilities and problems.

Social workers ask their clients to keep records for a number of reasons. Through such documents, workers can discover new information about the client-need-situation, and explore in-depth the client's innermost thoughts and feelings. Clients sometimes introduce important matters in their writing that they find difficult to talk about face-to-face. Client memoranda, then, may be useful in surfacing information that would otherwise remain hidden or be uncovered much later in the service process. Client memoranda can also be used in monitoring the client-need-situation between sessions with the practitioner. Clients may be asked to write about their sad feelings or family arguments, for example, documenting not just what occurred but also their own thoughts, feelings, and actions and those of others in the situation. In addition to supplying information, client memoranda can provide a learning experience for the client. Observing and writing can lead to greater self-awareness. By describing specific experiences in detail, the client learns about how he or she feels, behaves, and thinks. Client memoranda encourage clients to express themselves verbally and label their perceptions and reactions. Diaries and logs enhance the service transaction because keeping records can encourage the client to be more active in seeking information, expressing opinions, making decisions, and reaching conclusions. They serve as a tangible link between the worker and client when they are not together, and as a source of continuity and focus of discussion when they meet. The process of recordkeeping may even have a more general benefit, offering the client an opportunity to gain a sense of self-control as well as some control over the service process.

Client memoranda take two basic forms—diaries and logs. In both forms, the client documents relevant feelings, ideas, and experiences. The worker helps the client focus the content by asking the client to write about particular events, reactions, or environments. The worker also suggests when and how often entries should be made. The difference between diaries and logs is in their structure. A diary is open ended and idiosyncratic; the client decides what to write about and how to organize the material. A diary is an expressive document, allowing the client to talk about whatever comes to mind. A log is more structured; its content and organization are planned in advance. In preparing the log, the client's task is to document a narrow range of observations at specified times, in designated environments, and using a prepared form or format. The content of the log is limited to a few behaviors, feelings, or thoughts that are the focus of service; the task of documentation is similarly focused. Diaries and logs have quite different purposes, but can be used simultaneously or in sequence. Workers should consider which might be a better fit in a specific instance. A client's diary is likely to be highly individualistic, expressive, and inclusive. It may reveal a great deal about the client-need-situation but may not be clearly focused on the issues at hand. In con-

---

Exhibit 6.1   Excerpts from Client Memoranda

Excerpts from the Diary of a Teen-Age Girl

I really don't know what to write about. Keeping a diary of "who I am" seems like just another assignment from White [English teacher]. Sometimes it seems that no one really knows or cares who I am—especially me. . . . Today just happens to be one of those days . . . maybe because everyone tries to be so cheerful, so helpful, when I feel like— . . . Smile, smile . . . keep up the pretense of being anything, anyone, something, someone. . . .

Excerpt from the Log of a Teen-Age Girl

Circumstances Surrounding Fights with Mother				
What Happened Before	**When**	**Where**	**What**	**How I Felt**
Sleeping	8:30	Bedroom	She wanted me to get up	Tired, angry; ruined my day
Eating, reading the paper	10:00	Kitchen	She wanted me to clean up	Tired, angry; wanted to get out
Out	7:00	Kitchen	Where had I been?	Tired, mad; why did I come home???

---

trast, a log is likely to include specified information but not the client's moment-to-moment thoughts, feelings, or perceptions.

Preparing a diary or log can be a meaningful experience for a client, and can contribute to the worker-client relationship and the service process. However, practitioners should use them with discretion, carefully considering the following questions:

Should client memoranda be used?

Of course, client memoranda can only be used with the client's consent. Before introducing the idea of a diary or log, workers should consider both potential benefits and whether there might be adverse effects. On the one hand, the use of a diary or log might bring information into the service transaction, provide a beneficial experience for the client, and give focus to intervention. On the other hand, the memoranda may prove intrusive, especially in group or family processes. Writing about thoughts or feelings may seem overwhelming to clients who are experiencing personal crises. Recordkeeping may also be an unnecessarily difficult assignment for clients who are undergoing severe stress, are self-conscious about their writing or reading ability, or have limited language proficiency.

Practitioners should consider other factors as well. Memoranda are probably not well-suited for mandated or involuntary clients who, at least initially, may not trust the worker, and for others who have reasons to conceal their own or others' behavior. Culture may also be an important consideration. In some communities, revealing sensitive information to "outsiders" is a serious breach of norms (Woolfolk, 2003). Preparing written materials might intensify the client's concerns about divulging information or being betrayed, and may undermine a fragile worker-client bond. Clients with cognitive impairments or other disabilities may wish to participate, but may need assistance or guidance. These and other clients may benefit from newer technologies, like pocket voice recorders and voice recognition software so they can "talk" rather than "write" their memoranda. Indeed, many clients today are comfortable with written communication and self-disclosure via personal Web pages and blogs, text-messaging, and chat rooms.

The decision to use client memoranda should be based primarily on whether they will be meaningful to the client and can contribute to the service process. Logs are particularly useful in assessing contingencies of behavior, changes in the client-need-situation, and the effects of service. Diaries are especially useful in surfacing issues that are salient to the client but are difficult to acknowledge in face-to-face meetings. However, client memoranda have only limited value in supporting the practitioner's responsibility for accountability and recordkeeping.

If client memoranda are to be introduced, the worker should clearly outline their purpose, content, structure, and use. The client should be encouraged to discuss and think about the idea, initially and in subsequent meetings.

> **Poor**: "I want you to keep a diary. Okay?"

> **Better**: "I wonder what you think of the idea of keeping a diary of your experiences, ideas, and feelings. We've talked a lot today about your not knowing who you are and what you are 'supposed to be.' It seems that you keep changing, and so do your ideas and feelings. If you would write down, every night before you go to bed, just what you are thinking and feeling about who you are, we'll be able to talk about it when you come next time. Nothing fancy—just your thoughts and feelings in any form you like. What do you think?"

The practitioner should be prepared to answer the client's questions about what to write, how often to make entries, and who will see what is written. The practitioner should make clear that the client has considerable discretion as to what to include in memoranda, and can refuse to take part in the process or choose not to share some or all of their writings. Indeed, the decision to write and to share often becomes an important subject for discussion. Some clients who seem reluctant at first become fully immersed in preparing diaries or logs. Others who initially agree to prepare memoranda may forget or not follow through on the decision to do so.

Who should keep the diary or log?

When practitioners introduce the keeping of diaries or logs into couples, family, or group work, the situation becomes more complicated. Practitioners should be aware that the role of recordkeeper carries power with it. That is, whoever keeps a record has the opportunity to define the situation as well as the behavior and reactions of others. For example, a teacher who keeps a log of a pupil's behavior has an important role in defining that behavior. A family member who keeps a diary presents the family from her or his perspective. A diary or log presents only one view of complex interpersonal relationships and transactions between people and their environments. When the goal is to document varying perspectives or balance power, more than one person in the client-need-situation should be asked to prepare records. For example, the log presented in exhibit 6.1 is only one of two logs that were prepared by clients in the case. The mother and daughter were each asked to keep logs of their fights. In this way, the worker sought to encourage each to express her point-of-view while minimizing the potential disruptive effect of giving one of them the power to keep the record.

Where is the diary or log kept?

Practitioners should inform clients from the outset whether their memoranda will appear in the agency record and in what form. Most often, clients keep possession of their diaries. However, diaries do appear in the agency record, since practitioners are likely to describe some of the diary's contents and how it is used in the service process in their records. In contrast, clients are usually asked to prepare logs for the record. These logs are then used along with other information to identify changes and track movement in the client-need-situation over time. Whether or not they appear in the client's file, any memoranda that the worker retains become part of the official record. They may be accessible to others in and outside the agency or subject to subpoena (see chapter 9).

How should the memoranda be used?

Client memoranda can only be meaningful to the client and useful in practice if they are regularly discussed in meetings and sessions. Clients choose what they want to record and bring with them what they expect to share. If the practitioner fails to inquire about or leave enough time to discuss memoranda, however, the client may question the worker's commitment and lose interest in the process. Some workers discuss client memoranda informally during the course of interviews or meetings. Others reserve time for a more formal review, discussion, and evaluation of the memoranda and the contents. For example, the worker and client may use a chart to document information from client memoranda over time, comparing current with previous entries.

What are the possible limitations in the use of client memoranda?

Although client memoranda can be an important source of information, they are inherently subjective. Written from a single point-of-view, they provide valuable insights into the thoughts, feelings, and actions of the person keeping the diary or log. However, client memoranda should only be used in conjunction with other sources of information for assessment, intervention, and evaluation.

RECORDKEEPING IN PRIVATE PRACTICE

What records do I need to keep for my private practice?

For practical and ethical reasons, it is important to keep records in private practice, even when clients pay out-of-pocket for services. Records are useful in office management for scheduling, billing, and other administrative tasks. Even brief clinical records can help the practitioner recall details of a case and support continuity of services, especially when clients receive service intermittently or over a long period. For these reasons, some practitioners keep informal written notes about people, places, and events in the client's life; recurrent themes and dynamics in relationships; and hypotheses and plans for intervention. They review this material before sessions with clients, bringing to mind key issues that help to sustain empathy and immediacy in the relationship. They find that, over time, such notes reveal patterns and developments that might not otherwise have been apparent.

Most private practitioners today, however, keep more comprehensive records, documenting ongoing assessments and monitoring services and their impact over time. Such records identify specific diagnoses or problems; goals and plans; and specific indicators of movement over time to gauge whether the client-need-situation is improving and whether to continue or change the direction of services. As services draw to a close, these records often include an evaluation of service outcomes and their impact, as well as client satisfaction. Keeping thorough and systematic records can be decisive in practitioners' negotiations with and reimbursement by managed care and other third-party payers. In providing funders with information about the client-need-situation and the service process prior to, during, and following the termination of services, practitioners may be expected to use funders' forms, templates, outlines, or software.

Records are crucial to accountability and the worker's credibility should the client become involved in a legal matter (see chapter 9). Practitioners who assume that their clients will not end up in court (or, if they do, would not waive the worker's testimonial privilege) and those who choose not to keep records or neglect their recording, may find themselves in some difficulty. Although some clients are referred by the court, and others are involved from the outset in civil or domestic disputes, practitioners cannot always know in advance that their records will be subpoenaed or that they will be called to court to testify about current or former clients. When practitioners tell the court that they keep no records, relying instead on their memories for details about people and events, they may find not just their testimony but their professional reputations called into question. In fact, social work licensure laws in some states require practitioners to keep records.

For legal and ethical reasons, and to meet accountability standards, social workers in private practice are advised to keep records that include, at minimum:

- assessments of the client-need-situation, with *DSM* diagnoses, if appropriate;
- description of the service approach, with the rationale for its selection;
- decisions and actions taken that affect services or the client-need-situation, including those by the client, worker, funders, and other interested parties;
- service goals and plans, with timelines;
- indicators of movement, with systematic documentation of selected measures;
- any change in approach, goals, or plans, with the rationale for the change;
- appointment logs;
- full documentation of any critical event, such as a threat of violence, with the practitioner's response and actions taken;
- status of the client-need-situation at closing, with reasons for termination, and any referral or follow-up; and
- efforts to ensure that clients who need continuing services are not abandoned but receive services elsewhere.

Private practitioners should also consider designating a colleague to handle their records and other professional matters should they suddenly die or be incapacitated. Some practitioners may wish to make a "professional will," in which they outline in detail how their professional responsibilities should be handled in case of death, accident, or catastrophic illness (Clemens, 2006; Firestein, 1993). At minimum, however, practitioners should ask a colleague who is a licensed social worker or other professional to assist clients and handle confidential information in case of an emergency. A practitioner would enter into a consultation agreement with another licensed social worker so that client confidentiality would be preserved. Should an emergency occur, the consultant would be familiar with and have access to the practitioner's office, client list, and recordkeeping system.

Some private practitioners do not keep formal records, relying instead on handwritten notes. Most, however, keep systematic records, and many use computers to simplify their clinical recordkeeping and billing, and to transmit information to and from third-party funders. Practitioners can choose from a variety of available word processing and database software packages. Word processing software allows practitioners to create error-free letters, records, and forms and retrieve and revise information quickly. Office management software can simplify billing and scheduling, and signal due dates for reports and deadlines for authorization of services. Case management software can support assessment and diagnostic classification, treatment planning, goal and progress documentation, and report writing. Many private practitioners have adopted fully integrated business and practice management software (The Therapist, Therapist Helper, or TheraScribe, for example), which prompts them to include needed information and permits them to move easily between different recordkeeping functions without duplicating efforts. In addition, most software packages now incorporate security measures that deny access to unauthorized users and safeguard clients' protected health information.

Practitioners who provide services outside the context of a social service organization face special obligations. Private practice offers freedom from institutional constraints but leaves practitioners without institutional support or legitimacy. To some extent, practitioners can establish their legitimacy through licensure and certification. However, keeping records is an important standard of professional practice and a requirement of licensing laws in some states. Private practitioners who fail to keep thorough and timely records will find it difficult to demonstrate their competence, compliance with laws, adherence to best practices, and accountability to the client and community.

RECORDS AND MANAGED CARE

What kind of records do I need for clients who are covered under managed care?

Increasingly, clients who seek services from social workers in hospital and agency-based as well as private practice are covered under managed care arrangements. Managed care is intended to limit and use resources more efficiently (Austad & Berman, 1991; Van Dyke & Schlesinger, 1997). First used in health and mental health services, managed care arrangements are now used to distribute resources and deliver services in substance abuse, child welfare, and other areas of practice. Under managed care, costs may be contained by limiting benefit offerings or use of services, requiring referral and ongoing review, or negotiating lower payments or "shared risk" with providers. Originally intended as a fiscal measure, managed care has had a major impact on the way social service programs are administered, social work is practiced, and records are kept.

Managed care is distinctive from other mechanisms for financing social services in that oversight entities may be involved in day-to-day practice decisions. "Gatekeepers" may control access to as well as level and amount of care a client receives by authorizing and limiting services. "Watchdogs" may review and evaluate the quality, appropriateness, and cost-effectiveness of services. Sometimes external agents, like case managers employed by managed care organizations (MCOs), are responsible for authorizing and reviewing services. To claim reimbursement, social workers or their agencies must submit forms or electronic reports that document, at minimum, assessments, service goals and plans, service contacts, progress of service, and the client's status at various stages of the service process and at termination. Their records are also open to review by the MCO. Sometimes services are financed under performance contracts, which define standards of practice and service outcomes to be achieved. Sometimes the institution itself operates as a managed care organization, as, for example, in health maintenance organizations (HMOs). Here, internal panels undertake prospective and retrospective quality and utilization reviews.

Managed care places some restrictions on practitioners' discretion in decision making and action taking. Practitioners may be constrained as to the method, length, and focus of services delivered on behalf of clients. They may be expected to frame their assessments around a *DSM* diagnosis, functional assessment, or similar classification of the problem; focus on goals and plans that bring about change in the defined problem; and adhere to the managed care or contracting organization's practice guidelines or standards of care for services to clients with the relevant diagnosis or problem. For example, services to clients with the diagnosis of depression may be approved only for certain approaches to intervention (e.g., cognitive-behavioral) and for a predetermined number of sessions. In addition, such services will usually be authorized only if the diagnosis is covered under the contract or insurance agreement and service is deemed necessary and appropriate. Services are expected to focus on the diagnosed problem or symptom and be goal directed; other issues in the client-need-situation may not be addressed. Many managed care systems operate on the assumption that services will be brief but clients may return later for additional services, as they would for visits to a family physician.

Under managed care, services are intended to reduce problems or symptoms, and improve functioning to a tolerable level rather than remediate the full range of issues identified in a psychosocial assessment. Social workers worry that, under managed care, clients' complex and systemic problems may be neglected. While recognizing that other forms of financing can be very costly and result in maldistribution of services, social workers have raised questions about whether traditionally underserved groups actually benefit from managed care enrollment (Davis, 2001; Perloff, 1996). They are concerned about the potential for abuse in programs operating under financial incentives that can lead to the denial or delay of services (Reamer, 1997; Strom-Gottfried, 1998). They are disturbed by court decisions that limit consumers' rights to sue when they are denied access to appropriate, high-quality care (Kopels & Manselle, 2006). These concerns turn to alarm when poor clients are denied choice, enrolled in programs that offer inferior services, or barred from needed health, mental health, or substance abuse treatment (New York City Chapter, NASW, 1994; Warren, 1995). Social workers, like other managed care professionals, report being frustrated with limitations on services and time-consuming reviews. They are also troubled about potential risks to clients' privacy when information in their records is transferred via phone lines and retained in managed care companies' databanks (Chambliss, Pinto, & McGuigan, 1997).

Nonetheless, managed care offers some advantages over other forms of financing and rationing services. The adoption of managed care principles has already brought about important improvements in the way social workers conceptualize and deliver services. For example, due at least in part to managed care, contemporary services may focus on prevention and early intervention as well as remedial services. Services are more likely to be based on best practices and focused on producing discernible outcomes. Practitioner networks and integrated systems of care may improve access to and coordination of services. Clients may be more actively involved in making decisions about the services they receive and in evaluating those services.

Managed care programs differ widely. However, most include these components: (1) capitation and performance contracting, whereby practitioners, or organizations included in a managed care or preferred provider network, agree to specific financial incentives and service arrangements; (2) a system of preauthorization, utilization review, and case management to screen and track clients, and allocate and evaluate services; (3) a financial partnership in which the provider assumes some risk for overutilization or poor performance; and (4) a benefit package defining and limiting mandated and available services (Shueman, Troy, & Mayhugh, 1994; Wernet, 1999). Managed care contracts provide clients with a network of available services, but place constraints or offer incentives to limit cost, use, and choice.

Under managed care, clients may access social work services in several ways. A client may be referred to a practitioner by an MCO case manager or another provider in a managed care network. For example, at the suggestion of her physician, a client is referred by a case manager to a social worker who has been approved by the MCO as a preferred provider. The social worker completes an assessment, and submits the assessment plus a service plan to the case manager, who may request additional information, ask for justification, or propose alternatives. In general, services are authorized for, and must seek to alleviate, a focal problem. Although a full social work assessment might identify many current and long-term personal, family, and community problems, under managed care the worker and client must identify a specific problem that is to be the focus of service. The focal problem must be significant, acute, and disruptive to the client-need-situation. Services must be needed, and the service plan must be time limited and supported by evidence that it can alleviate or at least ameliorate the problem. Often, practitioners use practice guidelines issued by MCOs to identify focal problems and practice approaches that are likely to be authorized.

Once the plan is approved and services authorized for a specified number of sessions, the practitioner continues to communicate with the MCO about the implementation of the plan and progress toward achieving the goals. The case manager may authorize additional sessions based on a review of the client's record or other information supplied by the practitioner and the client. Sometimes services are terminated by mutual agreement. At other times, however, a client may want or need additional services after he or she has exhausted the financing available through managed care. Should this happen, the practitioner is ethically obligated either to continue providing services or assist the client in finding services elsewhere (NASW, 1999, 1.16[b]).

Clients may also access social work services as part of a managed care contract between a provider agency and an employer, public or private agency, or managed care network. The employer, agency, or network negotiates a preset, fixed fee with the provider agency to cover specific services for a group of clients. For example, members of a family who are receiving services from a large state child welfare agency may be referred for services to a mental health and a substance abuse treatment agency. Based on the managed care contract that has been negotiated in advance, the family receives whatever services are covered and deemed necessary.

Finally, clients may receive social work services through their HMO. Clients who are enrolled in an HMO under employer insurance, Medicare, Medicaid, or another benefit plan may receive services from social workers who are employed by or under contract with the HMO. Social workers may assist HMO enrollees with a full range of health, mental health, and community and family services.

Records are crucial to practice under managed care. Under managed care, "accountability means that the record confirms that the social worker is providing the service claimed and that the service is done in a professional, competent manner" (Callahan, 1996, p. 203). Managed care and contracting organizations expect full access to records of service to their enrollees or clientele. They may scrutinize records for information about the necessity for and level of care, delivery and utilization of services, and their effectiveness and efficiency. Indeed, performance contracts often include standards for the content and timeliness of records.

Records can help establish a positive relationship between a provider and a contractor or oversight entity that can carry over from client to client and program to program (Browning & Browning, 1996). Practitioners need to prepare their records knowing that they will be used in authorizing, monitoring, and evaluating services. Records need to be up-to-date, and demonstrate compliance with standards and managed care agreements. They should also show service quality and effectiveness, professional competence, and administrative integrity.

The Service-Centered approach to recordkeeping (outlined in chapter 2 and developed throughout this book) forms an excellent basis for recording under managed care. In addition, practitioners and agencies are advised to incorporate three special features into their managed care recording systems: (1) conformity to practice guidelines, (2) ensuring that specific information is documented, and (3) computerization of recordkeeping systems and clerical support.

PRACTICE GUIDELINES

Practice guidelines are recommendations regarding the most effective and efficient methods for delivering services for specified problems. Practice guidelines offer MCOs direction about what approaches to service are likely to achieve favorable outcomes within a limited time frame. Managed care organizations compare proposed plans of service with practice guidelines to ascertain whether services are necessary, appropriate, and likely to be successful. Practice guidelines are not blueprints to be followed by rote; rather, they are general standards against which services can be screened and evaluated. They are intended to describe "customary" or "best" practices.

Practice guidelines are usually developed from research findings and practice expertise, and are organized around specific diagnoses (Hetznecker, 1996). The practice guidelines for services to clients with the diagnosis of "depression," for example, might include (1) a thorough review of the client's history and an assessment based on *DSM* criteria, (2) a referral to a physician for health evaluation and possible medication, (3) a service plan based on an accepted approach to service, (4) a reasonable projection of the number and frequency of sessions required, (5) specific goals for changing behaviors or reducing symptoms, and (6) measures to be used in evaluating change in the focal problem.

The specific criteria that MCOs use in screening and reviewing cases are usually not directly available to providers. However, agencies and practitioners can learn more about practice guidelines through the National Committee on Quality Assurance (http://www.web.ncqa.org), which also publishes accreditation standards and quality assurance measures. They can also access systematic studies of research evidence on the effectiveness of various service approaches for specific client-need-situations online via the Cochrane (www.cochrane.org) and Campbell (www.campbellcollaboration.org) Collaborations. Using these and other resources, agencies and practitioners can develop their own protocols, sometimes called "clinical pathways" or "decision trees," outlining the decisions and actions to be taken in assessing and providing services to clients with specified focal problems or needs. These protocols can be used in developing forms or templates for recordkeeping and reporting, and in negotiating service contracts or preferred provider status with MCOs.

INCLUSION OF SPECIFIC INFORMATION

Records under managed care are subject to full review by the MCO, contracting agency, or authorized oversight entity. The record should present information about the client-need-situation and service process in a form that is accessible and useful to reviewers. Case managers and other reviewers will be especially interested in the soundness of the diagnosis; acuity of need; appropriateness, efficiency, and feasibility of the service plan; and impact of services delivered.

Social workers whose clients are covered under managed care should consider including the following information in their records:

Accountability
- client's identifying information;
- client's name or identification number on each page of the record;

- all entries signed off with practitioner's name, degree, date;
- informed consent to treat and for the service plan;
- informed consent for each release of information;
- documentation that the client has been informed about the limits of confidentiality, such as in situations involving danger to self and others, or abuse of children;
- date and number of contacts planned and/or used;
- missed sessions, including reasons for cancellation or failure to appear; and
- date of planned and actual termination.

Risk Assessment and Response

- high risk situations, such as suicide, assessed and regularly updated; and
- actions taken to reduce risk and monitor the situation.

Service Necessity

- observation of client-need-situation and description of focal problem;
- standardized and other assessment protocols;
- specific diagnosis or statement of problem that is to be the focus of services; and
- additional data on the level, acuity, and severity of the focal problem, and the need for the type and intensity of services planned.

Service Planning

- assessment of mental health, behavior, or other functional status;
- *DSM* diagnosis or other classification, as appropriate;
- identification of effective and feasible approaches to service;
- disclosure to client of service alternatives, risks, and benefits and evidence of effectiveness;
- goals and service plan clearly linked to alleviating focal problems or symptoms, but not necessarily addressing all issues surfaced in assessment;
- rationale for use of new or unusual approach to services;
- time frame for achieving goals, including frequency of contact;
- referrals and linkages to other services, e.g., for assessment and treatment of medical conditions; and
- plan for termination and follow-up.

Implementation

- adherence to empirically based practice guidelines, standards of care, and clinical pathways;
- regular entries regarding service process and any changes in the client-need-situation or service plan;

- observations of movement toward goals or barriers to change;
- repeated measures of service impact;
- homework between contacts; and
- use and impact of outside resources and referrals.

Termination
- measures of the focal problem;
- acuity of the problem at termination;
- movement toward achieving goals;
- functional status (e.g., role functioning) and quality of life;
- follow-up and referral plan, especially if continuing services are needed; and
- survey or other measure of client satisfaction.

COMPUTERS AND CLERICAL SUPPORT

Computers and clerical support are crucial to social work practice under managed care. Indeed, it would be nearly impossible today to operate a recordkeeping system under managed care without a computer. Many forms are now filed online. Moreover, not only does managed care increase the demand for paperwork. Agencies and practitioners also rarely receive financing from just one MCO, contract, or revenue source, each of which may have its own recordkeeping standards and forms. Computers can be used to ensure that crucial information about clients and services is properly documented, and to transfer this information to various forms and reports. Indeed, electronic reporting and recordkeeping is the wave of the future. The federal government's commitment to electronic documentation and information transfer suggests that hospitals, clinics, agencies, and practitioners receiving public funds under managed care programs will be under increasing pressure to computerize their recordkeeping systems.

Clerical support can also improve record management and be cost-effective. Private practitioners and small agencies may be able to manage their records with the use of inexpensive personal computers alone. However, even part-time clerical support can save practitioners time and improve case flow. Someone who is familiar with various forms and standards can assist practitioners in conforming to different MCO practices, and can communicate with various case managers, funders, and oversight entities. While it is possible to imagine an individual social worker in private practice preparing records, communicating with MCOs, and handling accounts without clerical support, his or her clinical productivity might suffer. For small agencies, clerical support can be an important asset; for large agencies with managed care contracts, clerical support is essential.

Chapter 7

Administrative Issues

The Cost of Recordkeeping

How can we reduce our recording costs?

The cost of recordkeeping is generated by:

- the time clerical workers, direct service workers, supervisors, and other administrators spend producing, storing, retrieving, and using information from records;
- the time practitioners and administrators spend developing, implementing, and evaluating record content, structure, and procedure;
- equipment (e.g., computer hardware and software);
- supplies (e.g., paper);
- facilities (e.g., storage space); and
- consultation, training, and support.

Agencies can reduce their recordkeeping costs by identifying ways to be more economical in any or all of these areas.

Studies of recordkeeping costs have usually focused on the time practitioners spend producing records. Prior to the 1980s, practitioners handwrote or dictated their records. Much of their recordkeeping involved preparing narrative records or reports. In 1953, Hill and Ormsby found that 32 percent (12.8 hours for a 40-hour week) of caseworkers' time in a family service agency was being spent on recording. In 1964, Goldman found that 21 percent (8.4 hours for a 40-hour week) of caseworkers' time in a children and family service agency was being spent on recordkeeping. In some agencies, workers reported spending as much as 50% of their time on recording and other recordkeeping tasks.

During the 1980s and early 1990s, agencies began computerizing their records, although few organizations had fully automated recordkeeping systems. Computers were intended to improve record quality, efficiency, and access. However, systems were expensive and complicated, and most social

199

workers did not have direct access to them. Most practitioners were still handwriting, typing, or dictating clinical notes. In 1980, the Records I survey (Kagle, 1984) found that agencies differed widely in the amount of time they attributed to record-related activities, from one hour to more than 15 hours per worker per week. On average, direct-service workers were spending four to seven hours per week preparing records; supervisors were spending three to five hours reviewing records. Based on data from 1981 and 1982, Edwards and Reid (1989) found that, following the introduction of a new recording system, child welfare workers were spending an average of 23.5 hours per week on recordkeeping, an increase of 9.4 hours per week from the previous year. Time spent providing services to clients decreased correspondingly, from 24.1 to 15.1 hours per week. During this period, few agencies experienced cost reductions as a result of computerization. The cost of equipment, training, and support was not offset by efficiencies in recordkeeping. Practitioners spent as much or more time producing and using records as before. Those with direct access to computer systems found them difficult and time-consuming to use. Reports prepared for administrative purposes did not include information relevant to practice, so workers often kept additional notes to supplement or make more accessible information in computerized agency records.

By the mid-1990s, computers had largely replaced other methods of producing records, and for storing and retrieving information about social work clients and services. Few agencies relied on typewriters or Dictaphones, and, although practitioners still kept handwritten notes, many had access to computers for administrative and clinical recording. During the following decade, the cost of computer hardware and software came down, and practitioners and clerical staff became skilled in using computers and other electronic devices. Nonetheless, in some agencies, recordkeeping costs remained high. Ever-increasing documentation requirements overwhelmed any efficiencies offered by computerization. Practitioners were expected to document more information more frequently. However, some agencies were able to use computers to reduce their recordkeeping costs and improve the quality and timeliness of recordkeeping. In these agencies, the time available for client services remained constant (Weaver, Moses, Furman, & Lindsey, 2003) and even increased (Velasquez, 1992) after computers were introduced. In general, agencies found that computers reduced the time workers spent on recordkeeping when they were used to simplify complex or repetitive tasks (e.g., calculating financial eligibility); when they replaced more time-consuming methods for producing records, like narrative recording, with checklists, fill-ins, or queries requiring brief responses; and when documentation requirements were constrained.

Of course, information about the time workers actually spend on recordkeeping is difficult to get and verify. Most agencies base their data on workers' reports of their activities, often called statistics. In many agencies, workers do not track their activities hour by hour; rather, they estimate their time use at the end of the day or week. Workers may overestimate time spent on recordkeeping, attributing "down time" between service activities, meetings, and other scheduled activities to the task. It is not unusual for practitioners to spend 20%–40% (one to two days per week) of their time on record-related activities. With some effort, this proportion can be reduced by half. Agencies and practitioners can simplify their recordkeeping systems, thereby reducing costs while preserving accountability, and free up resources for client services and other valued activities.

Some areas appear to be prime targets for time and cost-cutting:

1. *Eliminate redundancy.*

In some agencies, workers keep two or more sets of records that contain the same or similar information. They may keep a social work record and contribute to a medical record on the same client, or they may prepare personal notes as well as narrative reports for the official record. Where such practices exist, costs might be reduced if personal notes and supplementary records were limited to information that is not duplicated in the official agency or medical record.

Costs can also be reduced by eliminating redundancies within a record. Workers often repeat information from entry to entry. These redundancies can be decreased if workers review and update previous entries rather than repeat information that has already been recorded. The record as a whole, rather than the most recent entry, becomes the working record. To make information more accessible in lengthy records, workers can prepare brief summaries of previous entries at regular intervals.

2. *Discourage overdocumentation.*

When criteria for selecting information for the record are absent or unclear, workers may record too much. Many practitioners find that having well-constructed outlines of the information that is to be included in, or excluded from, narrative reports helps them limit the length of the record. Formats that include brief queries with space for the practitioner's response help to guide the process of preparing and organizing each entry while ensuring that needed information is documented. Moreover, when the space for their responses is limited, practitioners tend to provide briefer responses.

3. *Substitute brief forms, checklists, and outlines for open-ended narratives.*

Many agencies use a combination of forms and narrative reports in their recordkeeping systems. Whenever possible, they should consider replacing open-ended narratives with queries, fill-ins, and checklists. This simplifies the recording process, encourages documentation of important information, and minimizes narrative recording, which is the most expensive style. Queries and responses can be used, for example, to document information about the client's social network and use of resources in the environment at intake and throughout the service process. Checklists can be used to document referral information, family circumstances, or procedures followed in releasing confidential information. A simple fill-in form could be used to document the purpose of service and service goals and plans. Many of the forms and outlines in chapter 5 and elsewhere in this book can be adapted for these purposes.

4. *Provide templates for assessments, goals, service plans, tracking movement, and outcomes.*

Records are intended to individualize the client-need-situation by documenting not just shared characteristics, like those that are found on the face sheet, but also what is special and distinctive about the case. Nonetheless, recordkeeping can be simplified if agencies provide practitioners with an assortment of carefully designed prototypes for documenting each phase of service, based on shared characteristics and best practices for the clientele served by the agency. Depending on the specific client-need-situation, practitioners may follow, modify, disregard, or override a template in documenting their cases.

Exhibit 7.1 is a prototype that lists areas that are to be assessed for suicide risk.

5. *Streamline documentation of routine cases.*

Many agencies and programs use the same recording approach for all cases, regardless of their complexity or duration. In general, a recording format that is sufficiently detailed and open-ended to apply to complex, long-term cases is unnecessarily complicated and costly to produce in cases where services are brief, limited, and routine. In some social service agencies and departments, 25%–75% of services are routine and time limited, or terminated before the fifth contact (Kagle, 1987a). Agencies can realize significant savings if they develop a short form for documenting such cases.

Developing a short form for documentation of brief, time-limited, and routine services involves four basic steps. First, the organization establishes criteria for using a short form. They may choose cases in which the primary service is information and referral, the provision of resources, or planning a transition from one environment to another. Second, those involved in service delivery and program management outline the steps or procedures that are ordinarily taken in providing the designated services. Third, the organization develops a short recording form, using checklists with queries and responses to document such cases. The short form might focus on:

- demographic information about the client-need-situation;
- eligibility for services;
- reason or need for services;
- service decisions and actions, including referrals;
- a checklist of steps ordinarily taken in delivering the designated services, with space for indicating the date on which each step is completed;
- space to explain added or omitted steps;
- a checklist of steps taken in response to requests for or releases of information;

Exhibit 7.1   Assessment Prototype: Risk of Suicide

Check if assessed; document relevant information

( ) Previous attempts (description, methods used, actions, hospitalizations)

_____

_____

( ) Critical events (family, relationships, work, health)

_____

_____

( ) Major changes in habits, personality (withdrawal, giving away possessions)

_____

_____

( ) Recklessness (accidents, fights, self-abuse)

_____

_____

( ) Depression, other mental disorders

_____

_____

( ) Substance use

_____

_____

( ) Talking, hinting, threats, plan, intent, means

_____

_____

( ) Social isolation

_____

_____

( ) Family, network history of suicide

_____

_____

- a list of dates and times of all service contacts; and
- information about the status of activity and the client-need-situation at termination.

Finally, the form is tested out in practice, and then revised, before becoming a part of the agency's recordkeeping system.

Modifying the structure and content of records can simplify recordkeeping and reduce the time and resources agencies and practitioners spend on records. However, agencies may need to make additional investments if they are to realize further cost reductions while at the same time improving the quality of records and supporting administrative and clinical practice.

- *Clerical support.* Agencies sometimes seek to cut costs by eliminating clerical positions. Even when workers have direct access to computers and prepare their own clinical records, clerical support is crucial to managing record systems, preparing administrative documents, making appointments and assisting clients, managing transactions with funding and oversight agencies, and much more. When clerical services are inadequate, records are often incomplete, out-of-date, or backlogged. Workers are forced to assume tasks that can be performed more economically by clerical workers, and client services suffer. Cutbacks in clerical services can even lead to budget shortfalls when invoices are not filed in a timely manner and reimbursements for services fall behind or are denied.

- *Computers.* Today, computers are a necessary component of any recordkeeping system. They offer the most efficient way of producing records; storing, retrieving, and backing up information; managing administrative and clinical practice; gaining reimbursement for services; and communicating with funders and oversight agencies. However, the cost of purchasing or upgrading agency computer systems remains high. These costs include hardware; software (from one-third to twice as much as hardware); new recording forms and manuals; training; consultation; structural modifications, such as upgrading wiring; enhanced security; and maintenance. There are often hidden costs as well. For example, many agencies use the opportunity offered by the introduction of new systems to evaluate, modify, and improve their recordkeeping structures, policies, and procedures. Such improvements are often expensive, and may increase staff workload. On the positive side, the price of hardware and software continues to fall. Most practitioners and other staff are now skilled in computer use, and can adapt relatively quickly to new or improved systems. Storing information on computers, optical disks, or other media can substantially reduce the cost of warehousing paper records. Information stored on computers can be more easily, economically, and reliably retrieved, revised, backed up, and transmitted.

Postponing the purchase or upgrade of computer hardware and software can be false economies. When computers are unavailable, out of service, or difficult to use, workers delay or spend more time on recordkeeping. Failing to invest in computers can result in an increase in practitioners' workloads, a decrease in the quality of their records, and even a loss of revenue. Annual investments in computer systems are crucial to maintaining the quality and restraining the overall cost of recordkeeping.

- *Explicit guidelines for the content of records.* Creating and updating guidelines for records involves an investment of time and effort by practitioners and administrators, but can ultimately result in improved records and cost savings. Practitioners can only produce meaningful and accountable records if they have clear guidelines as to what should be included in, and what should be excluded from, their records. Manuals, forms, online guides, templates, and sample records not only improve the quality of records but also help reduce costs by decreasing the uncertainty that can lead workers to overdocument.

THE SECURITY OF RECORDS

How can we ensure that our records are secure?

To protect client privacy and the confidentiality of social worker-client relationships, and to prevent damage to or destruction of vital documents, practitioners and agencies have an obligation to maintain the security of their paper and digital records and the personal information they contain. Security requires a system of administrative, physical, and technical procedures against unwarranted access to, release of, or tampering with personal information. Everything from practitioners' notes to computerized records to information transferred electronically is vulnerable to security breaches. Moreover, anyone with access to an agency's records or the information they contain could potentially share or alter their contents.

Agencies cannot rely on professional confidentiality and discretion alone. They need to establish security policies and procedures that cover the full range of personnel who may have access to paper and computerized records, and describe in some detail authorized as well as unacceptable practices and uses. They need user policies that distinguish among various agency personnel and procedures that provide or limit access to records based on a user's role and responsibilities. They need mechanisms to ensure that important information is regularly reviewed, verified, and backed up. They need guidelines for conducting authorized transfers of information and preventing unauthorized releases. They need agreements with partner agencies and other external entities that protect the personal information they share. They need ongoing staff training and oversight programs. They need to keep staff, clients, and others informed about security policies and procedures, and about how to report security problems and concerns. They need a procedure for responding to security problems, and applying sanctions to personnel who fail to follow agency standards. Because security is continually evolving, they need to monitor, evaluate, and revise policies and procedures regularly.

Security is only as strong as its weakest component. For example, an agency may invest in a sophisticated computer system but fail to shred confidential documents or clean hard drives when discarding old computers. Physical security is crucial. Paper records are vulnerable to security breaches when they are not kept in secure environments. Even the most sophisticated computer systems are vulnerable when staff's compliance with security procedures is lax.

Security should be a high priority but must be balanced against cost and convenience. Highly secure systems can be expensive to implement and difficult to use. When, for example, access is limited by complicated or constantly changing passwords, practitioners may circumvent the system by posting the code on their computer screens or keep handwritten notes instead. The security of all or some records can be undermined when security measures are too burdensome.

Security is a moving target. Recordkeeping systems that may seem secure today will become vulnerable to security breaches over time as technology evolves and existing safeguards become obsolete. Agencies and practitioners must continually update their security policies, procedures, and technology.

The HIPAA Security Rule established standards for managing computerized protected health information securely. Many agencies and practitioners that are not directly involved in health or mental health treatment do not realize that if they transmit protected health information electronically, they are covered by HIPAA and are expected to comply with its regulations. Even agencies not currently covered by HIPAA mandates would be well-advised to update their security policies and procedures to comply with HIPAA guidelines (see chapter 8).

Once information is released to another agency or entity, its security can no longer be ensured. Prior to releasing information, practitioners and agencies should inform the client of any risks involved. Security breaches involving social work records have resulted more often from re-releases of information by receiving agencies, mistakes or errors of judgment, outdated systems, or lack of compliance with policies and procedures than from the efforts of those seeking unwarranted access to confidential materials.

> A health department statistician in Palm Beach County, Florida, sent an e-mail message to more than 800 county health department employees, attaching a highly confidential list of the names and addresses of 4,500 county residents with AIDS and 2,000 others who had tested positive for HIV. The statistician realized his mistake almost immediately and contacted his agency's information technology unit which shut down the system and tried to correct the problem. Still, it was difficult to determine how many recipients had opened the attachment and whether any had forwarded the e-mail on. This error occurred even though Health Depart-

ment employees receive training in confidentiality, and are required to sign a confidentiality agreement. (Daugherty, 2005)

Any document in which the client is identified should be physically safe-guarded from unwarranted access. Records, forms, and other documents containing client information should be accessible only to those directly involved in service provision or related administrative, consultative, or clerical roles. Records should be logged in and out to monitor access and locate the record for other users. Records should only be taken out of the agency for specific purposes, such as court hearings. The information that leaves the agency should be limited to what is necessary for that purpose. Any information that leaves the agency should be copied or backed up. Practitioners should be aware that records or notes left in cars or briefcases, or on laptops or other devices, are exceptionally vulnerable to loss, theft, or casual inspection.

> A social worker was called out of the office on a series of emergencies that affected her clients. She fell behind in her record-keeping. Knowing that her records needed to be up-to-date before her scheduled vacation, she took home the records of 17 of her cases. While she and her family were out, her home and the records were destroyed by fire. The agency had copies of identifying and billing information; the rest of the records were lost.

Records should be stored in low traffic areas. Records of closed cases should be stored electronically if possible, and in secure areas that are closed to the public. When laws and rules permit, agencies should consider abstracting important information, and then destroying the full records of cases that have been closed for a long time. Not only is storage of paper records costly, but retaining old records places client privacy at risk after most of the information in the record is out-of-date, irrelevant, or of doubtful value (see chapter 9).

Paper records and notes should be locked up when they are not in use and at the end of the work day. Records should never be left on the worker's desk or otherwise visible during interviews or meetings. Practitioners who share offices should be careful that others cannot look over their shoulder or read their work. Clerical staff who work in public areas should make special efforts to block personal information on forms and screens from view. Workers who are preparing records or notes outside of secure office environments should make sure that their writing cannot be carelessly observed.

> A client was scheduling an appointment with her social worker. She glanced at the papers on the appointment secretary's desk, and recognized the name of her pastor's wife. "Is Reverend J's wife being treated here too?" she asked.

Computerized records require special safeguards. Computer screens should be filtered or turned away from view, and computers should be set to time out or shut down automatically when the staff member is not present. Agencies should have clear and detailed policies and procedures that provide overall security while allowing varying levels of access to different personnel via password, fingerprint, smartcard, or other technology. Such systems can allow clerical workers in a hospital, for example, to make appointments, file reports, and retrieve some information from a patient's record without gaining unauthorized access to psychiatric or social service reports. These systems not only deter unwarranted access to sensitive personal information, they also can track how and when information is documented or inspected. For these systems to be effective, however, passwords, smartcards, and other authentication devices must not be shared and should be frequently changed.

Computers that are linked to the Internet to permit e-mail exchanges, information searches, and data transfers are especially vulnerable to security breaches. Every Internet connection needs a firewall and other means of security to protect against viruses, hackers, and other intruders. A single unprotected wireless link, for example, could allow outsiders access to an entire record system. A misdirected e-mail could send information to the wrong recipient, who could, in turn, pass the information along to others. Accidental installation of programs or applications could permit "backdoor" intrusions into computer operations or record systems (Backdoors, 2006). Just by downloading unapproved software, for example, a practitioner could allow outsiders to copy or edit a file, steal or delete a document, corrupt or control a computer, undermine or spy on operations, or shut down an entire recordkeeping system. For these and other reasons, some agencies do not permit practitioners to install their own software on agency computers or to have direct Internet access.

Practitioners who use cell phones, PDAs, or other mobile devices to support their practice may also unknowingly expose records or personal client information to security breaches. Devices that contain or provide access to confidential information via wireless connections are not only vulnerable to loss and theft, but can expose information by using unprotected channels. Agencies that do permit wired or wireless interchanges need strong firewalls and user authentication systems, and must continuously update security policies, procedures, and technology. Systems that have been in place for only a month or two may already be penetrable.

Agencies must ensure that confidential information that is being transferred to another agency or system is encrypted, and that the transfer medium (e.g., Internet, phone) is secure. The receiving agency should also have strong security measures in place. Agencies often assume but fail to confirm that other agencies and practitioners will safeguard confidential client information. This is not always the case. Information that a client disclosed in confidence to a practitioner in one agency could be disclosed by a second agency whose security policies and procedures are less stringent, despite the first agency's careful adherence to all legal and ethical requirements in the release of information. Furthermore, unless information is encrypted or otherwise masked, agencies and practitioners should use faxes very sparingly, and only when no other medium is available. Faxes are easily misdirected or intercepted. Moreover, fax machines are shared by many users. Many fax systems store data internally, so a fax that has reached its intended recipient could be reprinted by someone else hours or even days later.

> Mrs. G and her family were leaving the community. She asked that her records be sent to an agency in another state. A few weeks later she called her former social worker. She had just been informed that her social security number and other personal information had been published on the Web by the new agency.

Agencies and practitioners must also guard against human error and deliberate breaches of security. Anyone inside an organization with access to personal information could inadvertently or intentionally reveal confidential information without proper authorization or security protection. They could lose their laptops, mislay paper records, abscond with CDs, reveal information in e-mail messages, or post data on the Internet. Reports of major breaches in the security of confidential information sometimes reach the public, undermining trust in professional judgment and discretion (Gelman, Pollack, & Weiner, 1999). To guard against such breaches, agencies should monitor access to and use of records, auditing for unusual requests or high demand, for example. Agencies should take special precautions to screen new and temporary staff, and strictly limit their access to confidential materials. No one should be allowed full access to records or other confidential information until they have successfully completed security training and supervised practice, and then only with careful oversight. Agencies should ensure that experienced personnel receive regular in-service training to teach new policies and practices, and reinforce ethical principles and security procedures.

Given the increased complexity and high costs associated with maintaining the security of computerized record systems, some agencies and practitioners may wonder whether such systems are really better than old-style paper records. Computers certainly make recordkeeping more efficient, but they also make it easier to copy and disseminate information, sometimes without proper authorization. Moreover, information cannot always be purged or corrected once it is entered into a computerized system or database, because it may be replicated to online and offline storage for purposes of backup, archiving, and information sharing. However, agencies and practitioners may have too much confidence in the security of their paper records. Such records can not only be easily accessed by bypassing physical security, they also can be damaged, destroyed, hidden, or copied without much difficulty. In contrast, good computer systems are more difficult to get into, and they track who has had access and what changes have been made. Indeed, except for the vulnerability of systems with Internet connections, computer-based recordkeeping systems offer better security than traditional paper records. Until such security problems are resolved, some agencies may choose to block or strictly limit access to the Internet for its recordkeeping system. Others might consider separating their networks into two systems, one for records, and the other for Internet searches, e-mail, and other communication. In this way, agencies may be able to protect the security of their records while at the same time encouraging the flow of other information in and out of the agency via the Internet.

COMPUTERS AND RECORDS

How are social work agencies and departments using computers?

Since the first edition of this book was published in 1984, computers have become commonplace in social service agencies, as they have in businesses and homes across the United States and around the world. Computers simplify the process of documenting, storing, retrieving, reporting, and using information. They also can contribute to the service process and to case, program, and agency administration. Most social work agencies and departments today use computers for some aspects of recordkeeping, although they vary considerably in the degree to which computers are integrated into day-to-day practice. On one end of the continuum are agencies that use computers only for clerical tasks, like typing and printing forms and reports. On the other, are those that have fully automated recordkeeping systems. Most agencies fall somewhere in-between, using computers to support many aspects of recordkeeping, while also maintaining some paper records.

Like most businesses and organizations, social work agencies and departments have largely replaced typewriters with computers to perform word processing and other clerical functions. Computers are used not just to type narratives and fill out preprinted and online forms. They make it possible to retrieve, review, annotate, and revise records with relatively little effort. They make it easy to send out mass mailings; prepare reports from archived records; locate information, even when it is embedded in narrative reports; and store large amounts of information in a small space.

Computers can archive information in databases for quick and easy analysis and use. Any information that can be documented specifically and systematically can be selected, sorted, classified, compiled, and compared. For example, the Borage County Mental Health Clinic uses a database to support case management. Workers fill out a brief monthly case reporting form on each case. This form includes only nine variables. They are:

- worker providing each service contact;
- client identification (name or case number);
- source of referral;
- identified problems;
- service goals;
- date of each service contact;

- services provided at each service contact;
- status of goals at end of month; and
- status of goals at termination (if appropriate).

Exhibit 7.2 shows the monthly reporting form used by the Borage County Mental Health Center. The agency can then use this information to prepare a number of reports, including:

- individual case reports;
- active cases for each practitioner grouped by problem type, by number of service contacts, and by services provided;
- cases by problem type;
- service contacts per month by worker, problem type, and goals;
- quarterly and annual reports by case and worker;
- outliers, such as cases receiving no services in the previous month or receiving only one to two contacts before dropping out; and
- comparison of outcomes by services, problems, and number of service contacts.

Exhibit 7.3 is an example of an outlier report issued monthly for a worker at the Borage County Mental Health Clinic (see page 214).

The Records II study (Kagle, 1993), conducted in 1987 and 1988, found that social work agencies and departments were using computers for four important functions: business and office management; agency management; client tracking, decision support, and caseload management; and case records. Two decades later, these continue to be the primary uses for computers. However, vast improvements in computer technology and functionality have completely transformed the workplace. Whereas in the late 1980s, few practitioners had direct access to computers, today a large proportion of practitioners have computers on their desks. Computers and other technology are fully integrated into their lives and work.

1. Business and office management.

Computers play a crucial role in billing and other financial transactions, preparing routine forms and reports for oversight and funding agencies, scheduling appointments and meetings for clients and staff, storing and retrieving information, and much more. It would be hard to imagine a large or small agency, or even a practitioner with a small private practice, who could manage business or office functions without a computer. Indeed, agencies and practitioners that have not automated their business functions are under growing pressure to do so, as federal and state agencies, insurance companies, and oversight bodies request or require that billing and other information be exchanged electronically.

2. Agency management.

Supervisors, program managers, and agency administrators all rely on computers for information about programs, services, staff, and clients. Manag-

Exhibit 7.2   Monthly Case Reporting Form

Borage County Mental Health Clinic **Monthly Case Reporting Form**

Worker: Month/Year:

Client ID:

Part I (new cases only)

Source of Referral:
( ) Self
( ) Friend or family
( ) Physician or psychiatrist
( ) School
( ) Mental health agency
( ) Attorney
( ) Crisis line
( ) Unknown
( ) Other (specify) _____

Problem Type*:
( ) Interpersonal conflict
( ) Dissatisfaction in social relations
( ) Problems with formal organizations
( ) Difficulties in role performance
( ) Problems of social transition
( ) Reactive emotional distress
( ) Inadequate resources
( ) Other (specify) _____

Service Goals (up to three):
( ) Teach new skills
( ) Resolve interpersonal conflicts
( ) Link to community agencies
( ) Work through emotional difficulties
( ) Improve or change social environment
( ) Improve or change physical environment
( ) Find job, housing, and/or other resources
( ) Build social support network
( ) Other (specify) _____

* This list is based on the "Target Problem" typology used in task-centered practice. See
Reid and Epstein's (1972) *Task-Centered Casework*.

Exhibit 7.2 *(continued)*

<table>
<tr><td colspan="3" align="center">Borage County Mental Health Clinic
Monthly Case Reporting Form</td></tr>
</table>

Worker:	Month/Year:
Client ID:	

Part II (for all cases)

Date of Each Contact:
_____   _____
_____   _____
_____   _____
_____   _____
_____   _____
_____   _____
_____   _____
_____   _____
_____   _____
_____   _____
_____   _____

Services Provided During the Month:
( ) Case management
( ) Crisis intervention
( ) Behavioral intervention
( ) Psychosocial casework
( ) Group work
( ) Marital counseling
( ) Family therapy
( ) Information or referral
( ) Provision of resources
( ) Assessment or evaluation
( ) Other (specify) _____

Status of Each Goal at Last Contact During the Month:

Goal 1	Goal 2	Goal 3
( ) Achieved	( ) Achieved	( ) Achieved
( ) Improved	( ) Improved	( ) Improved
( ) No change	( ) No change	( ) No change
( ) Worsened	( ) Worsened	( ) Worsened
( ) Activity deferred	( ) Activity deferred	( ) Activity deferred

Part III (at closing only)

Service Outcome:
( ) All goals achieved
( ) At least one but not all goals achieved
( ) No goals achieved
( ) Client dropped out
( ) Services terminated by agency
( ) Services no longer needed
( ) Referral successful
( ) Referral unsuccessful
( ) Other (specify) _____

Exhibit 7.3   Outlier Report

Borage County Mental Health Clinic

Worker: Elgin   Month: July
Total Cases Open: 66
Total Cases No Services: 19

Client #	Problem Type	Goals	Last Recorded Contact
7-033	5	1, 3, 5	6/xx
7-142	4	1, 2, 8	5/xx
7-151	4	1, 5, 7	7/xx
7-158	1	2, 5	5/xx
8-096	3	2, 3	6/xx
8-113	7	1, 3	5/xx
8-132	5	5, 6, 7	5/xx
8-149	4	1, 8	6/xx
8-176	7	3	3/xx
8-209	1	2, 8	4/xx
8-217	4	3, 7	12/xx

ers can view information directly on computer screens or printed in routine or special reports. They use the information to make decisions about budgets and allocation of resources, performance, deployment of staff, and efficiency and effectiveness of services, for example. They may also identify clients' emerging needs and their appraisal of the services they received. Some agencies have Management Information Systems (MISs) that are used to collect, analyze, and disseminate information for decision support, planning and evaluating services, and measuring and monitoring service processes and outcomes.

Records used in administrative practice are also supported by computers. Personnel records and performance appraisals; business transactions and expense reports; minutes of staff, community, and board meetings; legal documents and interagency agreements; governance documents and policy manuals, to cite just a few examples, may all be prepared, revised, accessed, and stored online. Agency managers also use computers for internal communication (e.g., to announce new procedures or interact with staff) and for external communication (e.g., recruiting staff and fundraising).

3. Client tracking, decision support, and caseload management.

Computers assist direct-service workers in their practice. They not only provide easy access to information about policies, programs, and procedures. They can offer guidance in evaluating clients' eligibility for services, assessing and diagnosing client-need-situations, planning services, and analyzing movement, for example, via online practice guidelines, assessment tools, decision trees, goal statements, and treatment protocols (Gingerich & Broskowski, 1996). They can be used to monitor goals and movement over time, and archive detailed information in complex cases. Computers allow practitioners to review and evaluate their caseloads, using reports profiling open cases, service activities, and pending court action, for example. Computers also can assist practitioners in meeting administrative guidelines, prompting them when cases are due for routine review or closing, or where documentation does not meet quality assurance or reimbursement standards. Computers also make it possible for practitioners to communicate more efficiently with other service providers, and have access to up-to-date community resource files. For example, using a computer database of community resources, one social service department was able to assist practitioners in finding appropriate placements and shorten patients' overall length-of-stay in the hospital (Rock et al., 1995).

Computers are being used not just to track clients within agencies but also to assist practitioners and managers in making decisions about clients, caseloads, and workloads. Some communities have created interagency systems to track clients with special needs who receive services from several agencies or providers. For example, one community created a system linking case managers in 18 agencies who provide services to people living with HIV-related illnesses. Concerned about the security of such sensitive information, the agencies "designed a password-controlled wide-area network with a shared intake template and layered access to information." They also separated the network into two systems, one with severely limited access for sharing confidential information, and the other permitting freer exchanges for e-mail and other communication (Henrickson & Mayo, 2000).

Communities nationwide are developing shared information systems to identify, count, track, and identify the needs of and services provided to adults and children experiencing homelessness. Following the experiences of cities like Philadelphia and states like Massachusetts that had improved services to the homeless due to careful study and tracking, the federal government mandated that communities receiving federal funds develop Homeless Management Information Systems (HMISs) (Perls, 2005). However, developing such systems has been a formidable challenge because of the sheer complexity of the initiative (Gutierrez & Friedman, 2005). Large and small communities have had difficulty implementing HMISs due to high costs, technical problems, limited staff and resources, as well as privacy and security concerns (Roman, 2003).

4. Client records.

Almost all social work agencies now use computers to support record-keeping, but most continue to keep records on paper. Practitioners and support personnel enter information, prepare reports, and print materials for the client's file. These files may also contain practitioners' handwritten notes, legal documents, and other papers. Some agencies and practitioners have begun to make the transition to electronic records. With electronic records, practitioners can enter and access appointment, billing, and client data; service information; and clinical notes online or in print. Some public agencies and hospitals have made the transition to fully automated client records.

Here, the client's file is online. Practitioners and support personnel have computers on their desks or readily available, so they can enter and retrieve client information directly. Even in these agencies, however, practitioners may still rely on paper copies of client records.

The electronic client record is the wave of the future. Although only about 10% of hospitals were automated by 2006 (Colliver, 2006), the conversion from paper to digital records is accelerating. Over the past decade, the federal government has offered incentives and technical support to encourage public child welfare agencies and health care providers to convert to electronic records. The federal government is also promoting the development of a National Health Information Network, with the goal of developing a secure network for linking and exchanging information from electronic medical records. The stated purpose is to reduce costs, identify emerging needs, and remedy medical crises, as well as to make health information readily available in situations when paper records might be lost or destroyed, as in national disasters. However, high costs, privacy concerns, and technical problems, such as system incompatibility, remain (Kaushal et al., 2005; "New Threat," 2006).

Social work organizations have made great progress using computers to provide ready access to information in support of decision-making, especially at the management level. The next step in many agencies is to extend the benefits of automation to the practitioner. Of course, computers have made it easier for practitioners to document and access information. However, although computers have great potential for making recordkeeping more efficient, the introduction of computers in agency-based practice has often increased practitioners' workloads. The next step is to find ways in which computers can be used to streamline and reduce practitioners' recordkeeping tasks. For example, on-screen forms, checklists, templates, and queries can increase efficiency while ensuring that important information is documented. Clerical workers, rather than practitioners, could be responsible for filling out and filing forms. Computers could be used to compile information that otherwise might be the practitioner's responsibility, for example, preparing statistical reports, calculating service units, and analyzing monthly productivity data. Practitioners could have access to computers, so that they could review and update the record directly, referring to information already documented rather than repeating it in subsequent entries. Finally, working together, practitioners and managers could develop realistic guidelines for documentation that meet the agency's information needs while using the practitioner's time wisely and efficiently.

RECORDS IN RESEARCH

Our agency's records contain a wealth of information. Should we encourage their use in research?

Agency records have been the primary data source in a number of classic research studies that have had a significant impact on social work policy and practice. Mary Richmond (1917) based *Social Diagnosis* on her investigation of narrative case records in several social service agencies. David Fanshel (1975) based his study of parental visits to children in foster care on computerized data from child-care agencies in New York City. Contemporary studies of Temporary Assistance for Needy Families (TANF) reform (Cancian, Haveman, Meyer, & Wolfe, 2002), child welfare outcomes (Testa, Fuller, & Rolock, 2005), child support policy initiatives (Cassetty & Hutson, 2005), and health services impact (Albert, Simone, Brassard, Stern, & Mayeux, 2005), among many others, use agency administrative databases in their analysis of major policies and their impact on diverse clientele. Studies of records and recordkeeping practices in agencies nationwide have been an important source of information for this and earlier editions of *Social Work Records*.

In addition to their use in traditional research studies, agency managers use administrative data to analyze client characteristics and needs, service patterns and outcomes, and professional activities and productivity. Practitioners use qualitative or quantitative methods of inference to study single cases and clusters of similar cases to understand and evaluate service processes and outcomes. These studies are used to inform program and practice decisions, and in practitioner self-evaluation. When such studies are published, they add to the knowledge base of the profession.

Yet, in spite of their widespread use in research, records that have been kept for service purposes and under the conditions of practice have inherent weaknesses that limit the reliability and validity of the conclusions they can support. Records may be useful in describing clients and needs, evaluating programs and services, and generating hypotheses. However, they may be less suitable for making inferences or establishing causal connections.

Before initiating any study using records as a source of data, agencies and investigators need to undertake four important processes.

1. Assess whether information in records is suitable for the purposes of the research.

2. Complete an institutional review board (IRB) review.

3. Institute human subject protections, using HIPAA consent forms where appropriate.

4. Establish procedures to mask clients' identities and otherwise ensure that personally identifiable information is handled confidentially.

In assessing whether the agency's records are a good source of data for a particular study, agencies and researchers need to consider the questions researchers are seeking to answer. Records can be good sources of data to answer such questions as:

- Who are the agency's clients?
- Where do clients come from (referral in)?
- Where do clients go (referral out)?
- What services do clients receive?

- How are agency resources being used?
- How are clients, needs, purposes, goals, processes, and outcomes defined?

They may also be used to answer questions about adherence to established policies, procedures, and standards:

- Is the agency adhering to privacy guidelines?
- Are practitioners documenting needed information?
- Are records up-to-date?

Records are especially useful in generating hypotheses about relationships (correlations). For example:

- Which client groups are seeking out and selected for which programs, services, or practice modalities?
- How does goal setting relate to outcomes achieved?

However, unless the conditions of practice conform to the standards of control necessary for making causal inferences (see Campbell & Stanley, 1963; Kagle, 1982b), existing records are probably not a good source of data for such questions as:

- Are casework services effective?
- Do inpatient services produce better results than outpatient services?
- Did family therapy help the M family?

Many factors can undermine the suitability of agency records for research. Among the most important are:

1. *Time lag.* Frequently social work practice records are written long after the events they report. Both accuracy and specificity are adversely affected by a lag in time between the collection of information and its documentation.

2. *Subjectivity.* Much of the information social workers collect and document in their clinical records involves varying perspectives on problems, experiences, and circumstances. Clients' and others' recollections of events, points-of-view, values, and inferences are crucial to practice, but may be too subjective to support quantitative research. Information in administrative databases, such as birth dates, frequency of interviews, and the like, might seem more suitable for such purposes. However, names of family members may be misspelled, reported inaccurately, or change over time, making information difficult to verify and cases difficult to track (English, Brandford, & Coghlan, 2000; Garnier & Poertner, 2000). Even what appears to be objective and factual data may be flawed.

3. *The context of information gathering.* There are important differences between the "ground rules" necessary for data collection in research and those of social work practice. These differences may affect the suitability of records as the data base for research. For example, the

research interview differs considerably from the service interview. To maintain consistency, the research interview is carefully structured, using a preestablished protocol; in contrast, the practice interview evolves in response to what is salient in the client-need-situation and the service transaction. To minimize the interviewer's influence on the subject's responses, the research interviewer remains attentive but is a disinterested listener; in contrast, the practitioner not only is attentive but also guides, reacts, responds, and contributes. In practice, the relationship between the worker and the client is mutual and ongoing; in research, the relationship between research subject and interviewer or observer is time limited and circumscribed. In practice, the client is deeply involved in the direction of services and their outcome; in research, the client may be unaware of or unaffected by the results. Because of selective focus, interpersonal influence, and personal investment in the service transaction, the service interview may not produce information that is sufficiently detached to serve as the basis for research.

4. *Selectivity.* Social work recording necessarily involves selection. The most complete and detailed records omit some information. Not only do the worker and the information source exercise discretion in information gathering, but the worker also exercises discretion in deciding what to record. A structured record (standardized forms, checklists, and so on) can guide the selection process and encourage the documentation of needed information. Nevertheless, the recorder makes choices in documentation even when completing a form. One worker may choose to document an event, idea, or concern that another might entirely overlook or place in a different context. In addition, the criteria used in selecting information for case continuity and supervision may not meet the selection criteria for the planned research project. The agency's records may not contain the needed information, or the needed information may not appear with sufficient frequency or in adequate detail.

5. *Consistency.* Another consideration in using records in research is comparability. The content of a record may vary from entry to entry, client to client, program to program, and one service modality to another. Most important, records may vary from worker to worker. Some of these variations will be immediately apparent, as when narrative records take different forms or contain different information. Other variations are less apparent, such as when workers use different terms to describe the same phenomenon ("physical aggression" versus "playing") or define divergent phenomena using a common term ("depressed"). Unless records are standardized and terms are carefully defined, different workers may use different criteria in documenting, for example, program goals, client movement, and service

outcomes. Because of these differences, researchers should not assume but must verify whether records reflect shared meanings for frequently used terms, and document similar phenomena in a comparable manner.

6. *Ease of access.* A final and often decisive consideration is the accessibility of existing information. Information that is documented on a computer or form is more readily useable in research than are narrative reports. It is not surprising, then, that management records are more often used in research than are clinical records. Clinical records can be a rich source of information for qualitative studies, and may be transformed into quantitative data. It is important to remember, however, that information that is accessible is not necessarily accurate. Although information that can be easily quantified may appear to be appropriate for research, it may not actually be reliable or valid. Like other information in records, information that is readily accessible must be checked for accuracy, specificity, completeness, and consistency.

If records or other sources of client information are to be used in a study, the agency and investigator should undertake an institutional review. Institutional reviews are intended to evaluate the quality, likely benefits, and potential risks of proposed research, and ensure that investigators protect individuals who are the subjects of research from coercion or breaches of privacy. Most agencies that conduct or host research have established IRBs or committees on human research (CHRs) to evaluate research proposals and ensure that human subjects are protected. These committees can require changes, negotiate improvements, or deny approval, if warranted. Agencies that do not have review committees may wish to consult government publications and Web sites for information about IRB formation, operation, and guiding principles (www.hhs.gov/ohrp/). Because universities and colleges require institutional review of research involving human subjects, faculty and student researchers often undergo two levels of review before a study can begin, one in their own institution and another in the host agency.

Another important step may be to garner the client's or an authorized decision maker's informed consent for the client's records to be used in the study. Prior to the implementation of HIPAA, studies of clients' records often did not require their consent. Rather, consent was usually required only when clients' records were used in studies that also involved direct observation or intervention. Under HIPAA, however, when clients' personal health information (PHI) is to be collected and analyzed, many institutions now require the use of special HIPAA-compliant consent forms. Indeed, some institutions require two separate consent forms—one for access to PHI and another for the client to participate in the research (see, for example, http://www.research.ucsf.edu/chr/HIPAA/chrHIPAAconsent.asp).

If consent forms are required, they should describe the study and indicate that records will be used. In addition, they should specify:

- what specific information will be collected and analyzed;
- how the individual's identity and other personally identifiable information will be protected;
- what risks of disclosure might exist;
- the identities of those who will conduct the study and have access to the record; and
- a date on which the consent expires, how to revoke consent, and what, if any, consequences might ensue should the client fail to provide or revoke consent.

Unfortunately, using consent forms may actually compromise privacy. Agencies and investigators can protect other personally identifiable information via masking or coding; consent forms, which explicitly identify the client, must be retained as is. Therefore, agencies and researchers must make special efforts to limit access to these forms and store them securely.

Whether or not consent forms are used, agencies and investigators must establish procedures that protect personally identifiable information in records and research data from unwarranted access, use, and disclosure. Agencies and investigators may wish to consider the following guidelines and procedures:

- limiting access to and coding of personal information to the minimum necessary to support the research;
- limiting the number of staff or researchers who have direct access to the record as well as ensuring that they are well-trained to protect personally identifiable information in records and research data;
- if possible, masking or otherwise preventing direct access to and use of the client's name, social security number, case number, and other personally identifiable information;
- if personally identifiable information is necessary for the research (e.g., because information from several sources must be matched), limiting access to the information, coding it, limiting access to the code, and then destroying the data and the codebook when they are no longer crucial to the study and its analysis;
- ensuring that paper, computer, and media used in data collection, storage, and analysis are stored securely and used in areas with limited access;
- ensuring that personally identifiable information is not used in research reports or other presentations of the study's findings;
- seeking a "certificate of confidentiality" from a federal or state agency to protect against compelled disclosures of sensitive and personally identifiable information. If, for example, the information for the study includes criminal acts or use of illegal substances, investigators may seek such a certificate to protect the research data and the identity of research subjects from subpoena, court orders, or other legal processes (see http://www.grants.nih. gov/grants/policy/coc/faqs.htm);

- monitoring and reviewing data collection and analysis, and reviewing reports and other products, to ensure that personally identifiable information is handled confidentially and will not be intentionally or accidentally revealed; and
- ensuring that IRB and other procedures are being followed.

There are many good reasons for agencies to permit and even encourage research on their records. Such research can:

- support field work students' academic and professional development;
- build relationships with faculty members and academic institutions;
- contribute to knowledge in the field;
- discover strengths and weaknesses in existing programs, identify areas for growth, and suggest new directions;
- provide staff with opportunities for skill development and professional recognition;
- contribute to the agency's mission and strategic goals; and
- garner prestige and resources.

Nonetheless, many agencies are reluctant to become involved in such ventures. Many are concerned about the costs associated with sponsoring and implementing the research. Even when a study is supported by external funding and academic investigators supply resources for data collection, analysis, and dissemination, agencies are still responsible for masking personally identifiable information in records and monitoring the research to ensure that confidential information is protected. Moreover, agencies recognize that hosting research may involve extra work for professional and other staff, who may be asked to update and clarify information in their records, fill out additional forms or protocols, and meet regularly with investigators. Staff members are also involved in institutional review, which can be a time-consuming and contentious process. If client consent is necessary, agency staff may be responsible for explaining the research to clients or their authorized decision makers and ensuring that their consent is informed and not coerced. Finally, agencies may be concerned about a lack of control over the research process and its outcomes, and about the potential for negative finding or disputes with investigators about how findings will be presented, interpreted, and made public. Many of these issues can be negotiated in advance or resolved amicably. But agencies and investigators should expect the unexpected. By definition, research exposes customary practices and assumptions to careful analysis, and opens the door to new ideas and surprising discoveries. Research can offer the agency and the investigator new insights into old problems, but may expose weaknesses as well as strengths. Hosting research may involve additional work for practitioners, managers, and other staff. However, the results can contribute to the agency in meaningful ways and be well worth the effort.

CHAPTER 8

RECORDS AND THE LAW

Chapter 8 focuses on legislation and its impact on records. It first discusses the five principles of privacy—confidentiality, abridgment, access, anonymity, and security—and then presents a brief history of federal privacy legislation. It then describes various federal and state laws that influence or control the handling of records and the information they contain. The chapter includes a thorough treatment of the privacy aspects of HIPAA and its relationship to state law. The chapter concludes with a discussion of HIPAA, state law, and the records of specific client populations.

Social workers observe the intimate details of their clients' lives. In seeking and receiving service, clients are obliged to share information about themselves, their circumstances, and their relationships with people and social institutions. The knowledge gained by the worker is used in planning and delivering services most appropriate to the client's wishes and needs; in fact, the purpose and process of some therapeutic approaches is the revelation of thoughts, feelings, and experiences that the client usually hides from others. Without this information, individualized social work service would be impossible. Because client disclosures form the core of many social service transactions, they also form the core of the social work record.

The client's obligation to share personal information is predicated upon a reciprocal obligation on the part of the social worker and the organization: the obligation not to reveal personal information except under specific, socially valued circumstances. The confidential nature of the relationship between client, worker, and organization is an underlying right of the client and an ethical and legal responsibility for the worker and the organization. However, the right of clients to the privacy of their information has never been absolute, and, over time, their privacy rights have eroded. Today, the worker and the organization are expected to balance the importance of maintaining the privacy of information revealed in the context of the worker-client relationship against other, competing societal interests and values. For example, society has come to expect that certain information, such as when a client poses danger to other people, will be disclosed.

223

New technologies have also raised the potential for access to, and misuse of, information in the client's record. In response, federal and state governments and public and private institutions have developed policies and procedures intended to protect the individual's right to privacy by setting parameters on the flow of information about the client into, within, and out of the service relationship. The specific parameters vary by state, field of practice, funding source, service program, the profession of the service provider, and the client group. Despite these many variations, what is common to all exchanges of client information is the role that legal principles and rules play in governing information disclosure. State and federal law increasingly governs access to and disclosure of information contained in client records. Five basic privacy principles are expressed explicitly or implicitly within these laws.

BASIC PRIVACY PRINCIPLES

The five basic principles of privacy are: confidentiality, abridgment, access, anonymity, and security.

Confidentiality is the primary means through which clients' privacy is protected. Confidentiality means safeguarding from disclosure personal information that the client reveals or the worker learns in the context of providing services. The responsibility for confidentiality resides with the practitioner but depends on professional ethics, organizational policies and practices, the actions of other service providers inside and outside the organization, the integrity of funding and accrediting agencies, and the protections provided by the law.

The NASW Code of Ethics establishes the ethical standards under which professional social workers practice. The 1996 version of the Code of Ethics, which was revised in 1999, was the first major modification of the Code since 1979 and includes greatly expanded sections on Privacy and Confidentiality (1.07) and Access to Records (1.08). In fact, these two standards together contain a greater number of provisions than were contained in the entire, original version. The current Code offers social workers general guidance in protecting clients' confidentiality and obligates them to inform clients about the limitations on social workers' ability to protect confidentiality.

The responsibility of social workers to safeguard the confidentiality of client information is never absolute. In other words, both the NASW Code of Ethics and confidentiality protections provided by various laws contain exceptions to the duty to maintain confidentiality. These exceptions reflect socially valued purposes. For example, social workers may reveal information when it is needed to protect the client or others from serious harm, when the disclosure is mandatory under the law (e.g., child abuse reporting), when the organization is being audited or monitored by an oversight agency, or to assist clients in receiving services from other providers.

Abridgment protects client privacy by limiting the collection, documentation, and retention of personal information to what is necessary to meet the expectations for accountability, comply with relevant laws and policies, and support practice. Abridgment is based on the assumption that personal information that does not appear in records, and records that are not retained beyond their usefulness, are less vulnerable to unauthorized access and other privacy violations. Abridgment means that information that is revealed in the context of service delivery, but is not relevant to the purpose of service, is left out of the record. Information in the record that is inaccurate or incomplete is carefully corrected and amended. Records that are out-of-date and no longer useful are abstracted, destroyed, or expunged. Of course, information that has been disseminated to other agencies or appears in databases is difficult to correct or eliminate. For this reason, it is important to limit information in the record to what is necessary, accurate, and meaningful. In abridging their records, social workers are guided by the NASW (1999) Code of Ethics and by relevant privacy laws and agency policies.

Access to records by clients, their families, or their agents enhances client privacy by allowing the recipient of services to learn what information is being collected, documented, and stored, and how information is being interpreted and used by the agency. Although most clients do not desire to see their records, those who do have many different reasons for seeking access. Some are encouraged to review their records by agency policy or by their social worker; while others may initiate a request for access on their own or on the advice of an attorney, physician, or other advisor. Certain individuals need copies of their past records to show to their current service providers or to obtain reimbursement for services already received. Some wish to see their records prior to signing an authorization for release of information, whereas others wish to have a copy of their records following termination of services. Some wish to confirm what they have been told, whereas others seek access because they feel that information is being withheld from them. Still others are merely curious about what is being written about them or how they are perceived.

Anonymity protects privacy by permitting the use of client information for specific and valued purposes if the client's name and other identifying information are obscured. Indeed, many uses of the record do not require that the client be identified. Information from records can be monitored by oversight agencies, used in education and research, and presented to the public without disclosing the client's identity. Whenever possible, social service agencies should keep clients' identities anonymous by blocking out names, personal identifiers like social security numbers, and other revealing information when records are used in education or research. They can, for example, pool anonymous information for presentations inside and outside the organization, read from pertinent sections rather than allowing monitors direct access to client records, and abstract records for reports to funding and other outside agencies.

Security protects privacy through a system of administrative policies and procedures, and physical and technical safeguards, that prevent unwarranted access to records and unauthorized release of or tampering with the personal information they contain. In fact, efforts to protect privacy via confidentiality, abridgment, access, and anonymity are useless if records and their contents are not kept secure. Due to continuing advances in technology and ongoing threats to records security, agency policies, procedures, and practices need continual review and revision. (See chapter 7 for more information about the security of records.)

The five basic principles of privacy serve to regulate the use of information about the client-need-situation. Confidentiality limits the flow of information out of the professional relationship and the organization. Abridgment limits the flow of information from and about the client into, within, and outside the organization. Client access increases the flow of information from the professional relationship and the organization to the client and others acting on the client's behalf. Anonymity increases the flow of information within and out of the organization but without divulging the client's identity. Security prevents the flow of information to unauthorized recipients via administrative, physical, and technical procedures. Because of their importance in protecting privacy, these principles have been incorporated into the laws and regulations that seek to prevent unwarranted intrusions into the personal lives of individuals, most notably those who seek and receive health, mental health, and social services.

A Brief History of Federal Privacy and Records Legislation

Prior to the 1970s, there was minimal legal regulation of how practitioners and the agencies they worked for handled client information. In limited instances, state law regulated information kept in client records. Typically, however, client records and the information contained within them were not subject to legal standards. Instead, social workers relied on ethical principles to decide what information should be placed in the client record and to whom this information would be disclosed. It was not until 1965 that the federal government began to address issues of privacy and its relationship to client records. Congress created a special subcommittee to study issues related to privacy and automated personal data systems. The U.S. Department of Health, Education and Welfare (1973) (now Health and Human Services) issued a report entitled *Records, Computers and the Rights of Citizens*. This report contained a Code of Fair Information Practices. These practices were stated as follows:

- There must be no personal-data record-keeping systems whose very existence is secret.
- There must be a way for an individual to find out what information about him is in a record and how it is used.

- There must be a way for an individual to prevent information about him obtained for one purpose from being used or made available for other purposes without his consent.

- There must be a way for an individual to correct or amend a record of identifiable information about him.

- Any organization creating, maintaining, using, or disseminating records of identifiable personal data must assure the reliability of the data for their intended use and must take precautions to prevent misuse of the data.

An examination of these practices reflects the subcommittee's concern with many of the same privacy principles that were explained in the previous section. Practices one, two, and four deal with issues related to access. The third practice reflects concern with abridgement of information. Practices three and five speak to issues related to the security of client information, also protecting privacy. All of the practices demonstrate concern for the confidentiality of information. The Code of Fair Information Practices delineated in the 1973 report have been incorporated into all subsequent federal laws related to information collection and served as the basis for the Privacy Act of 1974.

Since the late 1960s, Congress has passed a variety of federal laws that are related to the privacy of individuals' information. Initially, the legislation was designed to provide access to records to the people who were the subjects of the records. At that time, the concern was that people should be able to know whether governmental entities held information about them and what content was included in their records. Additionally, in case the information was erroneous, the individual should have the right to correct any errors. The Freedom of Information Act (1966) established the public's right to obtain information contained in records and documents of federal government agencies. The Privacy Act of 1974 regulated the government's use of individuals' personal information. The Fair Credit Reporting Act (1970) gave consumers the right to know what information lenders had when making decisions about providing them credit and other services. The Family Educational Rights and Privacy Act (1974) allowed parents access to the educational records of their children. These laws opened up certain governmental records about individuals to the individuals themselves.

Since the 1980s, the emergence of computer and other technologies and the potential for misuse of personal data have led to public concerns regarding the privacy of personal information. As a result, the federal government has enacted legislation that addresses these technologies and their effect on privacy. Some laws focus on the way external technologies have intruded into the lives of individuals. For example:

- The Electronic Communications Privacy Act of 1986 protects individuals' telephone and electronic transmissions against government surveillance without a court order and from carriers of the messages.

- The Employee Polygraph Protection Act of 1988 prevents employers from using lie detector tests during preemployment screening or employment.
- The Telephone Consumer Protection Act (1991) restricts the use of telephone and facsimile machines to deliver unsolicited advertisements; the law was expanded in 2003 to include the do not call registry.

More recent federal legislation focuses on the impact of technology on the unauthorized dissemination of individuals' personal information. In many instances, personal information that has been placed in computer databases has been wrongfully shared with third parties, often for profit. Examples of laws designed to protect individuals from unauthorized disclosure of information include:

- The Video Privacy Protection Act (1988) prevents disclosure of personally identifiable video or audiovisual rental records.
- The Driver's Privacy Protection Act (1994) prohibits states from disclosing personal and health information submitted when obtaining driver's licenses.
- The Health Insurance Portability and Accountability Act (1996) limits disclosure of health and medical information without consent.
- The Children's Online Privacy Protection Act of 1998 protects the privacy of children under the age of 13 by requesting parental consent for the collection or use of any personal information on Web sites.
- The Identity Theft and Assumption Deterrence Act of 1998 criminalizes the unauthorized transfer or use of a means of identification.
- The Gramm-Leach-Bliley Act (1999) governs the collection and disclosure of customers' personal financial information by financial institutions.

The legislation enacted in the 1990s reflects the federal government's concern for individual privacy and its response to the use of technology by third parties to gain information about individuals. The federal government attempted to protect individuals from *outside* parties' unauthorized intrusions into their private information. However, the events of September 11, 2001, and continuing concerns about national security have led to the federal government increasing its *own* ability to enter into individuals' personal matters. The Uniting and Strengthening America by Providing Appropriate Tools Required to Intercept and Obstruct Terrorism (USA Patriot Act) Act of 2001, commonly known as the Patriot Act, increased the power of the government to investigate and conduct surveillance of personal information, including information contained in personal files on the Internet. Before the Patriot Act, the federal government's tendency was to protect individuals' personal privacy. The Patriot Act signals a reversal in this policy, ostensibly in response to overwhelming unease about terrorism.

All of the above-mentioned federal legislation protects privacy by opening up records to their subjects while limiting disclosure only to those people or entities that are authorized to receive them. These laws deal with a wide range of privacy-related subjects, including educational, health, and financial records. Social workers may not encounter certain of these laws, like the Gramm-Leach-Bliley Act or the Video Privacy Protection Act, because they have a limited relationship to social work practice or social work records. Other federal laws are much more relevant to the practice of social work and how records are maintained. These laws are discussed below.

IMPORTANT FEDERAL LAWS RELATED TO SOCIAL WORK RECORDS

Federal legislation applies to all federal social service agencies. The federal government can create federal social service programs and benefits and require its own agencies, such as the Social Security Administration or the U.S. Department of Health and Human Services, to follow its rules. Because the United States has a hierarchal system of government, the federal government also has power over state governments and can require states to meet certain conditions in order to receive federal funding. Certain federal legislation may also apply to state or local agencies that receive federal money or are licensed or regulated by the federal government. The converse is not true, however. State governments do not have the power to require the federal government or federal agencies to comply with their state laws.

By accepting federal dollars, state and local social service agencies are bound to follow applicable provisions of federal laws that pertain to privacy, and must protect client information as the federal government directs. This is true even when a state passes its own legislation that covers matters of privacy and client records. It is important that social workers who work with clients who receive benefits derived from federal law understand that both federal and state law may influence access to and disclosure of information in their records.

For example, the federal government enacted the Education for All Handicapped Children Act of 1975, now known as IDEA, which entitles children with disabilities to receive special education and related services. To receive federal funds to serve children with disabilities, a state government may enact its own legislation to ensure that the state is in compliance with the requirements of IDEA. In turn, local school districts that receive direct funding from the state and indirect funding from the federal government are required to follow both federal and state law in the provision of services to children with disabilities. One of the requirements of IDEA is that school districts must maintain confidentiality of special education records and provide parents access to their children's records. In circumstances where states have their own laws on special education records and parental access, a school social worker working in a local school district will follow both federal and state laws.

FREEDOM OF INFORMATION ACT

Enacted in 1966, the Freedom of Information Act (FOIA) is a federal law that establishes the public's right to obtain information contained in the records of federal government agencies. In 1996, FOIA was amended to allow for increased access to electronic records. The FOIA applies to documents held by the executive branch of the federal government, including cabinet and military departments, government corporations, departments, agencies, offices, and federal regulatory agencies. Through FOIA, anyone may scrutinize the activities of agencies such as the FBI, the U.S. Citizenship and Immigration Services, the Bureau of Prisons, and federal public social service agencies, such as the Social Security Administration or the Department of Veterans Affairs. People who seek agency records may be interested in diverse subjects such as public health, environmental issues, consumer product safety, labor practices, government spending, civil rights, foreign policy, and national defense (Adler, 1992).

The FOIA was the first major law that allowed individuals to acquire information about government actions and programs as well as information about themselves contained in records held by the federal government. Before 1966, if an individual wanted access to information possessed by a federal agency, the burden was on the individual to establish a need for the information. There were no established guidelines or procedures to assist the individual in gaining information nor was there a remedy for the denial of such access. The FOIA shifted the burden so that individuals are presumed to have the right to access governmental records and the government must then justify its need for secrecy.

Of course, the FOIA recognizes that there are legitimate reasons the government may have to restrict disclosure of some information. The FOIA attempts to balance individuals' rights to access information against the government's need to protect certain sensitive information. There are nine categories of information that are exempt from disclosure, such as information classified in the interest of national security, law enforcement investigation files, or information that would constitute an unwarranted invasion of someone else's personal privacy. While the FOIA does not grant an absolute right to examine government documents, it opens up governmental actions to public scrutiny. People who request information are entitled to the information they asked for, a redacted version of the information, or other response to their request. If the record cannot be released, the person who requested it is entitled to be told the reason for the denial and has the right to appeal the decision.

PRIVACY ACT OF 1974

The Privacy Act of 1974 governs federal government agency recordkeeping and disclosure practices. The practices contained within the Code of Fair Information Practices, as discussed earlier, were used to form the basis of the Privacy Act and were considered groundbreaking for the times. Today, these privacy practices seem commonplace to most social work practitioners because the practices are routinely included in most federal and state records legislation.

The Privacy Act allows citizens to learn how records about them are collected, maintained, used, and disseminated by federal agencies. The act permits individuals to gain access to most of their personal information in government records and to seek amendment of any inaccurate, incomplete, untimely, or irrelevant information. The Privacy Act regulates the federal government's use of personal information by limiting the disclosure of personally identifiable information, allowing consumers' access to information about them, requiring federal agencies to specify the purposes for collecting personal information, and providing civil and criminal penalties for misuse of information. The rights to inspect and to correct records are the most important provisions of the Privacy Act (Committee on Government Reform, 2005). Together with the FOIA, the Privacy Act permits disclosure of most personal files to the individual who is the subject of the files.

Social workers who work for federal social service agencies should be aware that their clients have the right to access and amend the records kept about them. For example, if a social work client believes that she has been denied Social Security disability benefits because of a mistaken calculation of her employment history, she can access her records held by the Social Security Administration, submit accurate documentation, and request that her records be corrected. Clients of Veterans Affairs may access their files to verify whether their service eligibility has been correctly determined.

Social workers can use the FOIA together with the Privacy Act to achieve the goals of service for their clients. For example, a client who is seeking political asylum in the United States and who has been denied that status can use both FOIA and the Privacy Act to acquire information from the Board of Immigration Appeals. As the social worker helps the client prepare for an appeal, they can check that the government's information about the client is correct and look at governmental reports regarding the grant or denial of asylum in the United States. Social workers who work with homeless populations can use the FOIA to access the records of the Department of Housing and Urban Development about the availability of low-income housing subsidy vouchers. If their clients live in a geographic area that is underserved, the social workers could then advocate for a more equal distribution of the vouchers.

FAMILY EDUCATIONAL RIGHTS AND PRIVACY ACT

The Family Educational Rights and Privacy Act (FERPA), also known as the Buckley Amendment, was enacted in 1974. The law applies to all schools that receive funds under a program of the U.S. Department of Education. FERPA allows parents access to the education records of their children. The term "education records" is defined broadly to mean information that is directly related to a student and maintained by a school. Prior to this law, parents had no right to view information schools kept about their children.

FERPA gives certain rights to parents; these rights then transfer to the student when the student becomes an "eligible student," which is defined as those who are 18 years of age or older or who attend a postsecondary school.

Parents or eligible students have the right to inspect and review education records and request that the school correct records that they believe to be inaccurate, misleading, irrelevant, or improper. If the school chooses not to amend the record, the parent or eligible student has the right to a formal hearing. Additionally, parents or eligible students have the right to place a statement in the record that sets forth their perspective about the disputed information. Whenever the contested information is released, the parents' or eligible students' statement is to accompany it.

Schools generally must have written permission from the parent or eligible student to release any personally identifiable information from a student's education record. However, written consent is not required to release education records to certain people or under specified conditions. FERPA allows disclosure without consent to teachers and other school officials with legitimate educational interests; to a school where the student is transferring; to accrediting, audit, or evaluation entities; to comply with a judicial order or lawfully issued subpoena; in connection with a health and safety emergency; and to state and local authorities specifically authorized to receive such information.

FERPA differentiates between directory information and other types of information contained in the student's education record. Directory information includes a student's name, address, telephone number, date and place of birth, honors, awards, and dates of attendance. Directory information does not require the consent of the parent or eligible student for its release, so long as they have had previous notice about the school's policy regarding disclosing directory information.

While FERPA does not specifically define the term education record, education records include more than information related to academic performance. Written records about students created by special educators, school health care personnel, school psychologists, and school social workers are also considered education records. The records created by these personnel are education records regardless of whether they are kept with the students' academic record or in the professionals' offices or files. Therefore, these records are subject to access by parents and eligible students and may be disclosed with their consent to outside entities.

School social workers complete social developmental studies as part of case study evaluations of students with disabilities. Social workers also provide individual and group counseling to students and document their efforts. These records are subject to FERPA's rules regarding access and disclosure. Accordingly, parents are allowed to see records of social work services provided to their children. Indeed, the fact that parents *do* have access to the social work component of their children's education records can prove problematic for school social workers and their clients. There are a number of sensitive issues that children, especially adolescents, may share with their social workers that they do not wish their parents or guardians to know about. This may include matters related to sexual activity; feelings they have about their parents or other significant people in their lives or themselves; and alcohol or drug use. In deciding what to document, social workers must keep in mind that parents have the right to access their children's education records and may choose to do so until the students become eligible adults.

School social workers can assist parents in using FERPA to access their children's education records. Parents may wish to see their children's education records if their children are not doing well in school or have social or behavioral problems. When a child brings home a report card that shows that the child's performance has declined, the parents may want to review their child's records to determine a cause. From examining the record, a parent may realize that his child is sitting at the back of the classroom, is having trouble seeing the board, and may need glasses. The parent may then take the child to the eye doctor. A child who has become sullen or withdrawn at home may lead the parent to believe that something may be occurring at school that is troubling to the child. By looking at the record, the parent may discover that her child is being bullied, is having difficulty in peer relationships, or is engaging in behaviors that are deemed inappropriate by the teacher or administrator. School social workers can then assist the parent in accessing appropriate resources in the school and community to improve the child's social development and educational performance.

FEDERAL ALCOHOL AND DRUG ABUSE RECORDS

In the 1970s, Congress passed two laws, the Comprehensive Alcohol Abuse and Alcoholism Prevention, Treatment and Rehabilitation Act of 1970 and the Drug Abuse Prevention, Treatment and Rehabilitation Act of 1972. In the 1990s, Congress reorganized and combined these separate laws into one law that covers both alcohol and drug abuse, referring to the problems jointly as substance abuse. The federal regulations that govern substance abuse records are known as the Confidentiality of Alcohol and Drug Abuse Patient Records (2007), or Part 2 regulations. Part 2 regulations are based on the idea that people with substance abuse problems are more likely to seek and successfully complete treatment if they are assured that their need for treatment and their personal information will not be disclosed to others (Lopez, 1994).

Part 2 regulations apply to federally assisted substance abuse programs. Individuals or programs that provide alcohol and drug abuse treatment, diagnosis, or referral for treatment are considered substance abuse programs. Part 2 regulations are stricter than most other confidentiality rules regarding records and restrict both the disclosure and the use of information. These federal regulations define records as any information that relates to a patient and is received or acquired by a federally assisted drug or alcohol abuse treatment program.

Part 2 regulations divide the disclosure of patient identifying information into three distinct parts: (a) situations where the patient provides written consent, (b) situations where disclosure is allowed without patient consent, and

(c) situations where disclosures are made pursuant to a court order. Under federal regulations, a substance abuse program may not disclose patient identifying information without the written consent of the patient. For example, if a social worker wants to arrange follow-up services in the local community for a patient who is receiving in-patient substance abuse treatment, the social worker must first obtain the patient's written consent before any information about the patient can be disclosed to the local provider. Even when the patient wants follow-up services and agrees that the information should be used, written consent must first be obtained. Any person or provider who receives information about a patient is also prohibited from making any further disclosure of the information unless the patient provides subsequent written consent.

Under some circumstances, patient consent is not necessary to disclose information contained in the records. One such circumstance is when substance abuse personnel suspect child abuse or neglect. Because social workers are mandated reporters, they are obligated by law to report their suspicions of child abuse and neglect. Part 2 regulations do not prohibit program personnel from making child abuse reports and confirming the reports in writing. However, the regulations *do* apply to the subsequent disclosure or use of the alcohol or drug abuse patient records in civil or criminal child abuse proceedings.

For example, a patient who is receiving treatment for his alcohol abuse tells his social worker that he is ashamed that he sexually abuses his child when he is severely intoxicated. The social worker is required to report this child abuse and may use what the patient told her in reporting the situation to the appropriate child welfare investigative agency. After the social worker makes the child abuse report, the state may bring juvenile court proceedings on behalf of the child or prosecute the father in criminal court for his behavior. To prove what the father did, the state's attorney may want the social worker to disclose information contained in the father's alcohol treatment record. However, without the father's consent or a court's order for the records' release, the social worker may mot use or disclose information about the father's sexual abuse of his child.

Another situation where patient consent is not necessary is for medical emergencies. Identifying information from patients' records may be disclosed without consent to medical personnel in an emergency to treat a condition that poses an immediate threat to the health of any individual. In an emergency situation, the person who discloses the information must make a written notation in the patient's record about the nature of the emergency and to whom disclosure was made. Patient consent also is not required for disclosures for the purposes of scientific research, audits, and evaluations. Additionally, if a patient commits a crime on program premises or against program staff, or threatens to commit such crimes, consent is not required to disclose this information to law enforcement officials. If a social worker witnesses a patient committing an assault against another patient or staff in a treatment program, the social worker is permitted to report this information to the police.

Part 2 regulations also contain detailed provisions for handling record disclosures when a substance abuse program receives a court order for records. Substance abuse records and the information contained within them are handled uniquely. Simply stated, a court order for substance abuse records allows disclosure to be made if the program also receives a subpoena for the records (see chapter 9). A court order alone does not compel disclosure. A subpoena alone does not compel disclosure. Instead, a social worker who has alcohol or drug abuse records about a patient cannot disclose those records unless he or she receives both a court order and a subpoena for the records.

The Part 2 regulations delineate different procedures when disclosure is sought for use in criminal versus noncriminal cases. Criminal cases involve crimes committed against people or property, such as robbery, assault and battery, murder, arson, or vandalism. Police or prosecutors may seek the records to investigate or prosecute patients for crimes they may have committed. Noncriminal matters would be for any other reason, like divorce, custody battles, or negligence and malpractice actions. Individuals who are involved in lawsuits may seek the records of people with substance abuse problems to assist them at trial. For example, in a divorce case, a wife may want to use the husband's alcohol records to demonstrate that, because of his problems, she should be granted custody of their children. Or, for example, in a negligence case where a mother sues a crib manufacturer because she believes the crib's faulty design led to the death of her child, the manufacturer may try to obtain the substance use records of the babysitter to shift the blame from the crib's design to the quality of the babysitter's care.

In noncriminal cases, an application for a court order must use a fictitious name to refer to any patient and may not contain any patient identifying information. These applications are often referred to as "John Doe" applications to protect patients' identities and are unique to substance abuse records. The patient and the person holding the records must be given notice and an opportunity to respond to the application. Before it may order the disclosure of confidential patient information, a court must find that there is "good cause" for the disclosure. Good cause means that the court must determine that there is no other effective way to obtain the information and that the need for disclosure outweighs any potential injury to the patient or the therapeutic relationship.

Social workers who provide services to people with substance abuse problems may find that they are asked to provide testimony in civil cases on their clients' behalf or for others who have interests adverse to those of the clients. Clients' substance abuse problems affect their marriages and other significant relationships, their employment, their judgment, and other important aspects of their lives. A social worker may be asked to provide testimony in a case where people are fighting over custody of children, where domestic violence protective orders are sought, where employment is terminated, or where guardianship or civil commitment is needed. However, unless clients provide written consent to the disclosure of their substance abuse records, social workers must receive both a court order and a subpoena before they are permitted to reveal information from the client records.

Social work clients who have addiction problems may commit crimes to support their substance habits or because their mental states are impaired by the presence of alcohol or drugs. When client records are sought in criminal cases for the purpose of investigating or prosecuting the client, the same general procedures regarding John Doe applications must be followed. Additionally, the court may authorize the disclosure and use of patient records only if certain, additional criteria are met. These other criteria are that the crime is extremely serious, causing or threatening to cause death or serious harm, and that the records sought are reasonably likely to disclose information of substantial value to the investigation or prosecution.

Orders authorizing the disclosure or use of patient records for criminal cases must limit disclosure to those parts of the patient's record that are essential to fulfill the objective of the order and to those people who are responsible for the investigation and prosecution of the crimes. Social workers may be asked to testify regarding the client's addiction and mental status as a defense to the crime or as a factor that may mitigate the punishment. If the client requests the use of the records, he or she should sign a written authorization for release of information. Otherwise, the social worker must make sure that there is a court order and subpoena and limit the information released to the least amount possible.

HEALTH INSURANCE PORTABILITY AND ACCOUNTABILITY ACT

Congress recognized the importance of protecting the privacy of health information by enacting Public Law 104-191, the Health Insurance Portability and Accountability Act of 1996 (HIPAA). HIPAA contains two major parts. Title I provides for the portability of health care insurance, so that workers and their families retain health insurance coverage when they change or lose their jobs. Title II of HIPAA covers the measures entities must take to simplify the administration of health care, which includes protecting the privacy and confidentiality of health care information. The final regulations governing health information privacy, also known as the "Privacy Rule," became effective on April 14, 2003.

The Privacy Rule

One of the most significant aspects of the Privacy Rule is that it creates minimum national standards (a floor) that apply to the individuals and entities that must follow its provisions. HIPAA does this by preempting state laws that govern health information, unless a state's law is considered to be more stringent, that is, more protective of privacy. In other words, the Privacy Rule creates basic principles that apply to almost all providers of health care and supersedes any state law that falls below federal standards. For example, if state law provides patients enhanced access to their records, limits outside parties' ability to obtain client information, or restricts the use of information that would be permitted under HIPAA, then the law is viewed as more stringent and takes priority over the federal rule.

To illustrate, under Alabama law prior to HIPAA, patients did not have the right to access their own medical records. Because HIPAA allows patients such access, Alabama's law yields to the provisions of HIPAA: Alabama patients are entitled to access their medical records under HIPAA. In contrast, although HIPAA requires covered entities to protect medical and health care information, many states treat mental health records more protectively than does HIPAA (Sullivan, 2004). In those states, covered entities would not simply follow HIPAA. Instead, they would follow HIPAA and also incorporate their state's more stringent requirements into their mental health practice. In effect, covered entities may discover that they need to follow both federal and state law. Where HIPAA is more protective of privacy, practitioners should follow HIPAA. When state law is more stringent than HIPAA, practitioners should follow state law. Practitioners may wish to consult knowledgeable authorities in situations where it is unclear whether federal or state law is more protective of privacy.

HIPAA applies to a broader range of providers and entities than most other laws. HIPAA requires "covered entities" to follow its provisions. A covered entity is (a) a health plan, (b) a health care clearinghouse, or (c) a health care provider who transmits any health information in electronic form. A health plan means an individual or group plan that provides or pays for the costs of medical care. A health care clearinghouse is a public or private entity that processes or facilitates the processing of health information.

Under HIPAA, a health care provider is defined as a provider of services that furnishes, bills, or is paid for health care in the normal course of business. Health care providers include professionals, such as social workers, psychologists, and psychiatrists, who were previously familiar with protecting patient information. Covered entities also include professionals, like dentists and pharmacists, who had limited previous experience with protecting patient privacy. Covered entities include doctors, therapists, nurses, psychologists, clinical social workers, acupuncturists, speech pathologists, physical and occupational therapists, chiropractors, dentists, and pharmacists as well as clinics, hospitals, and institutions. Almost all social workers or the agencies they work for are considered health care providers because they furnish, bill, or are paid for health care. Social workers may also work for "hybrid" agencies whose activities include both covered and noncovered health care functions. In that case, HIPAA rules apply to the covered functions of the agency.

Different hybrid agencies have reached different conclusions about their responsibilities under HIPAA. On the one hand, the Kentucky Cabinet for Health and Family Services (2006) (KCHFS) determined that its Division of Protection and Permanency and its Department for Medicaid Services were the only covered entities that fell under HIPAA. Because of the functions of these divisions, the KCHFS concluded that it was a "hybrid entity" and created a policy for those divisions required to be compliant with HIPAA. On the other hand, the Illinois Department of Children and Family Services (2003) determined that the entire agency was a covered entity because of its Medicaid billing systems. It then assessed the impact of the HIPAA privacy regulations as it affected the department's functions and provided instructions to its workers as to how they should comply with HIPAA.

To be considered a covered entity under HIPAA, a health care provider also must transmit health information in electronic form, whether it is done directly or through a third party, like a billing service. While a social worker may furnish health care to clients, if the social worker is a private practitioner who does not transmit health information electronically, she is not a covered entity and not required to follow the HIPAA privacy provisions. Of course, the social worker must still follow the NASW Code of Ethics and state law.

Protected Health Information

HIPAA also applies to a broader range of information than does most other laws. The Privacy Rule uses the term "protected health information" (PHI) to refer to individually identifiable health information transmitted by or maintained in any media, which includes electronic and paper records and oral communications. PHI means information that identifies an individual; that is created or received by a covered entity; and includes information about a person's health care, mental or behavioral health information, or the payment for those services. PHI does not include education records or the health clinic records of college students, as defined by FERPA, or employment records held by a covered entity in its role as an employer. Individually identifiable health information (IIHI) is a subset of health information that relates to the past, present, or future physical or mental health or condition of an individual.

Under HIPAA, the general rule is that covered entities may not reveal PHI without the authorization of a patient or their personal representative. The Privacy Rule views "authorization" differently than "consent" to disclose records. A valid authorization must contain certain core elements. These elements include: (a) a specific and meaningful description of the information to be used or disclosed; (b) the name or the class of people who can use or disclose the information; (c) the name or description of the person authorized to make the disclosure; (d) the purpose of the requested information; (e) the expiration date or event; and (f) the signature of the person authorized to make disclosure and the date of signing. In addition to these core elements, authorizations must contain statements (a) that inform authorized individuals of their right to revoke the authorization in writing and how this would be accomplished; (b) about whether signing the authorization places conditions on treatment, payment, enrollment, or eligibility for benefits; and (c) regarding the potential for the subsequent redisclosure of the individual's information to another entity outside the protections of HIPAA. HIPAA requires that authorizations be written in plain language and that individuals be given a copy of any authorizations they sign.

Although HIPAA typically requires that patients sign valid authorizations to disclose their PHI, it also provides for numerous situations where a covered entity may use or disclose PHI without the patients' authorization. HIPAA differentiates between "required" and "permissive" disclosures. HIPAA requires disclosure in only two situations: (a) to the client who asks for access to their PHI or (b) to the HHS if it requests the information to investigate a complaint. In other situations, HIPAA permits a covered entity to make certain disclosures without authorization. For example, under the Privacy Rule, a covered entity may disclose PHI for its own treatment, payment, or health care operations or to facilitate treatment, payment, or health care operations of another health care provider. Social workers who are covered entities can disclose information to other service providers to ensure that clients receive appropriate services or that the social workers or their agencies receive payment for services they render on behalf of their clients.

Disclosure is also permitted without patient authorization in situations where the patient or others may be at serious risk of harm. HIPAA allows for covered entities to disclose PHI to appropriate authorities that receive reports of child abuse or neglect. Additionally, HIPAA allows for covered entities to make disclosures to social service or protective services agencies that are authorized by law to receive reports about adults who are believed to be victims of abuse, neglect, or domestic violence. In these latter situations, the individual must agree to the disclosure. If the individual does not agree, the covered entity may use or disclose information if it believes the disclosure is necessary to prevent serious harm to the individual or other potential victims, or that the individual cannot agree because of his or her incapacity.

Similarly, the Privacy Rule allows a covered entity to use or disclose the PHI if it believes that disclosure is necessary to prevent or lessen a serious and imminent threat to the health or safety of a person or the public. If disclosure is made, it must be made to individuals who the covered entity believes are reasonably able to prevent or lessen the threat, including the person who is the target of the threat. Covered entities may also disclose information that would assist law enforcement authorities to identify or apprehend individuals when the covered entity learns from patient statements that the patients have participated in violent crimes or escaped from lawful custody.

Finally, there are other situations in which covered entities may disclose PHI without patient authorization. Other allowable disclosures include judicial and administrative proceedings, situations required by law, research, workers' compensation cases, fundraising, marketing, and health oversight activities (Sullivan, 2004). In certain of the above circumstances, the Privacy Rule requires that the covered entity apply a "minimum necessary" standard. In other words, the covered entity must make reasonable efforts to limit the use or disclosure of PHI to the minimum amount of information necessary to accomplish the intended purpose. The minimum necessary standard does not apply to disclosures made to the client, authorized by the personal representative, or furnished to providers for treatment purposes. Social workers can use this standard to practice in an ethical fashion by limiting the dissemination of information. When social workers receive overly broad requests for information, they can react by limiting their disclosures to that which is minimally necessary to meet the request. By restricting the information disclosed to the minimum necessary, social workers protect confidentiality.

Privacy Practices

HIPAA requires covered entities to follow certain administrative procedures to safeguard client information. One of these administrative requirements is that a covered entity must provide individuals with written notice of its privacy practices. The notice must explain to the individual when the covered entity will use or disclose PHI and provide examples of permitted and required uses. To illustrate, if a hospital will use PHI to coordinate appropriate health care upon the patient's discharge, the notice of privacy practices should state that the covered entity will release the protected health information to a home health agency or nursing home when it arranges subsequent care.

The notice of privacy practices must also contain a statement of an individual's rights with respect to PHI and a brief description of how individuals may exercise their rights. The specific rights that must be included in the notice are:

- the right to request restrictions on certain uses and disclosures of protected health information;
- the right to receive confidential communications of PHI;
- the right to inspect and copy PHI;
- the right to amend PHI;
- the right to receive an accounting of when and how the covered entity has disclosed PHI; and
- the right of an individual to receive the notice electronically.

The notice of privacy practices must also explain the specific duties of the covered entity to protect PHI and instruct individuals that complaints may be directed to the covered entity and the HHS if they believe their privacy rights have been violated.

Covered entities must demonstrate that they comply with HIPAA. Covered entities need to designate a privacy officer who is responsible for the development and implementation of the privacy policies and practices of the entity. The covered entity must also specify a contact person to receive complaints about matters discussed in the notice of privacy practices. Covered entities must also provide training to their workforce on their privacy policies and procedures, and develop a system of sanctions for personnel who violate these policies. Additionally, the covered entity must document any requests for accountings, that is, any disclosures of PHI in the previous six years. However, certain uses of PHI do not need to be accounted for, including disclosures made to carry out treatment, payment, and health care operations; disclosures made to the individual, pursuant to an authorization; or disclosures for national security or intelligence purposes.

The Security Rule

While the Privacy Rule protects the privacy of protected health information *in any form*, the Security Rule sets standards specific to guarding *electronic* PHI from unauthorized access, alteration, deletion, and transmission. HIPAA sets national standards for administrative, physical, and technical safeguards to protect the confidentiality, integrity, and availability of electronic PHI (e-PHI). HIPAA requires covered entities to take measures to secure e-PHI that it creates, receives, maintains, or transmits.

The Security Rule requires that covered entities implement certain administrative safeguards for e-PHI. These safeguards include conducting an analysis of the potential risks and vulnerabilities of e-PHI and implementing policies and procedures to reduce the risks; appointing a security official to develop and implement procedures; developing security awareness and training programs; creating sanction policies for workers who violate security policies; and developing contingency plans for responding to emergency situations that may damage systems containing e-PHI.

The HIPAA Security Rule requires physical safeguards as well. These safeguards require that covered entities implement policies and procedures to limit physical access to electronic information systems as well as provide access only to those who are allowed it. Covered entities also must develop procedures to control workstation use and security; ensure that the facility and equipment are protected from unauthorized physical access, tampering, and theft; and implement policies that govern the receipt and removal of hardware and electronic media into, within, and out of the facility.

Technical safeguards are also required. These include developing unique user names and numbers for identifying and tracking clients. Social security numbers may not be used. In addition, covered entities must create emergency access procedures for natural and man-made emergencies; implement procedures to automatically log off after a predetermined time of inactivity; and develop mechanisms to encrypt and decrypt e-PHI. HIPAA requires every provider who does business electronically to use the same health care transactions, code sets, and identifiers to refer to specific diagnoses and clinical procedures on claims and encounter forms.

Becoming HIPAA Compliant

HIPAA is significant in that, for the first time, the federal government has created minimum, national standards for protecting the privacy of PHI and e-PHI of all individuals who receive health care from covered entities. Although some states may have more stringent provisions within their laws, social workers and other providers who are covered entities will find that HIPAA's uniform standards exist throughout the country. HIPAA provisions apply across all practice settings to all health information that social workers and other health care providers transmit electronically. HIPAA provisions determine when records can be released, if client authorization is required prior to release, the type of information that is considered protected, mandate security measures, and create administrative duties of covered entities.

As mentioned, practitioners or agencies that do not directly transmit information electronically or have a billing service that does so indirectly on their behalf do not have to follow HIPAA. However, practitioners who are not covered entities may still wish to come into compliance with HIPAA. They may find that HIPAA's standards regarding the way that information and records should be handled may have an impact on their practice. For example, social workers who are not HIPAA compliant may find that they have difficulty accessing information about clients from HIPAA compliant practitioners. HIPAA compliant practitioners expect other providers to follow the provisions of HIPAA, not realizing that other providers may not be required to practice according to HIPAA. When HIPAA compliant entities receive a request for information from a non-HIPAA compliant professional, they may not disclose the information because the non-HIPAA compliant individual or organization is not using a correct authorization form or is asking for information that is protected under HIPAA. HIPAA compliant practitioners may worry that non-HIPAA compliant individuals or organizations will not properly handle protected information. HIPAA compliant professionals may mistakenly view non-HIPAA compliant individuals as unethical or unprofessional because they are not following HIPAA's provisions.

Social workers who are not HIPAA compliant may also find that they have difficulty in being a provider for certain insurers or being reimbursed for the services they provide unless they comply with HIPAA. One of the purposes of HIPAA is to bring standardization to the health care industry. As standardization increases, to receive insurance reimbursements insurers may require all providers to follow the safeguards brought about by HIPAA, whether or not they actually are covered entities. To illustrate, after HIPAA's enactment, Medicare changed its provisions to require providers with 10 or more full-time employees to submit claims electronically and to comply with HIPAA. Medicare did not differentiate between covered and noncovered entities. Instead, to receive Medicare reimbursement, providers must comply with HIPAA.

HIPAA providers must obtain a National Provider Identifier (NPI), a 10-digit number that is used by all health plans for providers to submit claims or conduct other transactions required by HIPAA. Social workers who are not required to comply with HIPAA may use paper forms to seek reimbursement for their services. However, they may encounter health plans that will not reimburse individuals who do not have an NPI. To obtain state funding, state laws may require non-HIPAA compliant individuals to use an NPI. Minnesota, for example, has already enacted such a law (Furlong, 2006).

Therefore, social workers who are not required to follow HIPAA may have financial incentives to comply. Because of financial motivations and the interests of their clients, all practitioners are encouraged to become HIPAA compliant.

HIPAA AND ITS RELATIONSHIP TO STATE LAWS

HIPAA created a system of national standards that safeguards access to and disclosure of protected health information. These national standards are the minimum requirements that agencies and practitioners who are covered entities must follow. However, across the states, there still remains a wide variety of legislation, regulations, and case law that influences social work practice regarding client records.

While HIPAA has established minimum practices, social workers keep a variety of other records that may not fall under the rubric of PHI. For example, social workers may be involved in community organization activities and document conversations they have with stakeholders during the process. School social workers keep records of the services they provide to children. Child welfare workers keep certain records that document services provided to a family. HIPAA may not pertain to these kinds of records whereas state law will.

HIPAA also does not override certain types of state records laws. As mentioned before, when state laws are more protective of privacy than HIPAA, the state law controls how records are handled. Additionally, when states require PHI to be reported to public health agencies for the purpose of preventing or controlling disease, injury, or disability; to collect information on vital events such as birth or death; to conduct public health surveillance, investigations, and interventions; or to report child abuse and neglect, HIPAA provisions yield to the requirements of state law.

Sometimes, states pass laws that cover the same type of subject matter that is handled by federal law, but apply its provisions to the state. For example, some states have their own Freedom of Information Acts or Privacy Acts that allow individuals access to the records of state governments and to the files of state agencies that contain information about them. In other situations, states pass laws that exactly mirror federal laws. For example, a state may pass its own student records law that is identical to the FERPA. The state does so to ensure that its citizens are aware of federal guarantees. Sometimes, a state may pass a law that is similar to a federal law but expands the law's provisions. In this way, the state can provide additional protections to its citizens, such as allowing the law to cover more people or speeding up the time frames for compliance. For example, the Illinois School Student Records Act (2007) allows parents the right to inspect and copy their children's records within 15 days of their request, rather than the 45 days allowed by FERPA. Other states, like Indiana and Iowa, have not enacted their own state student records laws and instead rely on FERPA.

In other situations, states may pass laws that impact individuals' rights to privacy but have no origin in existing federal law. For example, Oregon enacted the Death with Dignity Act (2006), which allows terminally ill Oregon residents to obtain prescriptions from their physicians and use the drugs to administer lethal medications to themselves. Other states, like California and Arizona, allow its citizens to use marijuana for medicinal purposes. Typically, these special laws reflect the will of the people and the value that the citizens of a state place on highly private personal matters related to health. These matters may include the protection of records related to sensitive topics, such as counseling for mental health issues, HIV/AIDS status, or genetic or other disease information.

A social worker who moves from one state to another may be surprised to learn that the new state handles issues of records differently than the former state. Social workers who live near a state border may find that they provide services to clients from another state. They may be surprised to learn that each state has distinctive ways of handling health, mental health, or other personal information. Not only must social workers be aware of the laws for all of the states in which they practice or their clients reside, they may also need guidance on how HIPAA requirements interplay with these state laws. Clearly, social workers cannot be expected to find and interpret these laws themselves. To learn about the requirements in their states, social workers should consult attorneys, seek consultation with their supervisors or other knowledgeable practitioners, and follow applicable agency guidelines and procedures.

HIPAA, STATE LAW, AND THE RECORDS OF SPECIFIC CLIENT POPULATIONS

HIPAA creates a floor for the handling of PHI. Many states also have created legislation to benefit certain populations that they view as vulnerable and in need of protection. Often, this legislation reflects concern for the privacy rights of these individuals and regulates consent to treatment, access to records, and disclosure issues. Social workers will come in contact with these clients and will need to be cognizant of their rights under federal and state laws. Social workers who work with children that are abused or neglected, provide services to children and adolescents, people with mental illness, people diagnosed with HIV/AIDS, or people who have guardians or other substitute decision makers should expect that both HIPAA and state laws will impact their practice. The following sections address HIPAA provisions as they relate to specific client populations and raise certain issues that may be handled by state law. Because of the complexity of whether HIPAA, state law, or both apply to how they keep their records, practitioners also should consult with knowledgeable people, such as attorneys, supervisors, and administrators, to learn how their state laws supplement or supplant HIPAA.

RECORDS AND CHILD ABUSE AND NEGLECT

To help reduce child abuse and neglect, Congress enacted the Child Abuse Prevention and Treatment Act (CAPTA) in 1974. CAPTA requires states to have a system in place to receive reports of child abuse and neglect. As a result, some states require reports to be made to a state-wide central registry, whereas other states have county-wide systems for reporting. Still other states require that serious physical or sexual abuse is reported to the police, while less serious abuse and neglect is reported to a government child welfare agency. States also require certain professionals who have contact with children to report suspected child abuse and neglect. In all states, social workers are mandated reporters who are obligated to contact the appropriate governmental authorities when they suspect child abuse or neglect may have occurred. No matter where the abuse is reported or who makes the report, records of child abuse and neglect reports are generated and maintained.

HIPAA does not create a conflict for social workers when they use PHI to make their mandated reports, nor does it preempt state law pertaining to child abuse reporting. It allows covered entities to disclose PHI without an authorization to a public health authority or other appropriate government organization authorized by law to receive reports of child abuse and neglect. Social workers who are covered entities can follow the laws in their state regarding child abuse reporting and still be in compliance with both their state law and the HIPAA Privacy Rule.

While HIPAA does not change the initial reporting of child abuse and neglect nor control the way child abuse reports are received and used by central registries, HIPAA may impact the later ability of child welfare personnel to obtain records of key people involved in a family's case. In addition to information regarding the children who are abused or neglected, child welfare workers often need to obtain physical or mental health information regarding parents, other adults or children in their homes, as well as prospective adult caretakers like foster or kinship care providers (Davidson, n.d.). Records that chronicle the services offered to, refused by, or given to parents and caretakers, and the results of those services, are often held by other agencies that provide services to the family. HIPAA and state law do apply to the records held by these other agencies.

Consider this example.

> A doctor in an emergency room reports suspected child abuse to a state central registry. The state child welfare agency (B) investigates the report and removes the child. B contracts with a private child welfare agency (L) to provide casework and reunification services to the family. Mom is a person with schizophrenia and sees a private psychiatrist for psychotropic medication and receives counseling from a social worker at the local mental health agency. The L caseworker wants a copy of the reports prepared by the psychiatrist and the mental health agency social worker regarding the services rendered. They each refuse to disclose the reports because mom will not sign an authorization for their release to B or to L.

In this example, under child abuse reporting laws in every state, the emergency room doctor is required to report suspected abuse to the proper child welfare authorities. State law mandates that a doctor disclose necessary information when he or she reports suspected child abuse. However, HIPAA also provides the mother with certain rights regarding her PHI. The mother has the right to authorize or refuse to authorize the disclosure of her PHI to anyone, including both the state and private child welfare agencies. Whether the child welfare agencies will be able to obtain copies of the psychiatrist's or social worker's reports will depend on the provisions of the laws of the state. If the mother will not authorize the disclosure, the child welfare agencies may need to get a subpoena and court order to obtain the records. Without the intervention of the court, the psychiatrist and social worker would not be able to turn over their records. The privacy protections of HIPAA have important implications for agencies that perform child welfare work when they seek records or information from covered entities such as hospitals, mental health clinics, psychologists, social workers, and other practitioners.

RECORDS AND MINORS

Social workers must become aware of their own state's legal requirements when working with children and their parents. Under certain circumstances, states may create exceptions to the general rule that parents are the decision makers for their children. Practitioners need to understand these laws to ensure that the appropriate person consents to treatment and to the access and disclosure of information contained in records.

Under the law, children generally are viewed as incompetent (not yet having the requisite mental capacity) to make decisions until they reach their majority. Every state establishes the age of majority, the age when a minor child becomes an adult for legal purposes. In most states, the age of majority is 18. Typically, when children become adults, they are granted all of the rights that adults have.

In certain states, minors may be emancipated from parental control before they reach the age of 18. Situations that may emancipate minors under state law are marriage, enlistment into the armed services, or becoming a parent. In some states, minors above a certain age, such as 16-years-old, can petition the court and demonstrate that they are mature enough to make their own decisions. In these situations, the court can set them free from parental control and give them certain rights that they can exercise on their own behalf.

Until minors become adults or are emancipated, however, the law typically gives their parents, guardians, or persons *in loco parentis* (persons acting in the place of the parents) the power to act on their behalf in all matters. HIPAA is consistent with this general rule: HIPAA treats parents, guardians, or those acting *in loco parentis* as the authorized representatives of their minor children. HIPAA refers to these authorized representatives as "personal representatives." Unless state law handles the matter differently, HIPAA provides that a covered entity must treat parents, guardians, and persons acting *in loco parentis* as the personal representatives of the minor in decisions related to health care and control over their children's PHI.

In some states, however, specific laws provide children with rights in particular situations. These rights tend to be given to adolescents, rather than younger children, and may include being able to make decisions regarding their medical and mental health treatment and access to and disclosure of information contained in their records. For example, in some states, like California, Michigan, and North Carolina, children above a certain age, such as 12-years-old, can make their own decisions concerning alcohol, drug, or mental health treatment, as well as birth control or abortion services. While HIPAA recognizes parents as the personal representatives for their children's PHI, HIPAA defers to state law when it provides greater rights to children in special situations. In a state where no law exists that grants rights to children, their parents, guardians, or persons *in loco parentis* would be responsible for treatment decisions and authorizations.

Generally, when state law grants certain rights to minors, the parents or guardians no longer have those rights. When state law confers rights to minors, HIPAA also defers to the state law and the minor is considered to be the person qualified to act with respect to PHI. When minors control access to the information in their records, they may deny their parents or guardians the right to see the contents. Parents or guardians may not understand that they are not entitled to see their children's records. They may demand that they be given access to their children's information. Practitioners must be aware of the laws that cover these complicated consent and treatment issues and be careful to gain consent from the appropriate person.

RECORDS AND ADULTS WITH COGNITIVE IMPAIRMENTS

Social workers often provide services to adults with mental retardation, adults with mental illness, adults with health conditions, and elderly people with Alzheimer's disease or dementia that may impact their ability to make decisions. Normally, once individuals are adults, they are responsible for their own decision making. However, reaching the age of majority is not the only condition for legally being able to make decisions. A person also must be considered capable of providing consent. Because of certain mental or cognitive conditions, some people may lack the ability to understand what is being told to them and to carefully consider the nature and purpose of a proposed treatment or service.

Depending on the severity of the impairment to their decision making, individuals may lack the ability to make competent decisions. For consent to be truly informed, people must be considered legally competent to agree to what is being asked of them. Generally, people must be able to provide consent voluntarily; understand the nature and purpose of proposed treatments; the risks or benefits of proposed actions; alternative treatments and their risks or benefits; and have the capacity to make and communicate their decisions. Both ethically and legally, social workers must receive informed consent to take actions on behalf of their clients.

Since the provision of social services is predicated upon the clients' ability to provide informed consent, clients also must be able to give their social workers consent when they authorize their workers to take any action, including the release of client records. When clients are unable to provide informed consent, there are a number of other individuals who may be empowered by law to act on the clients' behalf. State law determines who these individuals are and what powers they have to act on behalf of the individual. When clients are unable to provide consent, social workers may need to contact family members or friends to locate any people who have the legal authority to make decisions for clients. Social workers may also need to work with family members, social agencies, and the courts to establish decision makers.

Guardians (or conservators) of the person may be appointed by a court to manage the personal matters, such as treatment, medication, living arrangements, and social services, of individuals who lack the capacity to make the decisions for themselves. Guardians may also be appointed over the estate of an individual who lacks the cognitive ability to make decisions and be empowered by a court to handle matters such as money, property, and other financial holdings. State law determines whether the guardian has limited or total authority over the person who is impaired and if there are certain decisions that guardians are not allowed to make without court approval, such as involuntary sterilization or admission to a nursing home.

In some cases, people may make advance plans regarding how they want their personal or financial matters handled if they are determined to no longer be competent to make these decisions for themselves. An individual must have the requisite mental capacity to make these "advance directives" at the time the declarations are completed. Some people, such as those with severe mental retardation, those who are suffering from dementia, or those who are currently psychotic, would not have the ability to make these directives. Advance directives may include living wills and/or durable powers of attorney that express an individual's wishes regarding health care or property matters and that delegate their decision making to other people. Typically, living wills and durable powers of attorney do not require court involvement. The laws of a particular state, available resources, whether the individual engaged in advance planning, and the specific needs and functioning of the individual will determine which substitute decision-making possibilities are appropriate.

State law determines when other people can make decisions on behalf of adults who do not have the ability to consent to the use of their records. Social workers must ascertain who these individuals are and the limits of their authority. Under HIPAA, if state law gives someone, such as a guardian or a power of attorney, the power to act on behalf of an adult in decision making related to health care, covered entities must treat that person as the personal representative for the adult. They must provide the personal representative with the same rights to PHI as the adult would have. Personal representatives are entitled to receive PHI about the individual as well as provide any authorizations to disclose the information. However, to be considered personal representatives, individuals must have specific authority to act in regard to health care. Those who have been appointed as a guardian over property or have a power of attorney for matters other than health care are not viewed as personal representatives.

Unlike many state laws, HIPAA requires covered entities to provide a description of the personal representative's authority on the form used for authorizations. Therefore, social workers should verify the identity of personal representatives and their authority to act on behalf of an individual. For example, they should note on the authorization and in the client's record that the personal representative has been appointed as guardian over personal matters or is a power of attorney for health care.

Social workers may encounter situations where they suspect that their adult clients who lack decision-making ability are also abused, neglected, or endangered by their family members. In some instances, these same family members also serve as their personal representatives. Under HIPAA, if practitioners believe that these personal representatives are subjecting clients to domestic violence, abuse, or neglect, they can decide whether to limit the personal representatives' access to PHI.

Practitioners should be aware, however, that the ability to deny personal representatives' access to PHI might conflict with state law. In some states, guardians of adults are specifically given the right to access the medical or mental health records of disabled adults. In such cases, a social worker or organization cannot deny such access, even when they believe the guardian is abusive. Social workers whose practice involves adults with cognitive impairments should familiarize themselves with the laws in their states regarding the duties of guardians, powers of attorneys, or other legally recognized decision makers.

RECORDS AND MENTAL HEALTH

States often treat the records of people with mental health problems differently than the records of people with other medical conditions, placing stricter controls over access to and disclosure of mental health information to outside parties. Because of the stigma that still surrounds mental illness and because of the intimate details clients disclose to their therapists, people may be reluctant to seek treatment if they believe their information may be released to others without their consent. While people may understand their need to seek help for their mental health problems, they also may fear being exposed to discrimination or other negative social- and work-related consequences if their mental health conditions become known. At the same time, state legislatures are aware that some people with untreated mental health problems may engage in unpredictable, violent behavior and that these individuals and society as a whole would benefit from their receipt of mental health treatment.

The U.S. Supreme Court acknowledged that "[b]ecause of the sensitive nature of the problems for which individuals consult psychotherapists, disclosure of confidential communications made during counseling sessions may cause embarrassment or disgrace. For this reason, the mere possibility of disclosure may impede development of the confidential relationship necessary for successful treatment" (*Jaffee v. Redmond,* at 10). Accordingly, mental health information documented in records often receives heightened protections under state law and may be treated more stringently than other PHI under HIPAA.

Clients with mental health problems sometimes make threats to harm themselves or others. One of the more difficult issues for practitioners is determining whether these threats are merely threats or whether the client will act upon their words. Social workers often mistakenly learn that they have a "duty" to warn or protect third parties when their clients threaten physical harm. Warning or protecting another person often results in practitioners' disclosing information contained in clients' records.

While the "duty to warn" is often misunderstood (Kopels & Kagle, 1993), state legislation or case law may delineate practitioners' specific responsibilities when their clients threaten serious physical harm to themselves or others. HIPAA permits practitioners to use or disclose PHI to avert a serious threat to the health or safety of a person or the public so long as the use or disclosure is made to people who are reasonably able to prevent or lessen the threat, including the target of the threat. State law is often more stringent. For example, HIPAA allows disclosure to avert harm to the public: some states only allow disclosure to be made when threats are directed toward specifically identifiable individuals. Social workers who work with clients experiencing mental health problems must take steps to learn whether their state provides more stringent controls for access and disclosure of mental health records than does HIPAA and follow the stricter provisions.

RECORDS AND HIV/AIDS

To stem the spread of HIV/AIDS, certain states encourage people to voluntarily be tested to learn whether they have HIV infection. These states strictly limit access to and disclosure of information regarding the HIV/AIDS status of individuals. They do this so that people will not be deterred from testing because of potential negative consequences such as discrimination and job loss or the reactions of others who learn of their condition. These laws are based on the assumption that when individuals learn their HIV/AIDS health status, they are more likely to make positive decisions to seek appropriate treatment and to take precautions that will lessen the risk of infection for themselves and others. Prior to the enactment of HIPAA, the majority of states had some type of privacy laws that governed HIV/AIDS information.

Under HIPAA, HIV/AIDS information is not treated as a separate category of information. Rather, HIPAA considers HIV/AIDS related health information simply as a type of PHI. As PHI, HIV/AIDS information contained in records is subject to HIPAA's rules regarding access and disclosure. As in all situations where state law provides more privacy protections than HIPAA, social workers would follow the more stringent provisions.

For example, HIPAA allows the release of HIV/AIDS related records without the individual's authorization for the purpose of treatment, payment, and health care operations. However, New York and Illinois laws do not allow disclosure for this purpose. Because both of these states' laws are more protective of privacy than is HIPAA, HIPAA yields to state law. Therefore, in New York and Illinois, social workers who work with patients with HIV/AIDS would follow their respective state laws that govern HIV/AIDS. Social workers in other states would need to seek legal advice or other consultation to determine whether their states' laws also provide more protection for HIV/AIDS records than does HIPAA. In states where no laws exist related to the privacy of HIV/AIDS information, social workers would follow HIPAA provisions regarding PHI.

People with HIV/AIDS may come to social workers for problems related to their mental health. They may be depressed because they have a potentially fatal disease. Others may seek services because they need help coping with their feelings about a family member who has been diagnosed with HIV/AIDS. Practitioners would be well-advised not to place information about an individual's HIV/AIDS status in the record, and instead use more neutral language, such as, "John is depressed because of his brother's diagnosis with a potentially life-threatening illness." Depending on state law, the record of service may be considered to be a mental health record because of the counseling services provided for depression, an HIV/AIDS related record because of the diagnostic information of HIV infection, or simply PHI under HIPAA. Social workers would need assistance in determining which law applies. To protect client privacy, whenever possible, practitioners should omit the diagnosis from their records.

RECORDS AND THE COURTS

Chapter 9 focuses on records and their use in court proceedings. The chapter presents legal issues pertaining to subpoenas, records, personal notes, and privilege, and the impact of federal and state law on social workers' responses. It next looks at record retention under the law and presents content on how statutes of limitation influence retention. The chapter concludes with a discussion of expungement of records.

The previous chapter discussed important federal and state legislation that impacts the records that social workers create or maintain when they provide services to clients. The laws specify what constitutes a record; describe who has access to the records; prescribe who has control over the release of information, such as whether the client or an authorized person's permission is required prior to allowing release; and provide exceptions under which client consent is not necessary to release information.

It is also important to note what these laws do not do. These laws do not instruct social workers and other providers of services about the substance of their records. They provide no guidance as to the content, kind, or quality of the records that practitioners keep. In other words, legislation can inform social workers about what they need to do to comply with legal requirements regarding records. For example, legislation may inform social workers that they need an authorization form from clients to release their records and what specific information must be included in the form.

The laws also do not provide guidance as to what constitutes a "good" record. It is not the function of legislation or regulations to instruct professionals on what and how to record. The law does not delineate each instance when social workers must document contact with clients, which revelations made by clients are significant, when to log phone calls made or received about a client, when to note contacts made with other service providers or family members, what to note about relevant conversations with supervisors, consultants, or others, or the words to use in describing the client-need-situation and services provided. Instead, laws defer to professionals and their judgment in deciding whether, when, and what to record.

Social workers can become skilled at how to record from classes taken in their educational programs, their field instructors, their job supervisors, the knowledge gained from working in the field, and the needs or requirements of their organizations. They should learn that the records they do keep must be complete, accurate, relevant, and timely. As they gain experience, social workers also may rely on their professional ethics, judgment, and skills to determine the content of the record based on the purpose of service to a client.

However, social workers typically do not receive sufficient exposure in classes, field instruction, or even in their practice to the use of records in court. They may be surprised when they receive a demand for their records and realize they are unprepared as to how to respond. Practitioners should be aware that their records have the potential to be both used and scrutinized in legal proceedings. Social workers may find themselves revealing and explaining the content of their records in courts of law, licensing boards, or other professional tribunals. They may also find themselves needing to defend their credibility and professionalism. When social workers' records are called into question, so is the quality of the services they provided to their clients.

WHY RECORDS WOULD BE USED IN COURT

Social workers may not think about their records being used for purposes other than documenting the client-need-situation and the services provided. However, social work records and the material contained within them may be relied on to supply important information in court proceedings in which clients are involved.

When practitioners receive a subpoena for their records, they may be surprised by the very fact that they have received a subpoena. If they reflect on the reasons why they provided services to their clients, the purposes for being called into court may then become clear. In other circumstances, no matter how hard practitioners try to relate the purpose of service to a court proceeding, they may be unable to figure out why they or their records have been subpoenaed. In some situations, the purpose of service to the client is irrelevant to the purpose for which the record is used in court.

Consider these examples.

Example 1

A client is seeing a social worker for marital counseling. In the course of the therapy, the client reveals that she has been having an affair with her coworker. The social worker documents the affair in the record. Later, the client's husband sues her for divorce.

The husband's attorney subpoenas the social worker's records. The attorney is hoping to discover information about the wife's behavior that can be used to verify the grounds alleged in the husband's divorce petition. The information the wife revealed about her affair during the course of marital counseling relates to the problems for which she is seeing the social worker. It also relates to the divorce. In this situation, when the social worker receives a subpoena for the records, the marital conflict directly relates to both the purpose of service to the wife and to the legal issues in the divorce.

Example 2

A teacher notices that a student is not paying attention in class and has dropping grades. The teacher refers the student to the school social worker, who sees the child a number of times. During their sessions, the child reports that his parents are arguing, his father calls his mother "really mean names," and he is sad and worried because of their conflict. The social worker documents the student's statements in the record and provides services to the child to help him deal with his feelings related to his parents' arguments and conflict. Sometime later, when the social worker is no longer providing services to the child, the parents decide to divorce. Each seeks custody of their child. Their respective attorneys subpoena the social worker's records to look for information that will help their clients demonstrate that the child would be better off living with them.

In this example, the reason social work services were provided was to help the child improve his educational functioning. His concern about his parents' marital conflict interfered with this performance, was a subject of discussion between the student and the social worker, and was described in the record. In this situation, when the social worker receives a subpoena for the records, the parents' divorce is only indirectly related to the purposes for which she provided services to the child.

Example 3

A client is seeing a social worker because of marital conflict. The client reports to the social worker that he deals with the stress at home by getting drunk almost every night. The social worker documents the client's statements regarding his drinking. One night, as he leaves a bar, the client witnesses a fight. The police catch the assailant and the client identifies the assailant in a line-up. The assailant is prosecuted for the crime. The attorney for the assailant subpoenas the social worker's records about the client to provide proof that the client has a drinking problem and is not a reliable witness.

The information documented in the record about the client's drinking is directly relevant to the client-need-situation and the purpose of service regarding marital conflict. However, the attorney is not seeking the social work records to look for information regarding the client's marriage. Instead, the information is being sought to demonstrate that the client has a drinking problem and therefore cannot be relied upon to correctly identify the assailant in the criminal prosecution. Upon receiving the subpoena in this case, the social worker would be dismayed that her records would be used to discredit her client, especially when it is totally unrelated to the purpose of service.

In each of these examples, the client received social work services related to issues that arose from marital conflict. In each of these examples, the clients revealed information that is pertinent to the purpose of service. The clients' revelations regarding affairs, tensions in the home, and drinking would be properly documented in the clients' records because the statements provide valuable information about the client-need-situation. These statements are relevant to and congruent with the purpose of service and are appropriately included in the record.

Each of the examples differs in the way that the information documented in the social work record will be used in court. In example 1, the attorney seeks the social work record that documents marital conflict to prove that the affair is directly related to the subsequent divorce. In example 2, the attorneys seek the social work record that documents a child's school adjustment problems to use in the somewhat related purpose of child custody. In example 3, an attorney seeks the social work record that documents a client's drinking as a means of dealing with marital conflict for a reason totally unrelated to the purpose of service, that of defending a third party in a criminal case. Practitioners need to be aware that their records may be called upon to supply information in court proceedings, even in circumstances that have no apparent link to the purpose of service.

Clients are engaged in many life events that have the potential to lead to court involvement. Clients' marriages may end in divorce. They may give birth to or adopt children and later engage in custody fights about them. Clients may undertake activities that are against the law and that impact their work or school performance and relationships with others. Alternatively, clients may be victims of crimes, exploitation, or accidents. Clients may witness events between other people at their home, school, work, or other social environments that result in court actions. They may suffer from serious illnesses or debilitating health conditions or may have or develop mental or substance abuse conditions that impair their judgment or decision-making abilities or may make them dangerous to themselves or others. Clients may also feel that they have been harmed by the actions of their social workers.

In these and other situations, clients may become involved in court proceedings. Through their clients' involvement, social workers may become drawn into the proceedings. Social workers, through their records and their testimony, may be asked to provide information to the court about their clients. Social workers may provide background information about clients;

describe the services provided to clients and the results of those services; offer insight about client motivation, thoughts, and judgment; and explain environmental factors that affect clients' lives. Social workers may become involved in a case to corroborate and support their clients' positions. Sometimes, social workers must provide testimony that, although accurate, is contrary to the legal interests of their clients.

Social workers should realize that they may be called upon to supply information that arises from confidential relationships with clients. Of course, not all social worker-client relationships are confidential. For example, a social worker may be asked by a judge to meet with divorcing parents, and provide the court with a recommendation for a custody arrangement that would serve the best interests of the children. Or a social worker may be required to report to the court about whether a mandated client is participating in court-ordered services. In these examples, the worker-client relationship is not confidential. Both the worker and the client know that the worker will be providing information to the court. However, when social worker-client relationships are confidential, practitioners are ethically bound to protect the confidentiality of information they receive from and about their clients. When social workers receive subpoenas for their records, they also may incur legal obligations to reveal this confidential information.

Practitioners are aware of their ethical obligations to maintain confidentiality. They know that they cannot reveal any information to spouses, parents, family members, or others who may seek it without client consent. However, workers usually do not understand their legal obligations or how to handle situations in which they receive a request for their records in the form of a subpoena. The following sections are intended to help social workers understand how to fulfill their sometimes conflicting ethical and legal obligations when their communications with clients are confidential and their records are requested for use in court.

SUBPOENAS

A *subpoena* is a mandate for the submission of documents or the testimony of a witness in a court proceeding. Social workers may receive a *subpoena duces tecum*, which is a legal order to turn over documents or other written or electronic documentation. A *subpoena duces tecum* may seek material such as records, notes, tape recordings, or video recordings of sessions or other types of documentation, like computer files, diaries, and even art work.

Social workers may also receive a *subpoena ad testificandum*, which is a legal order that requires individuals to testify at a deposition, trial, or other official proceeding. The testimony that workers will be asked to supply derives from their interactions with clients and others, which also may be documented in the record. Typically, a deposition occurs before a trial and is held in a lawyer's office, with both sides to a dispute and their lawyers present. A court reporter records the questions lawyers ask and the answers given by the witnesses. A judge is not present but may be available by telephone to respond to queries of the attorneys. The purpose of the deposition is for the person being deposed (the deponent) to supply information that may be relevant to a pending court case. A *subpoena ad testificandum* may also require a social worker to attend a court hearing to provide testimony during a trial. In all situations where social workers receive subpoenas, they would be well-advised to consult with an attorney.

The receipt of a subpoena is particularly problematic for social workers and other mental health professionals. Subpoenas often seek the release of confidential information that practitioners know that they are precluded from disclosing. At the same time, subpoenas are documents that command compliance and threaten punishment for noncompliance. Social workers must respond to the receipt of subpoenas and not simply ignore them, assuming that their duty of confidentiality outweighs disclosure.

However, although social workers must respond to the subpoena, they need not necessarily turn over the requested documents or testify in court proceedings. Just because a subpoena is issued does not automatically imply that client records and the information within them ultimately will be disclosed. Judges may rule that attorneys are not entitled to such information, that the subpoenas are overly broad, or that the attorneys did not correctly comply with certain legal requirements in making their requests.

Social workers may be surprised to learn that some attorneys may not be aware of the social workers' obligation to maintain confidentiality or the special nature of the worker-client relationship. Attorneys are accustomed to issuing subpoenas in cases that do not involve confidential relationships between professionals and clients. These lawyers can be made aware of social workers' ethical and legal obligations not to disclose client information. Social workers or attorneys acting on their or their agency's behalf can inform the attorney who sent the subpoena that social workers' professional and legal obligations prevent them from disclosing any confidential information. Social workers are obligated only to show up at the designated time and location and answer questions about their own personal information, such as their name, age, address, and work history. Social workers may also claim a privilege to prevent the disclosure of any information related to a client. Sometimes, after lawyers learn that the information they desire will not be easy to obtain, they will not pursue the testimony. They may recognize that the information could be acquired elsewhere, is duplicative of other sources, is not worth the trouble, or is not truly important to the case.

Other lawyers may disregard social workers' professional obligations to protect confidentiality because they want the information to bolster their case and are unconcerned with why the social worker feels obligated not to comply. They may bully the social worker into believing that the law requires compliance with the subpoena. They may also threaten the social worker with being held in contempt of court.

Contempt of court can result when a person disrespects the court or willfully disobeys a judge's lawful order. An attorney who threatens a social worker with contempt is only threatening. Only a judge has the power to determine whether someone has engaged in contempt of court and institute punishment for the contemptuous action. Before a practitioner could be held in contempt of court because of failure to comply with a subpoena, he or she would be provided an opportunity to appear before a judge. The attorney would need to schedule a separate court proceeding, often called a hearing on a "rule to show cause." When a rule to show cause hearing is scheduled, judges expect that the person who may be found in contempt would attend. If the practitioner failed to show up, he or she would be found in contempt by the judge.

If the practitioner did attend the rule to show cause hearing, the practitioner would be given the opportunity to explain to the judge his or her reasons for refusing to comply with the subpoena. After the practitioner explained why he or she would not disclose the information, the judge would decide whether the practitioner was correct in keeping the information confidential. If the judge determined that the social worker had an obligation to protect the information, the judge would dismiss the contempt proceedings. Alternatively, the judge might determine that the social worker did not comply with the subpoena because the worker had an honest, but mistaken notion about the obligation to protect the information. The judge might then order the professional to reveal it. If the social worker then supplied the information, it would be unlikely that the judge would find the social worker in contempt. Being wrong about one's legal obligation is different than willfully disobeying a judge's order.

If the judge decided that the social worker should comply with the subpoena, the social worker would then have a choice. The worker could comply with the judge's order and disclose the information or could disobey the judge and refuse to supply the client's information. If the social worker continued to withhold the information, he or she might be held in contempt because the refusal would be considered willful disobedience of the judge's order.

A finding of contempt may be punished by a monetary fine or imprisonment. Usually, the imprisonment lasts as long as the person held in contempt (the contemnor) refuses to disclose the information. When the contemnor supplies the requested information, then he or she would be released from jail. In some situations, a judge might find a social worker in contempt, but not order imprisonment. The judge might allow practitioners to remain free while they appeal the judge's ruling. Some judges understand and may sympathize with practitioners who believe it is their ethical obligation to protect client information.

When a social worker receives a subpoena, there are a number of actions that he or she should take. First, the social worker should consult legal counsel to discuss the receipt of the subpoena and how best to respond. Next, the social worker should discuss the subpoena with the client. If the client is willing to sign an authorization for the release of information, this simplifies the situation and allows the practitioner to comply with the subpoena. Of course, the social worker would need to discuss with the client what types of information would be revealed and how this information could be used to help or harm the client. Only when the client is fully informed as to the consequences should the social worker gain the client's authorization to release information.

When a social work client is represented by an attorney, the social worker also should encourage the client to inform the attorney that the social worker received a subpoena. The client's attorney may be unaware that the subpoena was issued and thereafter take action on the client's behalf. If the attorney wants to discuss with the social worker the types of information the social worker might disclose, the client should be asked to sign an authorization form to allow the social worker to consult with the client's attorney.

If the client chooses not to sign an authorization to allow the social worker to release the information requested by the subpoena, ethical practice requires that the social worker act to protect the client's information. The NASW (1999) Code of Ethics requires social workers to take steps to protect the confidentiality of clients during legal proceedings. It states:

> Social workers should protect the confidentiality of clients during legal proceedings to the extent permitted by law. When a court of law or other legally authorized body orders social workers to disclose confidential or privileged information without a client's consent and such disclosure could cause harm to the client, social workers should request that the court withdraw the order or limit the order as narrowly as possible or maintain the records under seal, unavailable for public inspection. (107[j])

A social worker who receives a subpoena and whose client will not authorize the release of the information requested in the subpoena is ethically required to take action to protect the client's confidentiality. The action may include waiting until the court orders the social worker to disclose the information, claiming a privilege on behalf of the client before releasing any information, filing objections to a subpoena, seeking a protective order to limit the information that is provided, or filing a motion to quash (block) the subpoena (Polowy, Morgan, & Gilbertson, 2005). Because of the ethical obligation to protect confidentiality and the complexity of responding to a subpoena, a social worker may desire to retain her or his own legal counsel to assist with the response. Some malpractice insurance policies provide coverage for such a purpose.

HIPAA AND SUBPOENAS

HIPAA creates minimum legal requirements when subpoenas are issued for PHI. These requirements further complicate how social workers who are covered entities should handle the receipt of a subpoena. Under some circumstances, HIPAA allows practitioners to disclose PHI although their Code of Ethics or state law would not.

HIPAA permits covered entities to disclose PHI in the course of any judicial or administrative proceeding when a judge orders the disclosure. Judicial proceedings are held before a judge whereas administrative proceedings are conducted by administrative law judges (ALJs). Administrative proceedings include cases such as special education due process hearings or appeals of the denial of Social Security disability benefits. Under the Privacy Rule, when a judge or ALJ orders the disclosure of PHI, client authorization is not necessary.

HIPAA further permits covered entities to disclose PHI in response to a subpoena that is unaccompanied by a court order if certain additional procedures are followed. These procedures require the covered entity to receive "satisfactory assurances" by the party who is seeking the information. Receiving satisfactory assurances is defined by HIPAA to mean that the covered entity has received a written statement and accompanying documentation that demonstrates:

- the party requesting the information made a good faith attempt to provide written notice to the individual. If the person's address is unknown, then a notice must be sent to the person's last known address;
- the notice included sufficient information about the proceeding in which the PHI is requested to permit the individual to raise an objection to the court or administrative tribunal; and
- the time for the individual to raise objections to the court or administrative tribunal has elapsed and no objections were filed or any objections that were filed by the individual have been resolved.

A final way that HIPAA permits a covered entity to disclose PHI, based only on the receipt of a subpoena, is if the party seeking the information or the covered entity obtains a "qualified protective order." A qualified protective order means that a court or ALJ has ordered, or the parties have agreed, that the information disclosed will not be used for any purpose other than the particular proceeding. In addition, all copies of the PHI must be returned to the covered entity or destroyed at the end of the litigation.

In these limited situations, HIPAA allows disclosures in legal proceedings without client authorization. Regardless, social workers need to be aware that the NASW Code of Ethics requires them to take additional steps, as discussed in the previous section, to protect client records. Social workers can raise their professional ethics as a defense to the disclosure of records in court and administrative proceedings (Polowy et al., 2005).

SUBPOENAS AND STATE LAW

Social workers also should be aware that state laws might require more stringent standards than the minimum requirements of HIPAA. For example, New York law requires that subpoenas served on providers requesting medical records contain conspicuous, bold-faced type stating that the records will not be provided unless the subpoena is accompanied by a written authorization by the patient. In Illinois, subpoenas for mental health records must also be accompanied by specific court orders in certain types of court proceedings. Illinois places responsibility both on attorneys and on practitioners to handle subpoenas correctly; the attorney cannot serve nor the practitioner respond to a subpoena for mental health records that is not accompanied by a court order. Attorneys and practitioners who do not follow the provisions of Illinois law are subject to being sued for monetary damages (*Mandziara v. Canulli*, 1998). Practitioners in all states would be well-advised to seek legal or other advice on how to protect client privacy when a subpoena is received.

DEFINING THE RECORD UNDER THE SUBPOENA

When a *subpoena duces tecum* is received for client records, practitioners need to consider what actually constitutes the "record." Even when clients authorize their social workers to disclose their records to comply with a subpoena, social workers must determine what records to disclose. To ascertain what they can disclose, social workers should consult with supervisors, agency policy and procedures, and their attorneys before they release any information. Additionally, there are other factors to consider in determining what records are subject to subpoena. These factors include where records are kept, what documents constitute records, and how the law defines records.

Social workers' records of the services provided to clients may be stored on paper or in computers in various places throughout an agency. Records may be located centrally or dispersed in offices throughout the organization. For example, in some hospitals, records are kept centrally and personnel can document or review the records at workstations throughout the system. In some schools, various personnel keep their own records. There may be the social worker's file, the special education file, the student file in the admission and records office, the teacher's file, the disciplinary file, as well as other files kept by personnel who provide occupational, physical, or other specialized services. Regardless of who produces them, all of the files are considered part of the education record.

In many agencies, schools, and hospitals, record custodians are responsible for gathering and releasing the records from wherever they are kept. In those agencies, when a subpoena for the record is received by the agency or a worker, the subpoena is given to the record custodian to process. In other agencies, social workers may be responsible for assembling the records to respond to the subpoena. When the requested records relate solely to social work services, it is much easier for social workers to control the form of response by obtaining client consent, deciding which documents are released, or resisting compliance with the subpoena. However, even when they are not responsible for assembling the records, social workers need to protect their records from disclosure.

Subpoenas for records may seek all recorded information regarding a client. Social workers maintain documentation about their clients in a number of formats, however, and it may be difficult for practitioners to determine which documentation is subject to the subpoena. For instance, there may be mention of clients in daily logs, appointment books, calendars, day planners, and in interoffice staff communications to alert other shift personnel to client needs. The client's record may also contain memos, agency forms, releases of information, medical information, psychological evaluations, police reports, student grades, progress notes, discharge summaries, interim notes, treatment plans, and other documents created or maintained by the agency to assist in the provision of services to the client. A client's record may contain additional items that are useful tools for the practitioner, depending on the services provided. The client's folder may contain logs, journals, diaries, or art work created by them at the behest of their worker for therapeutic purposes. Some or all of these items may be considered part of the client's record and subject to the subpoena.

Practitioners think about records differently than the way the law treats records. For practitioners, a record is the documentation of services provided to clients, which may be created by various personnel of the agency and kept in various places throughout the agency. In contrast, under the law, a "record" is a general label for documents that are specifically defined by legislation or regulations and has no reference to any particular agency, practice, or mission.

Ultimately, the legal definition of a record will control what information gets released when clients authorize their records to be disclosed or a subpoena for records is received. Under the law, the definition of a record may be different in different practice settings. For example, a child welfare record would include different material than would a mental health record. If a social worker receives a subpoena for records, the social worker should consult agency memoranda or policies to determine whether the agency has a protocol for record release. Often agencies have such policies. However, these policies might be outdated. Therefore, the worker should also consult with agency managers and attorneys to determine what actions to take.

SUBPOENAS AND RECORDS DEFINED UNDER FEDERAL LEGISLATION

As discussed in chapter 8, federal legislation protects the privacy of individuals' information. Federal legislation often impacts the ways in which social workers decide what to document because they know that clients and others may have access to the records. One of the difficulties for social workers and other practitioners is that the term "records" is used in a number of federal laws but the meaning of the term varies by the particular law. In other words, there is no consistency between federal laws as to what "records" means. For example, a definition of what constitutes an education record differs from what constitutes a substance abuse record under federal law. A few illustrations from federal legislation and regulations will demonstrate that the federal government has no uniform way of defining records.

For example, the Privacy Act of 1974 uses an approach that carefully and specifically defines the types of information that comprise a record. Under the Privacy Act, a record means

> any item, collection, or grouping of information about an individual that is maintained by an agency, including, but not limited to, his education, financial transactions, medical history, and criminal or employment history and that contains his name, or the identifying number, symbol, or other identifying particular assigned to the individual, such as a finger or voice print or a photograph. . . . (§ 552[a])

In contrast, Part 2 takes a different approach to defining "record" by applying the term to a broad and inclusive range of information. Part 2 regulations define "records" to mean "any information, whether recorded or not, relating to a patient received or acquired by a federally assisted alcohol or drug program" (§ 2.11). Under Part 2 regulations, it appears that when clients make revelations to their workers, that information would be part of the record even if workers do not write it down.

However, Part 2 regulations do not specifically define what other material would be considered to be information. Instead, the closest definition to "information" is the term "patient identifying information." "Patient identifying information" means

> the name, address, social security number, fingerprints, photograph, or similar information by which the identity of a patient can be determined with reasonable accuracy and speed either directly or by reference to other publicly available information. The term does not include a number assigned to a patient by a program, if that number does not consist of, or contain numbers (such as a social security, or driver's license number) which could be used to identify a patient with reasonable accuracy and speed from sources external to the program. (§ 2.11)

The regulations suggest, then, that a Part 2 record consists not only of "patient identifying information," including fingerprints, social security numbers, and photographs, but also any information the patient reveals in the context of service, whether or not it is documented. Because of additional complications created by the regulations' restrictions on the use or disclosure of information, social workers are strongly advised to get legal consultation before revealing any records of individuals with alcohol or drug problems.

The Family Educational Rights and Privacy Act (FERPA) defines the term record by briefly stating what constitutes an "education record." It then excludes certain types of records from the definition of education records. Under FERPA (2007) regulations, education records means those records that are "(1) Directly related to a student; and (2) Maintained by an educational agency or institution or by a party acting for the agency or institution" (§ 99.3). FERPA then delineates what the term education record does *not* include:

> (1) Records that are kept in the sole possession of the maker, are used only as a personal memory aid, and are not accessible or revealed to any other person except a temporary substitute for the maker of the record.

(2) Records of the law enforcement unit of an educational agency or institution, subject to the provisions of § 99.8.

(3)(i) Records relating to an individual who is employed by an educational agency or institution, that:

(A) Are made and maintained in the normal course of business;

(B) Relate exclusively to the individual in that individual's capacity as an employee; and

(C) Are not available for use for any other purpose.

(ii) Records relating to an individual in attendance at the agency or institution who is employed as a result of his or her status as a student are education records and not excepted under paragraph (b)(3)(i) of this definition.

(4) Records on a student who is 18 years of age or older, or is attending an institution of postsecondary education, that are:

(i) Made or maintained by a physician, psychiatrist, psychologist, or other recognized professional or paraprofessional acting in his or her professional capacity or assisting in a paraprofessional capacity;

(ii) Made, maintained, or used only in connection with treatment of the student; and

(iii) Disclosed only to individuals providing the treatment. For the purpose of this definition, "treatment" does not include remedial educational activities or activities that are part of the program of instruction at the agency or institution; and

(5) Records that only contain information about an individual after he or she is no longer a student at that agency or institution. (§ 99.3)

As a final example, the Child Abuse Prevention and Treatment Act (1974) (CAPTA) defers to the states to define what is meant by a child abuse and neglect record. It merely provides that states must enact legislation to ensure that child abuse and neglect records are confidential and that their unlawful disclosure will be punished criminally: "The State must provide by statute that all records concerning reports and reports of child abuse and neglect are confidential and that their unauthorized disclosure is a criminal offense" (Child Abuse and Neglect Prevention and Treatment, 2007).

As can be seen by these examples, the definitions of records are not identical across federal laws. Social workers who previously responded to a subpoena for education records may believe they know how to comply when they receive a subpoena for another type of federally defined records, such as substance abuse records. They do not. Of course, on receipt of a subpoena, social workers should be in contact with their attorneys. Together, they can determine whether it is appropriate to comply with the subpoena and how records are defined under applicable law.

SUBPOENAS AND RECORDS DEFINED UNDER STATE LEGISLATION

Social workers who know how a record is defined under a specific federal law might assume that the same definition would be used when state law is applied. For example, a social worker who works in a school may believe that the state's definition of "education record" would be identical to that of the federal government. However, states define the term "record" in an even more varied manner than does the federal government. Even within a state, records may be defined differently under laws related to different types of services. For example, a subpoena that seeks "mental health records" under Pennsylvania law will be asking for different material than would a subpoena seeking "education records" under Pennsylvania law.

Social workers also should be aware of variations between states. For example, Pennsylvania's definition of a mental health record is different from that of Virginia. If a social worker receives a subpoena for mental health records, state law would determine what information is being sought. For example, a social worker who practices in Arizona would refer to Arizona law for the definition of mental health records.

> [Mental health records] means all communications that are recorded in any form or medium and that relate to patient examination, evaluation, or behavioral or mental health treatment. Records include medical records that are prepared by a health care provider or other providers. Records do not include:
>
> (a) Materials that are prepared in connection with utilization review, peer review or quality assurance activities. . . .
>
> (b) Recorded telephone and radio calls to and from a publicly operated emergency dispatch office relating to requests for emergency services or reports of suspected criminal activity. (Arizona Revised Statutes, 2007, § 36-501[40])

In contrast, if the social worker practices in Maryland and receives a subpoena for mental health records, state law regarding disclosure of mental health records refers the reader to the general law that covers confidentiality of medical records. In Maryland, a mental health record is a type of medical record. The Annotated Code of Maryland (2006) defines medical record as

> any oral, written, or other transmission in any form or medium of information that:
>
> (i) Is entered in the record of a patient or recipient;
>
> (ii) Identifies or can readily be associated with the identity of a patient or recipient; and
>
> (iii) Relates to the health care of the patient or recipient.
>
> (2) "Medical record" includes any:
>
> (i) Documentation of disclosures of a medical record to any person who is not an employee, agent, or consultant of the health care provider;
>
> (ii) File or record maintained . . . by a pharmacy of a prescription order for drugs, medicines, or devices that identifies or may be readily associated with the identity of a patient;
>
> (iii) Documentation of an examination of a patient regardless of who:

1. Requested the examination; or

2. Is making payment for the examination; and

(iv) File or record received from another health care provider that:

1. Relates to the health care of a patient or recipient received from that health care provider; and

2. Identifies or can readily be associated with the identity of the patient or recipient. (§ 4-301)

In Illinois, a receipt of a subpoena for mental health records will produce a different set of materials than in other states. In the Illinois Mental Health and Developmental Disabilities Confidentiality Act (2007),

> "Record" means any record kept by a therapist or by an agency in the course of providing mental health or developmental disabilities service to a recipient concerning the recipient and the services provided. "Records" includes all records maintained by a court that have been created in connection with, in preparation for, or as a result of the filing of any petition or certificate . . . and includes the petitions, certificates, dispositional reports, treatment plans, and reports of diagnostic evaluations and of hearings. . . . Record does not include the therapist's personal notes. . . . (§ 110/2)

Illinois' law defines mental health records to include documents that are kept by a therapist or an agency that provides mental health or developmental disabilities services or that are created in connection with the civil commitment of an individual. Under Illinois law, other information, known as personal notes, are not considered to be part of the record. Therefore, in Illinois, social workers who comply with a subpoena for "mental health records" would need to distinguish between records and personal notes.

PERSONAL NOTES

As noted above, Illinois' legislation draws a distinction between mental health records and personal notes. "Personal notes" is a distinctly defined term under Illinois law. However, the concept of personal notes is not unique to Illinois. The idea of keeping certain clinical notations separate from other parts of the record has existed throughout the history of social work recording.

Practitioners are concerned that if they document some client revelations in the official record they may not be able to protect client confidentiality. Practitioners believe that they may be able to offer heightened privacy to clients by keeping highly personal and sensitive information out of the client's agency record. By keeping the information in separate files, social workers believe they can protect client privacy by keeping individuals inside and outside of the agency from seeing the content. Additionally, when subpoenas are received for client information, practitioners believe that they can comply with the subpoena by releasing official agency client records and not their personal notes. Typically, personal notes are seen as being the personal property of the practitioner and not subject to being turned over in response to a subpoena. Practitioners often assume that, if information is kept out of the agency's records, it would not be subject to a subpoena. This may not be true.

Practitioners have other reasons for wishing to keep separate client files. Practitioners may wish to use a separate recordkeeping system to keep their clients from viewing their own files. Social workers may hope to shield clients from reading clinical observations that may be painful to them. Practitioners may also use these separate records to note important, yet unsubstantiated, information they would not wish the client or others to see. For example, they may use these other records to jot down their own hunches, speculations, gut reactions, reminders, and tentative diagnoses.

Practitioners use different terms to refer to the documents they keep separate from the official record. They may call these documents "dual records," "personal notes," "clinical notes," "unofficial records," or "informal records." Regardless of the terms used, the purpose is to somehow differentiate between two sets of records, one that can be shared with clients and others who have the right to see the information, and the other that is kept for the practitioner's own use. Here, we will refer to the difference between the two types of information as "records" versus "personal notes."

STATE LAW AND PERSONAL NOTES

In many states, practitioners can elect to keep personal notes in whatever manner they choose because no legislation exists that governs such notes. Social workers choose what information about the client-need-situation they feel should be placed in the official record. They also choose whether and what other information would be written down in a separate file and where that file would be kept.

In other states, keeping personal notes is controlled by laws. When laws govern personal notes, social workers lose some of their discretion about what information they can record separately from the agency record. Legislatures may define for practitioners what types of information may be considered personal notes and what information is properly considered a record. When practitioners keep personal notes in accordance with the legal requirements of their states, their personal notes are not subject to discovery during court proceedings. When practitioners do not keep their personal notes in accordance with the law, their personal notes may be considered to be records and subject to disclosure under a subpoena.

In 1979, Illinois became the first state to create a legal distinction between records and personal notes. Practitioners in Illinois may choose but are not required to keep personal notes to the extent they deem them useful or appropriate. Illinois' legislation on personal notes is considered pioneering and has influenced other states' records laws.

In Illinois, three categories of information are considered personal notes:

(i) information disclosed to the therapist in confidence by other persons on condition that such information would never be disclosed to the recipient or other persons;

(ii) information disclosed to the therapist by the recipient which would be injurious to the recipient's relationships to other persons; and

(iii) the therapist's speculations, impressions, hunches, and reminders. (Illinois Mental Health and Developmental Disabilities Confidentiality Act, 2007, § 110/2)

The first category is information that is disclosed to the social worker by someone other than the client on the condition that the information will not be shared with the client. For example, a wife may tell her husband's social worker that she is having an extramarital affair and is ambivalent about staying in the marriage. If the social worker were to write this information in the client's record, the husband would then have access to the information if he reviewed his file.

The second category is information that clients tell their social workers that may be harmful to the clients' relationships with other people in their lives. For example, a child may tell her social worker that her mother is really mean to her father and calls him bad names every time he drinks. If the social worker believes that the mother or father may want access to the child's records, the social worker may view the child's revelation as potentially harmful to the child's relationships with her parents and document it in personal notes rather than the record.

The third category of information includes the therapist's hunches, speculations, and impressions. For example, if the social worker suspects that a teenager has an eating disorder, but needs more information to confirm or contradict this hypothesis, he may place the information in personal notes. If the teenager or her parents sought access to her records, or if the information were subpoenaed, the tentative diagnosis would not be part of the available information.

In all of these examples, by placing the information in personal notes rather than records, the therapist has limited clients' and others' access to sensitive personal information. Social workers who use this provision improve the quality of their records by excluding unsupported or tentative suppositions from them. This information, if it is important for the worker to consider, can be placed into the practitioners' personal notes until the diagnoses or speculations are verified, and then documented formally in the record.

When practitioners in Illinois keep personal notes, those notes are required to be kept separate and apart from the client's file and shared with no one but the social worker's supervisor, a consultant, or an attorney. At any time, if the personal notes are shared with people other than those delineated, the personal notes automatically become part of the record. If personal notes contain only the three categories of information that are defined under the law as personal notes, and if the practitioner has not shared the notes, the notes are considered to be the personal property of the practitioner and not subject to discovery. This means that when social workers receive subpoenas for their records for use in depositions or trials, only information that is part of the client record would be subject to disclosure. Their personal notes would not need to be disclosed.

Because of the distinction between records and personal notes, Illinois social workers may be able to afford heightened privacy to their clients. However, just because social workers keep documents they designate as personal notes does not necessarily mean that the documents are, in fact, personal notes. In reality, attorneys may subpoena both records and personal notes. The determination of whether the material a social worker calls personal notes is truly personal notes is made by the judge presiding over the case and not by the practitioner.

In *In re Estate of Bagus* (1998), a woman who was seeing a psychiatrist committed suicide. Her husband requested a copy of her records but the psychiatrist refused to release them, claiming that all the records he kept were actually personal notes, and that he alone was entitled to determine what were records and what were personal notes. The husband sued to compel the doctor to produce the records. The question before the trial judge was who determines whether documents constitute personal notes or records, the therapist or the judge. The judge's decision was that he should make this determination. The psychiatrist appealed. The appellate court ruled that one of the functions of a trial judge is to supervise the discovery of information. The trial judge has the power to determine which documents are personal notes and, therefore, are not subject to disclosure, and which documents are records and may legitimately become part of the case. The judge makes this determination by examining the content of the documents designated as personal notes, comparing it to the legal definition of personal notes.

Other states also differentiate between records and personal notes. For example, in Maryland, personal notes are defined as information that is:

1. The work product and personal property of a mental health provider; and

. 2. Except as provided in subsection (d)(3) of this section, not discoverable or admissible as evidence in any criminal, civil, or administrative action.

(ii) Except as provided in subsection (d)(2) of this section, a medical record does not include a personal note of a mental health care provider, if the mental health care provider:

1. Keeps the personal note in the mental health care provider's sole possession for the provider's own personal use;

2. Maintains the personal note separate from the recipient's medical records; and

3. Does not disclose the personal note to any other person except:

A. The mental health provider's supervising health care provider that maintains the confidentiality of the personal note;

B. A consulting health care provider that maintains the confidentiality of the personal note; or

C. An attorney of the health care provider that maintains the confidentiality of the personal note.

(iii) "Personal note" does not include information concerning the patient's diagnosis, treatment plan, symptoms, prognosis, or progress notes. (Annotated Code of Maryland, 2006, § 4-307[6][1])

Maryland's legislation has many similarities to Illinois law. Like Illinois, Maryland considers personal notes to be the personal property of the practitioner and not subject to use in court proceedings. Similarly, personal notes in Maryland must be kept separate from the record, in the sole possession of the practitioner, and not shared with others, except the practitioner's supervisor, consultant, and attorney.

Unlike Illinois, which includes three categories of information in its definition of personal notes, Maryland's law does not delineate what is considered to be personal notes. Instead, Maryland excludes certain material from its definition of personal notes. According to Maryland legislation, therapists' personal notes do not include information regarding patients' diagnoses, treatment plans, symptoms, prognosis, or progress notes. While Maryland practitioners may be aware that they can keep personal notes and that certain information is not considered to be a personal note, they have much less legislative guidance than Illinois practitioners as to what actually constitutes a personal note.

The law in the District of Columbia also allows mental health professionals to keep personal notes. Personal notes are defined as "(A) mental health information disclosed to the mental health professional in confidence by other persons on condition that such information not be disclosed to the client or other persons; and (B) the mental health professional's speculations" (District of Columbia Mental Health Information Act, 2007, § 7-1201.01[13]). Like social workers in Illinois and Maryland, social workers in DC must not file personal notes in the client's mental health record. However, unlike Illinois and Maryland, the law in the District of Columbia prohibits social workers from sharing their personal notes with supervisors or consultants. In fact, the only instance when mental health professionals can share personal notes is when the practitioner needs the notes or the information contained within them to defend a malpractice case or breach of confidentiality lawsuit that a client files against him or her.

The above examples demonstrate that certain state laws permit practitioners to keep personal notes that are separate from the official record. These laws define the scope of personal notes and permit practitioners to document but exclude certain types of sensitive information from the formal record. In turn, the personal notes become unavailable to those to whom the records are generally available, including clients and the courts. Practitioners must ensure that they learn whether their state has created such a distinction, what the distinction entails, how the information should be stored, and with whom it can be shared. To protect client information contained in personal notes from being released under a subpoena, practitioners must explicitly follow their respective state laws.

Psychotherapy Notes under HIPAA

HIPAA adds another layer of complexity for social workers who wish to keep personal notes in addition to the official record. As discussed previously, HIPAA creates national minimum standards in the handling of protected health information for practitioners who are covered entities. When the Department of Health and Human Services issued its final version of the HIPAA Privacy Rule, it recognized the value of personal notes. It stated that:

> psychotherapy notes are primarily of use to the mental health profes-
> sional who wrote them, maintained separately from the medical record,
> and not involved in the documentation necessary to carry out treatment,
> payment, or health care operations. . . . Unlike information shared with
> other health care providers for the purposes of treatment, psychotherapy
> notes are more detailed and subjective and are . . . subject to unique pri-
> vacy and record retention practices. In fact, it is this separate existence
> and isolated use that allows us to grant the extra protection without caus-
> ing an undue burden on the health care system. (Standards for Privacy of
> Individually Identifiable Health Information, 2000)

By enacting the psychotherapy notes provisions of HIPAA, the federal government aids practitioners in their ability to protect client privacy because they legally can keep certain information separate from the official record. HIPAA creates the concept of personal notes for federal law, using the term psychotherapy notes to describe them.

Under HIPAA (2007), psychotherapy notes are defined as:

> notes recorded (in any medium) by a health care provider who is a men-
> tal health professional documenting or analyzing the contents of conver-
> sation during a private counseling session or a group, joint, or family
> counseling session and that are separated from the rest of the individual's
> medical record. Psychotherapy notes excludes medication prescription
> and monitoring, counseling session start and stop times, the modalities
> and frequencies of treatment furnished, results of clinical tests, and any
> summary of the following items: Diagnosis, functional status, the treat-
> ment plan, symptoms, prognosis, and progress to date. (§ 164.501)

Psychotherapy notes receive special treatment under HIPAA. To release psychotherapy notes, clients must sign specific authorization forms. Authorizations for the release of psychotherapy notes cannot be combined with authorizations for the release of PHI. When practitioners receive requests for the "complete medical record" or "all client records" accompanied with signed authorizations, their psychotherapy notes cannot be released. To release the psychotherapy notes, separate signed authorizations that specifically request the disclosure of psychotherapy notes also are required ("Social Workers and Psychotherapy Notes," 2006).

Certain exceptions exist to the requirement that client authorization is necessary to release psychotherapy notes under HIPAA. Client authorization for the use or disclosure of psychotherapy notes is not required in situations where the originator of the notes wants to use them; the notes are needed for the oversight of the person who originated them; the notes are used by the covered entity to train its students, trainees, or practitioners to practice or improve their skills in group, joint, family, or individual counseling; the notes are used by a coroner or medical examiner; or the notes are required to avert a serious and imminent threat to the client's health or safety.

Psychotherapy notes have received a higher level of protection than PHI because HIPAA requires clients to sign specific, additional authorizations for the release of psychotherapy notes. Ironically, HIPAA does not permit individuals to access their psychotherapy notes. Because clients cannot view the contents of their notes, they do not have adequate knowledge of what these notes contain. If they sign an authorization, they cannot be sure about what information will be released. For this reason, practitioners may wish to discuss the contents of their psychotherapy notes with clients to ensure that clients can make an informed decision about whether they should authorize their disclosure ("Social Workers and Psychotherapy Notes," 2006).

HIPAA's inclusion of the concept of psychotherapy notes is also beneficial for practitioners in states that do not have laws that recognize or offer special status to personal notes. HIPAA provides practitioners with a legal justification for keeping sensitive client information out of the clients' official records. Because psychotherapy notes require separate client authorization, insurers who need records for their routine business functions and other third parties, such as business associates, are not entitled to see the psychotherapy notes when they review the client's official record.

However, HIPAA's inclusion of the concept of psychotherapy notes may add confusion for practitioners who work in states that *do* have laws defining personal notes. Psychotherapy notes under HIPAA are not the same as personal notes under state laws. Legal definitions determine what information is covered and protected under the respective laws. If practitioners and their agencies are covered entities under HIPAA, they will need to examine both HIPAA and state law. They must make a determination as to whether HIPAA's psychotherapy notes provisions are more stringent than the state's personal notes definition and which law prevails. There are several areas where the laws may conflict. These include: with whom notes can be shared, what types of information fall under the definitions of psychotherapy notes or personal notes, whether clients can view notes about them without jeopardizing their status as personal notes, and whether the client needs or is lawfully able to consent to the release of the notes. Clearly, practitioners cannot be expected to make this determination without help. In trying to resolve these complexities, practitioners should seek assistance from attorneys who are knowledgeable about the release of confidential information; supervisors and consultants; agency policies; and their professional associations, such as the National Association of Social Workers.

PRIVILEGE

As mentioned earlier in the discussion about responding to subpoenas, under some conditions, social workers may be able to claim a privilege against disclosing client information in a deposition or in the courtroom. A privilege, also known as "testimonial privilege," allows a person who has information regarding a case not to disclose it in judicial or administrative proceedings. Generally, when a privilege exists, information that would otherwise be relevant and valuable as evidence is unavailable for use in legal proceedings.

Privileges are created when a relationship between two individuals is deemed worthy of special legal protection, more than normally exists in the adversarial system of justice. The American justice system is based on the notion of two sides, which are adversaries, each using witnesses and supporting documentation to bring up all of the relevant facts that bolster their position in a case and that discredit that of their opponent. The judge or jury's job is to sort through all of the facts to reach a decision that reflects the truth. Even though the privileged information would prove helpful to a judge or jury to consider, the privileged relationship is protected at the expense of the evidentiary value of the information. In general, because privileges prevent relevant information from being revealed, they are generally disfavored in the law.

The concept of confidentiality is different than the notion of privilege. Confidentiality is an ethical duty that social workers possess because of their adherence to the NASW Code of Ethics or other ethical codes. Confidentiality also may become a legal duty when legislatures write into laws that certain types of professionals must protect their clients' information. For example, HIPAA creates a legal duty to maintain the confidentiality of protected health information. Social workers and other practitioners' have ethical and legal obligations to maintain the confidentiality of client information. These obligations exist independently of any privilege they may have.

Alternatively, privilege is a legal concept that pertains to disclosing information in court. When a judge acknowledges that a professional has a privilege, or stands in a privileged relationship to another person, the privilege keeps the testimony from coming into evidence in courtrooms, or in the proceedings that precede them, such as depositions. Privilege allows practitioners to keep confidential information from being revealed publicly in a legal proceeding.

Privileges are created in a number of ways. In some circumstances, legislatures enact a statutory privilege for certain relationships. For example, a legislature may pass a law that grants privilege to rape crisis counselors so that they do not have to testify about what rape victims tell them. Judges can also create privileges. For example, a judge may determine that a domestic violence counselor stands in a privileged relationship with an abused woman. By recognizing a privilege, the domestic violence counselor will not have to reveal what the woman told her.

Legislatures and courts have various ways to determine whether a privilege should be recognized between individuals. One common method to determine whether a privileged relationship should be recognized is by applying the criteria developed by Wigmore, a legal scholar. Wigmore posited the following principles to consider when determining whether a privilege should be established.

(1) The communications must originate in a confidence that they will not be disclosed.

(2) The element of confidentiality must be essential to the full and satisfactory maintenance of the relation between parties.

(3) The relation must be one which in the opinion of the community ought to be sedulously fostered.

(4) The injury that would inure to the relation by the disclosure of the communications must be greater than the benefit thereby gained for the correct disposal of litigation. (Wigmore, 1961)

Wigmore's criteria examines the relationship between certain individuals, whether the communications between them originated in an atmosphere where confidentiality is expected, whether confidentiality is essential to the maintenance of the relationship, the value that society places on the relationship, and its need for confidentiality.

All states recognize privileged relationships between certain categories of individuals. The most commonly recognized privileged relationships are between attorneys and their clients, doctors and their patients, clergy members of all faiths and their parishioners, and husbands and wives. In all of these relationships, the privilege reflects societal views that confidentiality between these parties is so important to the public good that protecting the relationship is elevated over the need for evidence in court.

During the 1970s, the U.S. Supreme Court submitted proposed rules for privileged communications in federal court cases. The Court proposed nine categories of privileged communications that it believed Congress should establish, including those between doctors-patients, spouses, clergy-parishioners, and psychotherapists-clients. The proposed psychotherapist-patient privilege only included physicians and psychologists engaged in the diagnosis or treatment of mental or emotional conditions, including drug addiction. Social workers and other mental health professionals were excluded from the proposed privilege. Ultimately, Congress did not adopt any of the Supreme Court's suggested privileges. Instead, it substituted a general rule of evidence (Rule 501 of the Federal Rules of Evidence) that instructs courts to determine on a case-by-case basis whether a privilege exists.

In 1996, the U.S. Supreme Court decided the case of *Jaffee v. Redmond*. The question before the Supreme Court was whether a psychotherapist-patient privilege should be recognized under Rule 501, and if so, should the privilege also be extended to social workers. In *Jaffee v. Redmond*, an Illinois police officer (Redmond) was involved in a shooting that resulted in the death of an individual, Ricky Allen. The police officer sought counseling from a licensed clinical social worker, Karen Beyer, who saw Redmond for 50 sessions. Allen's family (Jaffee) sued Redmond, the police department, and the village (the defendants) in federal court, claiming that Redmond used excessive force in the shooting. They sought access to the notes of the counseling sessions Beyer had with Redmond for use in cross-examining Redmond.

Beyer received subpoenas for her records and was ordered by the court to disclose their contents. Both in depositions and at trial, Beyer refused to comply with the court's orders. Beyer's refusal to comply with the judge's orders was based on her ethical beliefs. Additionally, she believed that the psychotherapist-patient privilege should apply to her relationship with Redmond. If her relationship was deemed privileged, she would not be required to release the contents of her records. At the trial, the judge instructed the jury that Beyer had no lawful justification to refuse to disclose the information contained in her notes and that they could presume that the notes contained information unfavorable to Redmond. The trial judge based his ruling on the fact that the rules of privilege, as they had been initially proposed, did not include social workers in the psychotherapist-patient privilege. While the judge believed that a psychotherapist-patient privilege might exist for psychiatrists and psychologists, he did not believe social workers to be included. The jury ruled in favor of the Jaffee family.

The defendants appealed to a federal appellate court. Unlike the trial judge, the appellate court recognized a psychotherapist-patient privilege and its application to social workers. In reaching its decision, the appellate court looked to state law. It attached particular significance to the fact that Illinois' legislation expressly recognized a privileged relationship between social workers and their clients.

The Jaffee family then appealed the case to the U.S. Supreme Court. The Court agreed to decide the case, in part because there was a lack of uniformity in federal courts about the existence of a psychotherapist-patient privilege and to which professionals it should apply. The Court stated that the question it would decide was "whether a privilege protecting confidential communications between a psychotherapist and her patient promotes sufficiently important interests to outweigh the need for probative evidence" (*Jaffee v. Redmond*, at 9–10).

In its decision, the U.S. Supreme Court acknowledged the importance of maintaining confidentiality in a therapeutic relationship and the harm to the relationship if sensitive information were disclosed. The majority wrote:

> Effective psychotherapy, by contrast, depends upon an atmosphere of confidence and trust in which the patient is willing to make a frank and complete disclosure of facts, emotions, memories, and fears. Because of the sensitive nature of the problems for which individuals consult psychotherapists, disclosure of confidential communications made during counseling sessions may cause embarrassment or disgrace. For this reason, the mere possibility of disclosure may impede development of the confidential relationship necessary for successful treatment. (at 10)

The Court found that a "psychotherapist-patient privilege will serve a 'public good transcending the normally predominant principle of utilizing all rational means for ascertaining truth,'" and ruled that "confidential communications between a licensed psychotherapist and her patients in the course of diagnosis or treatment are protected from compelled disclosure" under federal law (at 15).

The majority of the justices concluded that the federal privilege should also extend to confidential communications made to licensed social workers in the course of psychotherapy. It noted that social workers provide a significant amount of mental health services to the poor and those of modest means who could not afford the assistance of psychiatrists and psychologists. Since the goals of the counseling sessions serve the same public purpose, the Court stated that the reasons for recognizing a privilege for treatment by psychiatrists and psychologists apply equally to treatment by social workers. Therefore, the Court ruled that the conversations between the police officer and the social worker, and the notes taken during those counseling sessions, were protected from compelled disclosure in court.

Jaffee v. Redmond is extremely important to the social work profession because it established a psychotherapist-patient privilege in federal court that applies equally to social workers, psychologists, and psychiatrists. When courts uphold the psychotherapist-patient privilege, social workers who provide counseling or treatment will not be forced to disclose information contained in their clients' records during trials and the proceedings that occur prior to court, such as depositions. Of course, for the privilege to apply, the social worker, psychologist, or psychiatrist must be licensed in their respective professions.

The psychotherapist-patient privilege established in the *Jaffee* case only applies to lawsuits that occur in the federal court system. When social work clients become involved in lawsuits that have a basis in federal laws or regulations, social workers can assert the psychotherapist-patient privilege so that client records and the information contained within them will not be disclosed. Examples of the types of cases that would be brought under federal law are cases that pertain to constitutional issues; discrimination based on disabilities, gender, race, religion, or age; problems in the employment, housing, and education settings; and the denial of benefits under federal programs such as Social Security or Veterans Affairs.

In state court cases, the *Jaffee* psychotherapist-privilege does not apply. When social work clients become involved in lawsuits that have a basis in state laws or regulations, state law applies. Examples of the types of cases that would be brought under state law include issues related to divorce, child custody, abuse and neglect, criminal and juvenile justice matters, domestic violence, guardianship, and mental health commitment. Almost all states offer some form of privileged communications to social workers, although the scope of the privilege varies. Social workers must learn the law in their respective states regarding the extent of the social work privilege.

Social workers are cautioned not to overrely on the fact that *Jaffee* or state law recognizes a privilege that protects their records and the information contained within them from disclosure in court proceedings. Even when professionals have privileged communication that is recognized by federal or state law, there are exceptions in which privilege does not apply. Often, these exceptions are outlined in the legislation that creates the privilege or are crafted by judges in response to specific situations where the practitioners' testimony is desired.

For example, social workers usually cannot claim privilege in cases where the law requires them to take action to protect clients and others. In cases of child abuse and neglect, when civil commitment is sought, or when warnings must be given to protect others, practitioners may not be able to claim privilege. Additionally, practitioners may be asked by the court to examine individuals and provide the court with their opinions about certain important issues in a case. For example, practitioners may examine individuals' psychological status, their competence to stand trial, or their suitability to return to employment. Practitioners may also be asked to determine which parent would be the better custodian, whether an individual is in need of a guardian, or whether an individual requires psychiatric hospitalization. In these situations, privileged relationships are not recognized because the professionals do not have an ongoing therapeutic relationship with the individuals and their services are provided for the benefit of the court. In these situations, social workers should advise the individuals that the information they provide will be reported back to the court so that the individuals do not mistakenly believe that what they say will be kept in confidence.

In other situations, judges may simply overrule any privilege practitioners may have. Judges may do this when they feel that the need for the information outweighs the benefits bestowed by the privilege. In a child custody case, for example, a judge may decide that the best interests of a child cannot be determined without access to all of the information in a case. The social worker in the case, whose records contain information about a parent's mental health, drug use, or other problems, might find that the records will be ordered disclosed, despite a privilege. When judges do not recognize their privilege, social workers must decide whether they will resist disclosure and face contempt proceedings or comply with the judges' demand for the information.

Judges may also determine that clients have waived their privilege. Waiver means that the client has voluntarily relinquished his or her right to have certain material treated as privileged. Courts may find that clients waive their privilege when they claim that someone's conduct has psychologically harmed them. For example, a client sues her employer for sexual harassment, claiming that the harassment caused her to suffer serious emotional harm for which she sought treatment from a social worker. Most courts would rule that the client waived the social work privilege because the client placed her mental state at issue in the lawsuit. By suing for compensation for the emotional harm she experienced as a result of sexual harassment, the client could not claim that she was injured without also allowing the content of her disclosures to the social worker to be used as evidence. For the same reason, clients are also deemed to have waived privilege when they sue their therapists.

RESPONSES TO REQUESTS FOR RECORDS

As can be seen, the receipt of a subpoena raises many complex issues. Practitioners must determine how they will respond to the subpoena, what information is being sought, whether the requested information is in records or personal notes, and whether privilege applies. Practitioners must also remember their ethical obligations to protect client privacy in addition to any legal requirements the law may impose. All of these issues are complicated by intricate state and federal laws.

Most social workers will need help in navigating the complexities involved with the receipt of a subpoena. Practitioners should become aware of the requirements of federal and state laws in their fields of practice and always act to protect clients' privacy. Because of the intricacies of the laws, social workers should consult with attorneys, supervisors, agency policies and procedures, and other consultants to determine the best way to deal with the receipt of a subpoena. In determining the proper way to respond, social workers should:

- remember that there is an ethical duty to protect clients' records and communications;
- consult with an attorney, supervisor, agency policies and procedures, and consultants to determine the best response;
- determine what the subpoena is asking for (testimony and/or records);
- seek the client's authorization for the disclosure of information;
- take steps to protect the client's information (such as waiting until ordered to testify, or seeking protective orders or motions to quash) absent client authorization;
- make sure that disclosure is limited to the minimum information necessary;
- ensure that personal notes are not included in the records; and
- assert a social worker-client privilege, if applicable.

RETENTION OF RECORDS

Social workers and the organizations they work for often wonder how long they are legally required to retain client records once services to clients have been terminated. On the one hand, maintaining client records indefinitely undermines confidentiality; the mere existence of the records brings with it the potential for unwarranted access. Additionally, storage problems, such as space, cost, and security, may influence the decision about how long records should be kept (see chapter 7). On the other hand, many practitioners, agencies, and departments would prefer to keep the records of their closed cases indefinitely, so that the client's history is available should the client later return for services. They may also like to review historical documentation of the services rendered and how the client-need-situations were resolved. Agencies may create policies and procedures that instruct their employees regarding how long the agency expects records to be retained. Practitioners may also look to their ethical codes and federal and state law to determine any record retention requirements.

The NASW (1999) Code of Ethics offers limited guidance as to the length of time records should be maintained. While the Code advises practitioners to store records following the termination of services to ensure reasonable future access, it does not specify the amount of time social work records should be retained, and instead defers to state law. The Code provides that "records should be maintained for the number of years required by state statutes or relevant contracts" (3.04[d]) and directs social workers to maintain their records according to the laws of the states in which they practice.

LEGISLATION AND RECORD RETENTION

None of the federal legislation discussed in chapter 8 contains provisions regarding how long records must be retained. Under HIPAA, covered entities must be able to provide individuals with an accounting of disclosures of PHI. HIPAA requires covered entities to maintain information about when and to whom they disclosed PHI for six years. However, HIPAA does not prescribe a time period for retention of PHI.

State law is the best source for practitioners to discover any record retention requirements. In some states, laws or regulations require social workers to retain records for a certain period of time. For example, Florida law requires that designated health care professionals maintain written records regarding their clients. Florida's regulations further specify that licensed clinical social workers, along with marriage and family therapists and mental health counselors, must maintain client records for seven years after the last contact with the client. In other states, social workers are listed among health care professionals who must maintain records for a set period. For example, in Maryland, health care providers, which include social workers, may not destroy medical records, including mental health records, for five years after the record was made. In Maryland, if the patient is a minor, the record cannot be destroyed until three years after the patient attains the age of majority.

In still other states, laws or regulations specify how long social workers must retain certain categories of records. For example, Colorado requires social workers or their agencies to retain records on each of their social work/psychotherapy clients for up to 10 years following termination of services. Colorado divides client records into two distinct categories—full records and summary records. Full client records (including identifying information; reason for the social work/psychotherapy services; date of each client contact; information on all referrals; name, date, and administrator of any tests administered; information on all mandated reports made; and fee information) are to be kept for five years after termination. Summary records (including client identifying information as well as the name of the social worker; reasons for the social work/psychotherapy services; and the dates of the first and last contact with the client) must be retained until five years after the expiration of the full record retention period.

When states have laws on record retention, they can be found within social work licensing statutes or regulations, medical records statutes, or hospital recordkeeping laws ("Social Workers and Record Retention Requirements," 2005). However, as of 2005, only 19 states had record retention provisions that offer social workers guidance on how long to retain records ("Social Workers and Record Retention Requirements," 2005). Unfortunately, in the majority of states, no explicit guidance is available. Social workers must look to other sources for direction as to how long they should retain their records. In these situations, social workers may want to consult their attorneys, determine whether agency policy covers record retention, check with experienced social work practitioners, see how allied professionals handle retention, or seek guidance from professional organizations to determine how long they should retain records. Professional liability carriers that provide malpractice insurance for social workers may also provide guidance or have requirements regarding record retention.

LAWSUITS AND RECORD RETENTION

The decision regarding how long client records should be retained is complicated by their potential use in lawsuits in which the services provided by the social worker are relevant to the case. As discussed earlier, social work clients may become involved in court proceedings. These lawsuits may pertain to events in their own lives or in the lives of others. Clients also may bring suit against the social worker and the agency.

Social workers and their agencies may require records to document the quality of services, efforts expended by the worker, decisions regarding services offered and their alternatives, as well as statements made by clients and third parties. Records may be crucial factors in the resolution of a lawsuit. Whether to provide information in cases involving clients or to defend the actions of workers or agencies, social workers and their organizations should retain client records at least as long as the potential for litigation exists as determined by law.

Statutes of Limitation

The law places a limit on how long a person has to file a lawsuit against those who they feel have wronged them. Statutes of limitation are laws that set forth the maximum amount of time that is permitted for the initial filing of a case. If a case is not filed within the proper period, the case will be dismissed. Statutes of limitation are based on the notion of fairness. Over time, since a person's memories can fade or evidence can be lost, it becomes more difficult to prosecute or defend a case. Also, individuals should be able to predict with some certainty that, at a future point, they can no longer be sued for their actions. Therefore, to resolve issues fairly, limitations are placed on when litigation can be initiated.

Statutes of limitation vary between states. Legislatures determine what they believe to be an appropriate statute of limitations period in various situations. For example, Hawaii provides litigants a six-year statute of limitation for breach of contract, while Ohio has a 15-year limitation on such actions ("Social Workers and Record Retention Requirements," 2005). In Louisiana, malpractice suits must be filed within one year whereas Minnesota allows a four-year limitation period.

Statutes of limitation also vary within a state, based on the type of case that is filed. There are a multitude of legal theories that serve as justification for lawsuits. Claims based on property and commercial transactions tend to have longer statute of limitation periods than do personal injury actions such as malpractice, negligence, libel, slander, defamation of character, invasion of privacy, or false imprisonment.

When lawsuits are brought against practitioners, they are likely to be based on a breach of contract or personal injury claim. Even these claims have different statute of limitation periods. For example, in Kentucky, contract cases must be initiated within 15 years, whereas malpractice cases have a one year statute of limitation. In Indiana, contract cases must be initiated within 10 years whereas malpractice cases must be filed within two years. In both Alabama and New Hampshire, actions against health care providers, whether based on contract or malpractice issues, must be filed within two years ("Social Workers and Record Retention Requirements," 2005).

Social workers should retain their records for the longest applicable statute of limitation period in their state. They should be aware that lawyers may craft lawsuits based upon any legal theory that is available to them. If the statute of limitations for one legal theory has expired, lawyers will select another legal theory for which the statute of limitations has not expired.

Consider this example:

> A female social worker sees a husband and wife for marital counseling to improve their communication and their marriage. During one of the counseling sessions, the wife unfairly accuses the social worker of being in love with her husband and having a sexual relationship with him. The social worker rightfully denies the accusations and refocuses the wife on how her jealousy impacts her marriage. A few months later, the husband files for divorce.

> After the divorce, the wife decides to sue the social worker and the agency for "causing" her divorce. She discusses with her attorney her desire to sue the social worker for her "unethical"

actions. The wife's attorney will choose among the legal theories, conscious of the statute of limitation periods in the state. Depending on the state and the time that has passed since the wife decided to take legal action, the attorney will choose the bases for the lawsuit. If the wife lives in Wyoming, for example, she can only file her lawsuit for malpractice (the social worker breached her duty of appropriate care) within two years. However, if the wife uses breach of contract as the basis for her claim (the social worker did not provide marital therapy as contracted), she has 10 years in which to sue the social worker. To defend against such a lawsuit, the social worker and her agency are advised to keep the records for at least 10 years following termination of services in case the longer of Wyoming's statute of limitation periods applies.

Tolling of Statutes of Limitations

Additionally, statutes of limitation are often "tolled" under specified circumstances. Tolling stops the time clock for filing a lawsuit. Generally speaking, statutes of limitation are tolled when people have certain characteristics that interfere with their ability to file lawsuits. For example, as noted in chapter 8, children under the age of majority and adults who have conditions such as dementia, mental retardation, or mental illness may have their statutes of limitation tolled because they are incompetent under the law. In some states, individuals who are on active military duty or are imprisoned will also have their statute of limitation periods tolled.

In these situations, the statutes of limitation are tolled for the period during which that individual is viewed as disabled under the law. Legislatures often provide additional periods of time for these individuals to file their lawsuits once they are no longer considered to be under a legal disability. For example, when children reach adulthood, they have an additional time period, such as two years, to file their lawsuits. A person who has been institutionalized because of a mental illness may have the statute of limitation period extended by the length of the hospitalization.

Other individuals, for example, those with severe retardation or dementia, may be viewed as permanently disabled under the law. For these individuals, the statute of limitation period may never expire and lawsuits can always be filed. For example, Hawaii law states that, when there are two or more disabilities existing at the same time, statutes of limitation do not begin to run until all of the disabilities are removed (Hawaii Revised Statutes, 2006, § 657-15). If a client were a child and had profound retardation, statutes of limitation would never attach. While the child would eventually reach adulthood, the profound retardation would still exist, the disability would continue, and lawsuits could always be filed.

Many of the clients for whom social workers provide services may have the statute of limitation periods tolled because they are "disabled" under the law. Indeed, some individuals, because of their disabilities, may never have the limitations period tolled. That means that they, or someone acting on their behalf, could file lawsuits at any time during their lives. Social workers who work with people who are considered disabled under the law are advised to retain their records beyond any relevant statute of limitation period. Since there is no limitation on when such lawsuits could be filed, their records need to be available indefinitely.

EXPUNGEMENT OF RECORDS

Social workers create records that are used to document the services they provide with and on behalf of clients. These records are often transferred or released to other organizations. Social work records may also become part of court files through clients' voluntary submissions, court-ordered examinations or services, or as a result of subpoenas. When social workers testify or their records are entered into testimony, this information also becomes part of the court record.

The expungement and sealing of court records removes certain records from being publicly available. These terms are sometimes used interchangeably, but involve different procedures. Expungement deletes a court record through its physical destruction—the expunged record no longer exists. In contrast, when court records are sealed, the physical documents still exist, although access to them is limited to specific users, such as judges, prosecutors, and law enforcement personnel.

Individuals who have criminal records but no longer engage in criminal behavior may wish to expunge their records. They may find that having a criminal history causes them to be subject to discrimination based on their past behavior. They may be unable to secure employment as well as be ineligible to receive public benefits like food stamps and TANF. In other situations, immigrants who have criminal arrest records may be subject to deportation from the United States. Because of the severe consequences, most states have passed legislation that allows individuals to expunge their criminal court records. Typically, expungement can be sought when specified time periods have elapsed and the individuals have maintained clean criminal records.

For example, Ohio provides for the expungement of the arrest records of first-time offenders. In many states, such as New Jersey, people can petition to have their criminal convictions expunged after a certain period of time without further convictions. Minnesota allows people who were arrested but not convicted to have their records returned to them. Colorado and many other states allow individuals to clear their juvenile delinquency records once they are adults and have not committed additional criminal acts.

The expungement of records may also occur in other types of court cases. In adoption cases, for example, many states seal the court proceedings that contain the original birth certificate, agency reports, and other documents to make them unavailable to the public, including the adoptee. To gain access to the court records once they are sealed, individuals have to petition the court and prove that they have good cause to unseal the records, such as for a medical emergency.

Records that are held by public social service agencies or public institutions may also be expunged. For example, in Massachusetts, as in some other states, public assistance records are to be destroyed 10 years after the termination of service to the client. In schools, records of children's names, addresses, and phone numbers, grades, attendance records, classes attended, grade level completed, and year completed are kept indefinitely. However, records that contain information of a more personal nature, such as medical, disciplinary, or special education files may be expunged after a specific period of time. In some states, before they are destroyed, the records are offered to the parents for their future use.

In 38 states and certain U.S. territories, laws or regulations provide for the expungement of the records held by public agencies that investigate child abuse and neglect ("Review and Expunction," 2005). In most states, unsubstantiated reports of child abuse/neglect can be expunged from the central database; the time frames for expungement range from immediately upon determination to up to 10 years. In a few states, cases that are investigated but not substantiated are never permitted to be placed in the central registry database.

Typically, substantiated reports of child abuse and neglect cannot be expunged for 5–10 years from the time of substantiation ("Review and Expunction," 2005). In situations where the abuse or neglect was especially heinous, such as where the death of a child results, records may be retained for much longer without being expunged. For example, in Illinois, when children have died or have been sexually penetrated, reports must be maintained for 50 years. Before they can be expunged, records of other serious physical injuries, sexual molestation, or sexual exploitation must be retained for 20 years after the abuse is substantiated.

BIBLIOGRAPHY

Abel, C., & Johnson, W. (1978). Clients' access to records: Policy and attitudes. *Social Work, 23*(1), 42–46.

Addison, L. (1985, November). Mental health information: Shrinking plaintiffs' privilege. *Texas Bar Journal,* 1222–1224.

Adler, R. A. (1992). Step-by-step guide to using the Freedom of Information Act. American Civil Liberties Union Foundation. Retrieved July 18, 2007, from http://www.skepticfiles.org/aclu/foia.htm

Albert, S., Simone, B., Brassard, A., Stern, Y., & Mayeux, R. (2005). Medicaid home health services and survival in New York. *The Gerontologist, 45*(5), 609–616.

Alexander, M., Siegel, C., & Murtaugh, C. (1985). Automating the psychiatric record for care review purposes: A feasibility analysis. *Computers in Human Services, 1*(4), 1–16.

American Hospital Association. (1978). *A reporting system for hospital social work.* Chicago: Author.

American Medical Association. (1978, March 23). Statement presented to Hon. Herman E. Talmadge, regarding Privacy Protection Study Commission and recommendations thereon of the Department of Health, Education and Welfare. Washington, DC.

American Psychiatric Association. (2000). *Diagnostic and statistical manual of mental disorders (DSM-IV-TR)* (4th ed., Text Rev.). Washington, DC: Author.

Ames, N. (1999). Social work recording: A new look at an old issue. *Journal of Social Work Education, 35*(2), 227–337.

Annotated Code of Maryland, Health-General Article, § 4-301 *et seq.* (2006).

Applying computers in social service and mental health agencies: A guide to selecting equipment, procedures, and strategies. (1981). *Administration in Social Work,* 5(314).

Aptekar, H. (1960). Record writing for the purposes of supervision. *Child Welfare, 39*(2), 16–21.

Arizona Revised Statutes, Public Health Safety, § 36-501(40) (2007).

Austad, C. S., & Berman, W. H. (Eds.). (1991). *Psychotherapy in managed health care: The optimal use of time and resources.* Washington, DC: American Psychological Association.

Backdoors. (2006). Retrieved March 23, 2006, from http://www.2–spyware.com/backdoors-removal.

Baird, B. N. (1996). *The internship, practicum, and field placement handbook: A guide for the helping professions.* Upper Saddle River, NJ: Prentice Hall.

Barbeau, E. J., & Lohmann, R. A. (1992). The agency executive director as keeper of the past. *Administration in Social Work, 16*(2), 15–26.

Barker, R. (1986). Spelling out the rules and goals: The written worker-client contract. *Journal of Independent Social Work, 1*(2), 43–49.

Barker, R. (1987). To record or not to record: That is the question. *Journal of Independent Social Work, 2*(2), 1–5.

Beck, A., Kovacs, M., & Weissman, A. (1979). Assessment of suicidal intention: A scale for suicide ideation. *Journal of Consulting and Clinical Psychology, 47,* 343–352.

Beinecke, R. (1984). PORK, SOAP, STRAP, and SAP. *Social Casework, 65*(10), 554–558.

Bell, C. (1978). *Accessibility of adoption records: Influences on agency policy.* Ann Arbor, MI: University Microfilms.

Bernstein, B. E. (1977). Privileged communications to the social worker. *Social Work, 22*(4), 264–268.

Bloom, M., & Fischer, J. (1982). *Evaluating practice: Guidelines for the accounting professional.* Englewood Cliffs, NJ: Prentice-Hall.

Blount, A. (1985). Mental health center approach. In D. Campbell & R. Draper (Eds.), *Applications of systemic family therapy.* Orlando: Grune & Stratton.

Bongar, B. (2001). *The suicidal patient: Clinical and legal standards of care* (2nd ed.). Washington, DC: American Psychological Association.

Bonney, N., & Streicher, L. (1970). Time-cost data in agency administration. *Social Work, 15*(4), 23–31.

Bork, K. (1953). A staff examination of recording skill (Parts 1 & 2). *Child Welfare, 32*(2), 3–8; (3), 11–14.

Boyd, L., & Hylton, J. (1978). Computers in social work practice: A review. *Social Work, 23*(5), 368–371.

Bristol, M. C. (1936). *Handbook on social case recording.* Chicago: University of Chicago Press.

Brodsky, S. (1972). Shared results and open files with the client. *Professional Psychology, 3*(4), 362–364.

Browning, C. H., & Browning, B. J. (1996). *How to partner with managed care.* Los Alamitos, CA: Duncliff's International.

Bunston, T. (1985). Mapping practice: Problem solving in clinical social work. *Social Casework, 59*(4), 225–236.

Burgess, E. W. (1928). What social case records should contain to be useful for sociological interpretation. *Social Forces, 6*(4), 524–532.

Callahan, J. (1996). Documentation of client dangerousness in a managed care environment. *Health & Social Work, 21*(3), 202–207.

Camenga, M. (1974). *A guide to record keeping and social services: A system for child development programs.* Atlanta: Humanics Press.

Campbell, D., & Stanley, J. (1963). *Experimental and quasi-experimental designs for research.* Chicago: Rand McNally.

Cancian, M., Haveman, R., Meyer, D., & Wolfe, B. (2002). Before and after TANF: The economic well-being of women leaving welfare. *Social Service Review, 76*(4), 603–641.

Cassetty, J., & Hutson, R. (2005). Effectiveness of federal incentives in shaping child support enforcement outcomes. *Children & Youth Services Review, 27*(3), 271–289.

Cerveny, K., & Kent, M. (1983–1984). Evidence law: The psychotherapist-patient privilege in federal courts. *Notre Dame Law Review, 59,* 791–816.

Chambliss, C., Pinto, D., & McGuigan, J. (1997). Reactions to managed care among psychologists and social workers. *Psychological Reports, 80,* 147–154.

Child Abuse and Neglect Prevention and Treatment, 45 C.F.R. § 1340.14 (2007).

Child Abuse Prevention and Treatment Act, P.L. 93-247 (1974).

Children and Family Research Center. (2001). *Report on child safety and permanency in Illinois for FY 2001.* Urbana: School of Social Work, University of Illinois at Urbana-Champaign.

Children's Online Privacy Protection Act of 1998, 15 U.S.C. § 6501 (2000).

Christian, W., & Hannah, G. (1983). *Effective management in human services.* Englewood Cliffs, NJ: Prentice-Hall.

Clemens, N. A. (2006). Until death do us part. *Journal of Psychiatric Practice, 12*(2), 113–115.

Cohen, M., & Garrett, K. (1995). Helping field instructors become more effective group work educators. *Social Work with Groups, 18*(2/3), 135–145.

Colliver, V. (2006, March 24). Digital records crusader: SF doctor promotes electronic health data. *San Francisco Chronicle,* p. D-1.

Committee on Government Reform. (2005, September 15). *A citizen's guide on using the Freedom of Information Act and the Privacy Act of 1974 to request government records* (Report 109–226). Washington, DC: U.S. Government Printing Office. Retrieved July 18, 2007, from http://www.fas.org/sgp/foia/citizen.pdf

Comprehensive Alcohol Abuse and Alcoholism Prevention, Treatment and Rehabilitation Act of 1970, 60 U.S.C. § 4541 (1970).

Confidentiality of Alcohol and Drug Abuse Patient Records, 42 C.F.R. § 2.1 *et seq.* (2007).

Confidentiality of health and social service records: Where law, ethics, and clinical issues meet. (1976, December). Proceedings of the Second Midwest Regional Conference, Chicago, IL.

Corcoran, K., & Gingerich, W. (1992). Practice evaluation: Setting goals, measuring and assessing change. In K. Corcoran (Ed.), *Structuring change: Effective clinical practice for common client problems* (pp. 28–47). Chicago: Lyceum.

Courtney, M. E., & Barth, R. (1996). Pathways of older adolescents out of foster care: Implications for independent living. *Social Work, 41*(1), 75–83.

Daugherty, J. (2005, February 22). E-mail gaffe reveals HIV, AIDS names. *Palm Beach Post.*

Davidson, H. (n.d.). The impact of HIPAA on child abuse and neglect cases. Retrieved July 18, 2007, from http://www.familyrightsassociation.com/bin/white_papers-articles/impact_of_hipaa_on_child_abuse.htm

Davis, K. (2001). The intersection of fee for service, managed health care and cultural competence. In N. Veeder & W. Peebles-Wilkins (Eds.), *Managed care services: Policies, programs, and research* (pp. 50–73). New York: Oxford University Press.

Death with Dignity Act, Oregon Revised Statutes, 127.800 *et seq.* (2006).

Delgado, R. (1973). Underprivileged communications: Extension of the psychotherapist-patient privilege to patients of psychiatric social workers. *California Law Review, 61,* 1050–1071.

Demlo, L., Campbell, P., & Brown, S. (1978). Reliability of information abstracted from patients' medical records. *Medical Care, 16*(12), 995–1005.

District of Columbia Mental Health Information Act, § 7-1201.01(13) (2007).

Driver's Privacy Protection Act, 18 U.S.C. § 2721 (1994).

Drug Abuse Prevention, Treatment and Rehabilitation Act of 1972, 21 U.S.C. §1101 (1972).

Dwyer, M., & Urbanowski, M. (1965). Student process recording: A plea for structure. *Social Casework, 46*(5), 283–286.

Education for All Handicapped Children Act of 1975, P.L. 94-142 (1975).

Edwards, R., & Reid, W. (1989). Structured case recording in child welfare: An assessment of social workers' reactions. *Social Work, 34*(1), 49–52.

Electronic Communications Privacy Act of 1986, 18 U.S.C. §2510 (1986).

Eliot, T. (1928). Objectivity and subjectivity in the case record. *Social Forces, 6*(4), 539–544.

Employee Polygraph Protection Act of 1988, 29 U.S.C. § 2900 (1988).

English, D., Brandford, C., & Coghlan, L. (2000). Data-based organizational change: The use of administrative data to improve child welfare programs and policy. *Child Welfare, 29*(5), 499–515.

Fair Credit Reporting Act, 15 U.S.C. § 1681 (1970).

Family Educational Rights and Privacy Act, 20 U.S.C. § 1232g (1974).

Family Educational Rights and Privacy Act, 34 C.F.R.§ 99.3 *et seq.* (2007).

Family Service Association of America Task Force on Privacy and Confidentiality. (1977). *Position paper on privacy and confidentiality.* New York: Family Service Association of America.

Fanshel, D. (1975). Parental visiting of foster children: A computerized study. *Social Work Research and Abstracts, 13*(3), 2–10.

Fein, E. (1975). A data system for an agency. *Social Work, 20*(1), 21–24.

Feinstein, A. (1973). The problems of the problem-oriented medical record. *Annals of Internal Medicine, 78*, 751–762.

Firestein, S. K. (1993). On thinking the unthinkable: Making a professional will. *The American Psychoanalyst, 27*(4), 16.

Fisher, C. (1972). Paradigm changes which allow sharing of results. *Professional Psychology, 3*(4), 364–369.

Foster, L. (1980). State confidentiality laws: The Illinois act as model for new legislation in other states. *American Journal of Orthopsychiatry, 50*(4), 659–665.

Fox, R., & Gutheil, I. A. (2000). Process recording: A means for conceptualizing and evaluating practice. *Journal of Teaching in Social Work, 20*(1/2), 39–55.

Freed, A. (1978). Clients' rights and casework records. *Social Casework, 59*(8), 458–464.

Freedom of Information Act, 5 U.S.C. § 552 (1966).

Frings, J., Kratovil, R., & Polemis, B. (1958). *An assessment of social case recording.* New York: Family Service Association of America.

Furlong, A. (2006, July 11). The national provider identifier: What every dentist should know. *The American Dental Association News.* Retrieved July 18, 2007, from http://www.ada.org/prof/resources/pubs/adanews/adanewsarticle.asp?articleid=2009

Gambrill, E. (1999). Evidence-based practice: An alternative to authority-based practice. *Families in Society, 80*(4), 341–350.

Gambrill, E. (2003). Evidence-based practice: Sea change or the emperor's new clothes? *Journal of Social Work Education, 39*, 3–23.

Gansheroff, N., Boszormenyi-Nagy, I., & Matrulla, J. (1980). Clinical and legal issues in the family therapy record. In J. Howells (Ed.), *Advances in family psychiatry.* New York: International Universities Press.

Garfield, G., & Irizarry, C. (1971). The record of service. In W. Schwartz & S. Zalba (Eds.), *The practice of group work.* New York: Columbia University Press.

Garfinkel, H. (1968). *Studies in ethnomethodology* (pp. 186–207). Englewood Cliffs, NJ: Prentice-Hall.

Garnier, P., & Poertner, J. (2000). Using administrative data to assess child safety in out-of-home care. *Child Welfare, 29*(5), 597–613.

Garvin, C. (1981). *Contemporary group work* (pp. 202–205). Englewood Cliffs, NJ: Prentice-Hall.

Gelman, S., Pollack, D., & Weiner, A. (1999). Confidentiality of social work records in the computer age. *Social Work, 44*(3), 243–262.

Giglio, R., Spears, B., Rumpf, D., & Eddy, N. (1978). Encouraging behavior changes by use of the client-held record. *Medical Care, 16*(9), 757–764.

Gingerich, W. (1985). Three software programs from applied innovations for the human services clinician. *Computers in Human Service, 1*(3), 83–91.

Gingerich, W. J., & Broskowski, A. (1996). Clinical decision support systems. In T. Trabin (Ed.), *The computerization of behavioral healthcare* (pp. 11–38). San Francisco: Jossey-Bass.

Gobert, J. (1976, January). Accommodating patient rights and computerized mental health systems. *North Carolina Law Review, 54*, 153–187.

Godwin, P. (1988, August). Could your medical records wreck your life? *Better Homes and Gardens*, 40–42.

Goldman, M. (1964, July). An agency conducts a time and cost study. *Social Casework, 45*(7), 393–397.

Goodman, M., Brown, J., & Deitz, P. (1992). *Managing managed care: A mental health practitioner's survival guide*. Washington: American Psychiatric Press.

Gramm-Leach-Bliley Act, P.L. 106-102, 113 Stat. 1338 (1999).

Gutierrez, O., & Friedman, D. (2005). Managing project expectations in human services information systems implementations: The case of homeless management information systems. *International Journal of Project Management, 23*, 513–523.

Hamilton, G. (1936). *Social case recording*. New York: Columbia University Press.

Hamilton, G. (1946). *Principles of social case recording*. New York: Columbia University Press.

Hartman, A. (1978). Diagrammatic assessment of family relationships. *Social Casework, 59*(8), 465–476.

Hartman, B., & Wickey, J. (1978). The person-oriented record in treatment. *Social Work, 23*(4), 296–299.

Haselkorn, F. (1978). Accountability in clinical practice. *Social Casework, 59*(6), 330–336.

Hawaii Revised Statutes, § 657-15 (2006).

Health Insurance Portability and Accountability Act (HIPAA), P.L. 101-191, 110 Stat. 1936 (1996).

Health Insurance Portability and Accountability Act (HIPAA), 45 C.F.R. Part 160, Part 164 (2007).

Hedlund, J., Vieweg, B., & Cho, D. (1985). Mental health computing in the 1980s. *Computers in Human Services, 1*(1), 3–33; *1*(2), 1–31.

Helms, D. J. (1975). A guide to the new federal rules governing the confidentiality of alcohol and drug abuse patient records. *Contemporary Drug Problems, 4*(3), 259–283.

Henrickson, M., & Mayo, J. R. (2000). The HIV cybermall: A regional cybernetwork of HIV services. *Journal of Technology in Human Services, 17*(1), 7–26.

Henry, D., DeChristopher, J., Dowling, P., & Lapham, E. V. (1981). Using the social history to assess handicapping conditions. *Social Work in Education, 3*(1), 7–19.

Henry, S. (1981). *Group skills in social work*. Itasca, IL: Peacock.

Hepworth, D. H., Rooney, R. H., & Larsen, J. A. (2004). *Direct social work practice: Theory and skills* (7th ed.). Belmont, CA: Wadsworth.

Herzlinger, R. (1977). Why data systems in nonprofit organizations fail. *Harvard Business Review, 55*(1), 81–86.

Hetznecker, W. (1996). Are practice guidelines useful in managed care? In A. Lazarus (Ed.), *Controversies in managed mental health care* (pp. 41–54). Washington, DC: American Psychiatric Press.

Hill, G. (1971). *Ethical practices in the computerization of client data: Implications for social work practice and record keeping.* Washington, DC: National Association of Social Workers.

Hill, J., & Ormsby, R. (1953). The Philadelphia cost study. *Social Work Journal, 34,* 165–178.

Hochwold, H. (1952). The use of case records in research. *Social Casework, 33*(2), 71–76.

Hodge, M. H. (1977). *Medical information systems: A resource for hospitals.* Germantown, MD: Aspen Systems Corporation.

Holbrook, T. (1983, December). Case records: Fact or fiction? *Social Service Review,* 645–658.

Hollis, F. (1967). Explorations in the development of a typology of casework treatment. *Social Casework, 48*(6), 335–341.

Hollis, F., & Wood, M. (1981). *Casework: A psychosocial therapy* (3rd ed.). New York: Columbia University Press.

Hoshino, G., & McDonald, T. (1975). Agencies in the computer age. *Social Work, 20*(1), 10–14.

Houghkirk, E. (1977). Everything you've always wanted your clients to know but have been afraid to tell them. *Journal of Marriage and Family Counseling, 3*(2), 27–33.

Hudson, W. (1982). *The clinical measurement package.* Homewood, IL: Dorsey Press.

Human Research Protection Program, University of California at San Francisco. HIPAA consent form guidance. Retrieved May 31, 2007, from http://www.research.ucsf.edu/chr/HIPAA/chrHIPAAconsent.asp

Hurley, M. (1985). Duties in conflict: Must psychotherapists report child abuse inflicted by clients and confided in therapy? *San Diego Law Review, 22,* 645–668.

Identity Theft and Assumption Deference Act of 1998, 18 U.S.C. § 1028 (1998).

Illinois Department of Children and Family Services. (2003). Health Insurance Portability and Accountability Act. Policy Guide 2003.05. Retrieved November 5, 2006, from http://dcfswebresource.prairienet.org/policy_guides/2003.05.php

Illinois Mental Health and Developmental Disabilities Confidentiality Act, 740 ILCS 110/2 (2007).

Illinois School Student Records Act, 105 ILCS 10/1 *et seq.* (2007).

In re Estate of Bagus, 294 Ill. App. 3d 887; 691 N.E. 2d 401; 229 Ill. Dec. 291 (2nd Dist. 1998).

Individuals with Disabilities Education Improvement Act of 2004, P.L. 108-446, 20 U.S.C. § 1400 *et seq.* (2007).

Itzin, F. (1960). The use of tape recordings in field work. *Social Casework, 41*(4), 197–202.

Ives, K. (1978). Revising an agency's service information system. *Administration in Social Work, 2*(1), 111–115.

Ivey, A. (1987). *Intentional interviewing and counseling.* North Amherst, MA: Microtraining Associates.

Jackson, J. (1987). Clinical social work and peer review: A professional leap ahead. *Social Work, 32*(3), 213–220.

Jaffee v. Redmond, 518 U.S. 1 (1996).

Jayaratne, S., & Levy, R. (1979). *Empirical clinical practice.* New York: Columbia University Press.

Johnson, H. (1978). Integrating the problem-oriented record with a systems approach to case assessment. *Journal of Education for Social Work, 14*(3), 71–77.

Joint Commission on Accreditation of Healthcare Organizations. (2001). *Standards.* Chicago: Author.

Kadushin, A. (1963). Diagnosis and evaluation for (almost) all occasions. *Social Work, 8*(1), 12–19.

Kagle, J. D. (1982a). Social work records in health and mental health organizations: A status report. *Social Work in Health Care, 8*(1), 37–46.

Kagle, J. D. (1982b). Using single subject measures in practice decisions: Systematic documentation or distortion? *Arete, 7*(2), 1–9.

Kagle, J. D. (1983). The contemporary social work record. *Social Work, 28*(2), 149–153.

Kagle, J. D. (1984a). Restoring the clinical record. *Social Work, 29*(1), 46–50.

Kagle, J. D. (1984b). *Social work records.* Homewood, IL: Dorsey Press.

Kagle, J. D. (1987a). Preventing clients from dropping out of treatment. *Journal of Independent Social Work, 1*(3), 31–43.

Kagle, J. D. (1987b). Recording in direct practice. *Encyclopedia of social work* (18th ed., pp. 463–467). Washington, DC: National Association of Social Workers.

Kagle, J. D. (1988). *How to overcome worker resistance and improve your agency's records.* Paper presented at the National Association of Social Workers' Meeting of the Profession, Philadelphia, PA.

Kagle, J. D. (1989). *Privileged communication: A client right and a professional principle.* Paper presented at the annual program meeting of the Council of Social Work Education, Chicago, IL.

Kagle, J. D. (1990). Teaching social work students about privileged communication. *Journal of Teaching in Social Work, 4*(2), 49–65.

Kagle, J. D. (1991). Essential recording: A new approach to teaching practice and recording. *Arete, 16*(2), 28–33.

Kagle, J. D. (1993). Recordkeeping: Directions for the 1990s. *Social Work, 38*(2), 190–196.

Kagle, J. D. (1996). *Social work records* (2nd ed.). Long Grove, IL: Waveland Press.

Kagle, J. D., & Kopels, S. (1994). Confidentiality after Tarasoff. *Health and Social Work, 19*(3), 217–222.

Kaiser, B. (1975). Patients' rights of access to their own medical records: The need for a new law. *Buffalo Law Review, 24*(2), 317–330.

Kane, R. (1974). Look to the record. *Social Work, 19*(4), 412–419.

Karls, J., & Wandrei, K. (1992). P-I-E: A new language for social work. *Social Work, 37*(1), 80–85.

Kaushal, R., Blumenthal, D., Poon, E. G., Ashish, K. J., Franz, C., Middleton, B., Glaser, J., Kuperman, G., Christino, M., Fernandopulle, R., Newhouse, J. P., Bates, D. W., & The Cost of National Health Information Network Working Group. (2005). The costs of a national health information network. *Annals of Internal Medicine, 143*(3), 165–173.

Kelley, V., & Weston, H. (1974). Civil liberties in mental health facilities. *Social Work, 19*(1), 48–54.

Kelley, V., & Weston, H. (1975). Computers, costs, and civil liberties. *Social Work, 20*(1), 15–19.

Kentucky Cabinet for Health and Family Services (KCHFS). (2006). The Health Insurance Portability Act of 1996. Retrieved November 5, 2006, from http://chfs.ky.gov/dcbs/dcc/hipaa.htm

Kiresuk, T., & Garwick, G. (1979). Basic goal attainment procedures. In B. Compton & B. Galaway (Eds.), *Social work processes* (2nd ed.). Homewood, IL: Dorsey Press.

Kiresuk, T., & Sherman, R. (1968). Goal attainment scaling: A general method for evaluating comprehensive mental health programs. *Community Mental Health Journal, 4*, 443–453.

Knapp, S., VandeCreek, L., & Zirkel, P. (1987). Privileged communications for psychotherapists in Pennsylvania: A time for statutory reform. *Temple Law Quarterly, 60*(2), 267–292.

Knox, F. (1965). *The Knox standard guide to design and control of business forms.* New York: McGraw-Hill.

Knox, F. (1981). *Managing paperwork: A key to productivity.* New York: Thomond Press.

Kopels, S., & Kagle, J. D. (1993). Do social workers have a duty to warn? *Social Service Review, 67*(1), 101–126.

Kopels, S., & Manselle, T. (2006). The Supreme Court's pre-emptive strike against patients' rights to sue their HMOs. *Social Work in Health Care, 43*(1), 1–15.

Kraemer, K. L., Dutton, W., & Northrop, A. (1980). *The management of information systems.* New York: Columbia University Press.

Kreuger, L. (1987). Microcomputer software for independent social work practice. *Journal of Independent Social Work, 1*(3), 45–58.

Kreuger, L., & Ruckdeschel, R. (1985). Microcomputers in social service settings: Research applications. *Social Work, 30*(3), 219–224.

Kucic, A. R., Sorensen, J., & Hanbery, G. (1983). Computer selection for human service organizations. *Administration in Social Work, 7*(1), 63–75.

Laska, E., & Bank, R. (Eds.). (1975). *Safeguarding psychiatric privacy: Computer systems and their uses.* New York: John Wiley & Sons.

Lazarus, A. (Ed.). (1996). *Controversies in managed mental health care.* Washington, DC: American Psychiatric Press.

Levi, J. (1981). The log as a tool for research and therapy. *Social Work, 26*(4), 333.

Levine, R. (1976). Child protection records: Issues of confidentiality. *Social Work, 21*(4), 323–324.

Levitan, K., Willis, E., & Vogelgesang, J. (1985). Microcomputers and the individual practitioner: A review of the literature in psychology and psychiatry. *Computers in Human Services, 1*(2), 65–84.

Levy, C. (1979a). Code of ethics. *NASW News, 24*(2), 6–7.

Levy, C. (1979b). NASW ethics task force. *NASW News, 24*(1), 9.

Lindenthal, J., Jordan, T., Lentz, J., & Thomas, C. (1988). Social workers' management of confidentiality. *Social Work, 33*(2), 157–158.

Lindsay, A. (1952). *Group work recording.* New York: Association Press.

Little, R. (1949). Diagnostic recording. *Journal of Social Casework, 30*(1), 15–19.

Lopez, F. (1994). *Confidentiality of patient records for alcohol and other drug treatment.* Technical Assistance Publication Series 13, DHHS Publication No. (SMA) 95-3018. Retrieved July 17, 2007, from http://www.treatment.org/TAPS/TAP13/tap13chap1.html

Lorents, A. (1982). Small computers: The directions of the future in mental health. *Administration in Social Work, 6*, 57–68.

Lowe, B., & Sugarman, B. (1978). Design considerations for community mental health management information systems. *Community Mental Health Journal, 14*(3), 216–223.

Lueger, R. J., Howard, K. I., Martinovich, Z., Lutz, W., Anderson, E. E., & Grissom, G. (2001). Assessing treatment progress of individual patients using expected treatment response models. *Journal of Consulting and Clinical Psychology, 69*(2), 150–158.

Lusby, S., & Rudney, B. (1973). One agency's solution to the recording problem. *Social Casework, 54*(10), 586–590.

Lutheran Social Services of Wisconsin and Upper Michigan. (1987). *Eval-U-Treat: A unified approach to program evaluation and direct service delivery.* Milwaukee, WI: Lutheran Social Service.

Mair, W. C. (1977). Computer abuse in hospitals. *Hospital Progress, 58*(3), 61–63.

Mandziara v. Canulli, 299 Ill. App. 3d 593; 701 N.E. 2d 127; 233 Ill. Dec. 484 (1st Dist. 1998).

Margolin, L. (1997). *Under the cover of kindness: The invention of social work.* Charlottesville: University of Virginia Press.

McCormick, M. (1978). Privacy: A new American dilemma. *Social Casework, 59*(4), 211–220.

McCullough, L., Farrell, A., & Longabaugh, R. (1986). The development of a microcomputer-based mental health information system: A potential tool for bridging the scientist-practitioner gap. *American Psychologist, 1*(2), 207–214.

McKane, M. (1975). Case-record writing with reader empathy. *Child Welfare, 54*(8), 593–597.

Meldman, M., McFarland, G., & Johnson, E. (1976). *The problem-oriented psychiatric index and treatment plans.* St. Louis: Mosby Company.

Meyer, R., & Smith, S. (1977). A crisis in group therapy. *American Psychologist, 32,* 638–643.

Miller, D., & Thelen, M. (1986). Knowledge and beliefs about confidentiality in psychotherapy. *Professional Psychology: Research and Practice, 17*(1), 15–19.

Mitchell, R. (1984). *The client record: A tool for optimizing quality mental health service and malpractice prevention.* Paper presented at the annual meeting of the National Council of Community Mental Health Centers, New Orleans, LA.

Monnickendam, M., Yaniv, H., & Geva, N. (1994). Practitioners and the case record: Patterns of use. *Administration in Social Work, 18*(4), 73–87.

Munro, M. M. (1951, October). Integrating casework and supervision through case records. *Social Work Journal,* 184–187, 197.

Munson, C. (2001). *The mental health diagnostic desk reference* (2nd ed., pp. 289–303). New York: Haworth.

Mutschler, E. (1987). Computer utilization. *Encyclopedia of social work* (18th ed., pp. 16–26). Washington, DC: National Association of Social Workers.

Mutschler, E., & Cnaan, R. (1985). Success and failure of computerized information systems: Two case studies in human service agencies. *Administration in Social Work, 9*(1), 67–79.

Mutschler, E., & Hasenfeld, Y. (1986). Integrated information systems for social work practice. *Social Work, 31*(5), 345–349.

National Association of Social Workers. (1973). *Legal regulation of social work practice.* Washington, DC: Author.

National Association of Social Workers. (1975). *Policy on information utilization and confidentiality* (pp. 214–219). Washington, DC: Author.

National Association of Social Workers. (1979). NASW code of ethics. *NASW News, 25,* 24–25.

National Association of Social Workers. (1989). *Standards for practice of clinical social work.* Washington, DC: Author.

National Association of Social Workers. (1999). *NASW code of ethics.* Washington, DC: Author.

National Institutes of Health, Office of Extramural Research. Frequently asked questions about certificates of confidentiality. Retrieved June 4, 2007, from http://grants.nih.gov/grants/policy/coc/faqs.htm

Nelson, J. (1981, Summer). Issues in single-subject research for non-behaviorists. *Social Work Research and Abstracts, 17,* 31–37.

Neuman, K. M., & Friedman, B. D. (1997). Process recordings: Fine-tuning an old instrument. *Journal of Social Work Education, 33*(2), 237–243.

The new threat to your medical privacy. (2006, March). *Consumer Reports.* Retrieved June 14, 2006, from http://www.consumerreports.org/cro/health-fitness/health-care/electronic-medical-records-306/overview/index.htm

Newkham, J., & Bawcom, L. (1982). Computerizing an integrated clinical and financial record system in a CMHC. *Administration in Social Work, 6,* 97–111.

Newman, F. L., & Sorensen, J. E. (1981). *The program director's guidebook for the design and management of client-oriented systems.* Belmont, CA: Wadsworth.

New York City Chapter, NASW. (1994). *An evaluation of Medicaid managed care: Social work issues and recommendations.* New York: Author.

Noble, J. (1971). Protecting the public's privacy in computerized health and welfare information systems. *Social Work, 16*(1), 35–41.

Northern, H. (1969). *Social work with groups.* New York: Columbia University Press.

Nugent, W. R. (2000). Single case design visual analysis procedures for use in practice evaluation. *Journal of Social Service Research, 27*(12), 39–75.

Nurius, P., & Mutschler, E. (1984). Use of computer-assisted information processing in social work practice. *Journal of Education for Social Work, 20*(1), 83–94.

O'Brien, J. (1983). *Computers and information processing in business.* Homewood, IL: Richard D. Irwin.

O'Brien, N., McClellan, T., & Alfs, D. (1992). Data collection: Are social workers reliable? *Administration in Social Work, 16*(2), 89–99.

Odem, M. E. (1995). *Delinquent daughters: Protecting and policing adolescent female sexuality in the United States, 1885–1920.* Chapel Hill: University of North Carolina Press.

Pannor, R., & Peterson, M. (1963). Current trends in case recording. *Child Welfare, 42*(5), 230–234.

Pardeck, J. (1986). Microcomputers in clinical social work practice: Current and future uses. *Family Therapy, 13*(1), 15–21.

Pardeck, J., Umfress, K., & Murphy, J. (1987). The use and perception of computers by professional social workers. *Family Therapy, 14*(1), 1–8.

Pawlak, E., & LeCroy, C. (1981). Critical incident recording for supervision. *Social Work with Groups, 4,* 181–191.

Payne, M. (1978). Social work records. *Social Work Today, 9*(32, 33).

Perlman, G. (1988). Mastering the law of privileged communication: A guide for social workers. *Social Work, 33*(5), 425–429.

Perloff, J. D. (1996). Medicaid managed care and urban poor people: Implications for social work. *Health & Social Work, 21*(3), 189–195.

Perls, L. (2005). *The homeless management information system.* Congressional Research Service Reports for Congress. Retrieved [insert date if possible], from http://digital.library.unt.edu/govdocs/crs/data/2005/upl-meta-crs-7973/RS22328_2005Nov21.pdf

Phillips, B., Dimsdale, B., & Taft, E. (1982). An information system for the social case-work agency: A model and case study. *Administration in Social Work, 6,* 129–143.

Pinkus, H. (1977). Recording in social work. *Encyclopedia of social work.* Washington, DC: National Association of Social Workers.

Poertner, J., & Rapp, C. (1980). Information system design in foster care. *Social Work, 25*(2), 114–121.

Polowy, C., & Gorenberg, C. (1997). *Client confidentiality and privileged communications: Office of general counsel law notes.* Washington, DC: National Association of Social Workers.

Polowy, C. I., Morgan, S., & Gilbertson, J. (2005). *Social workers & subpoenas.* Washington, DC: National Association of Social Workers.

Popiel, D. (1980). Confidentiality in the context of court referrals to mental health professionals. *American Journal of Orthopsychiatry, 50*(4), 678–685.

The Privacy Act of 1974, 5 U.S.C. § 552a (1974).

Privacy Protection Study Commission. (1977a). *Personal privacy in an information society.* Washington, DC: U.S. Government Printing Office.

Privacy Protection Study Commission. (1977b). *Privacy law in the states.* Washington, DC: U.S. Government Printing Office.

Prochaska, J. (1977). Confidentiality and client records. *Social Casework, 58,* 371–372.

Promislo, E. (1979). Confidentiality and privileged communication. *Social Work, 24*(1), 10–13.

Rapp, C. (1987). Information utilization for management decision making. *Encyclopedia of social work* (18th ed., pp. 937–944). Washington, DC: National Association of Social Workers.

Rapp, C. (1998). *The strengths model: Case management for people suffering from severe and persistent mental illness.* New York: Oxford University Press.

Rawley, C. (1938–1939). A functional examination of recording. *The Family, 19,* 298–305.

Reamer, F. G. (1986). The use of modern technology in social work: Ethical dilemmas. *Social Work, 31*(6), 469–472.

Reamer, F. G. (1987). Informed consent in social work. *Social Work, 32*(5), 425–429.

Reamer, F. G. (1997). Managing ethics under managed care. *Families in Society, 78*(1), 96–101.

Reamer, F. G. (2005). Documentation in social work: Evolving ethical and risk management standards. *Social Work, 50*(4), 325–334.

Reid, W. J., & Epstein, L. (1972). *Task-centered casework.* New York: Columbia University Press.

Reid, W. J., Kenaley, B. D., & Colvin, J. (2004). Do some interventions work better than others? A review of comparative social work experiments. *Social Work Research, 28*(2), 71–81.

Rein, M. (1975). *A model for income support programs: Experience with public assistance and implications for a direct cash assistance program.* Cambridge, MA: Abt Associates.

Review and expunction of central registries and reporting records. (2005). Child Welfare Information Gateway. Retrieved July 18, 2007, from http://www.childwelfare.gov/systemwide/laws_policies/statutes/registry.cfm

Reynolds, M. (1976). Threats to confidentiality. *Social Work, 21*(2), 108–113.

Reynolds, M. (1977). Privacy and privilege: Patients', professionals', and the public's rights. *Clinical Social Work Journal, 5*(1), 29–42.

Richmond, M. (1917). *Social diagnosis.* New York: Russell Sage Foundation.

Richmond, M. (1925). Why case records? *Family, 6,* 214–216.

Robinson, E., Bronson, D., & Blythe, B. (1988, June). An analysis of the implementation of single-case evaluation by practitioners. *Social Service Review,* 285–301.

Rock, B. D., Beckerman, A., Auerbach, C., Cohen, C., Goldstein, M., & Quitkin, E. (1995). Management of alternative level of care patients using a computerized database. *Health & Social Work, 20*(2), 133–139.

Roman, N. (2003, November/December). Tracking the homeless: An overview of HMIS. *Shelterforce Online, 132.* Retrieved June 26, 2006, from http://www.nhi.org/online/issues/132/WNV.html

Rosen, A., & Proctor, E. (2000). *Developing practice guidelines for social work intervention: Issues, methods and research agenda.* New York: Columbia University Press.

Rubin, E. (1976). The implementation of an effective computer system. *Social Casework, 57*(7), 438–444.

Russell Sage Foundation. (1970). *Guidelines for collection, maintenance, and dissemination of pupil records.* New York: Author.

Sackheim, G. (1949). Suggestions on recording techniques. *Journal of Social Casework, 30*(1), 20–25.

Sacks, H. (1975). Title XX—A major threat to privacy and a setback for informed consent. *Connecticut Medicine, 39*(12), 785–787.

Sacks, H. (1976). Strategies and remedies for confidentiality deficits in title XX and title IV D legislation. *Connecticut Medicine, 40*(2), 471–473.

Saleeby, D. (1996). The strengths perspective in social work practice: Extensions and cautions. *Social Work, 41*(3), 296–305.

Saleeby, D. (2002). *The strengths perspective in social work practice.* Boston: Allyn, Bacon.

Sauer, A. (1978). *Procedures for operating a service delivery information system.* New York: Family Service Association of America.

Savrin, P. (1985). The social worker-client privilege statutes: Underlying justifications and practical operations. *Probate Law Journal, 6,* 243–276.

Schoech, D. (1979). A microcomputer-based human service information system. *Administration in Social Work, 3*(4), 423–440.

Schoech, D. (1987). Information systems: Agency. *Encyclopedia of social work* (18th ed., pp. 920–931). Washington, DC: National Association of Social Workers.

Schoech, D., & Aranglo, T. (1979). Computers in the human services. *Social Work, 24*(2), 96–103.

Schoech, D., & Schkade, L. (1980). Computers helping caseworkers: Decision support system. *Child Welfare, 59*(9), 556–575.

Schrier, C. (1980). Guidelines for recordkeeping under privacy and open-access laws. *Social Work, 25*(6), 452–457.

Schwartz, G. (1989). Confidentiality revisited. *Social Work, 34*(3), 223–226.

Seaberg, J. (1965). Case recording by code. *Social Work, 10*(5), 92–98.

Seaberg, J. (1970). Systematized recording—A follow-up. *Social Work, 15*(3), 32–41.

Sechrest, L., McKnight, P., & McKnight, K. (1996). Calibration of measures for psychotherapy outcome studies. *American Psychologist, 51*(10), 1065–1071.

Shaw, D. R. (1981). *Your small computer: Evaluating, selecting, financing, and operating the hardware and software that fits.* New York: Van Nostrand Reinhold.

Sheffield, A. E. (1920). *The social case history: Its construction and content.* New York: Russell Sage Foundation.

Shueman, S. A., Troy, W., & Mayhugh, S. L. (1994). *Managing behavioral health care.* Springfield, IL: C.C. Thomas.

Shuman, D., & Weiner, M. (1982). The privilege study: An empirical examination of the psychotherapist-patient privilege. *North Carolina Law Review, 60,* 893–942.

Siegel, C., & Fischer, S. K. (1981). *Psychiatric records in mental health care.* New York: Brunner/Mazel.

Silverman, M., & Rice, S. (1995). Ethical dilemmas of working with individuals who have HIV disease. *Journal of Gay & Lesbian Social Services, 3*(4), 53–68.

Simmons, J. (1978). A reporting system for hospital social service departments. *Health and Social Work, 3*(4), 102–112.

Sircar, S., Schkade, L., & Schoech, D. (1983). The data base management system alternative for computing in human services. *Administration in Social Work, 7*(1), 51–62.

Smith, S. (1986–1987). Medical and psychotherapy privileges and confidentiality: On giving with one hand and removing with the other. *Kentucky Law Journal, 75,* 473–555.

Smith, S. R. (1986–1987). Privileges and confidentiality. *Kentucky Law Journal, 75,* 475–557.

Social workers and psychotherapy notes. (2006). National Association of Social Workers. Retrieved July 18, 2007, from http://www.socialworkers.org/ldf/legal_issue/200606.asp

Social workers and record retention requirements. (2005). National Association of Social Workers. Retrieved July 18, 2007, from https://www.socialworkers.org/ldf/legal_issue/200510.asp

Sorosky, A., Baran, A., & Pannor, R. (1978). *The adoption triangle: The effects of the sealed record on adoptees, birth parents, and adoptive parents.* Garden City, NY: Anchor Press.

Sosin, M. (1986). Administrative issues in substitute care. *Social Service Review, 60*(3), 360–375.

Southard, E. E., & Jarred, M. (1922). *Kingdom of evils.* New York: Macmillan.

Spano, R., Kiresuk, T., & Lund, S. (1977). An operational model to achieve accountability for social work in health care. *Social Work in Health Care, 3*(2), 33–42.

Spevack, M., & Gilman, S. (1980). A system for evaluative research in behavior therapy. *Psychotherapy: Theory, Research and Practice, 17*(1), 37–43.

Standards for Privacy of Individually Identifiable Health Information, 65 F.R. 82652 (2000).

Stiffman, A. R., Staudt, M., & Baker, P. (1996). Family preservation services: An example of the use of records to answer questions about outcome and client characteristics. *Community Alternatives, 8*(2), 56–69.

Streat, Y. (1987). Case recording in children's protective services. *Social Casework, 68*(10), 553–560.

Strom-Gottfried, K. (1998). Informed consent meets managed care. *Health & Social Work, 23*(1), 25–34.

Strom-Gottfried, K., & Corcoran, K. (1998). Confronting ethical dilemmas in managed care: Guidelines for students and faculty. *Journal of Social Work Education, 34*(1), 109–119.

Sullivan, J. M. (2004). *HIPAA: A practical guide to the privacy and security of health data.* Chicago: American Bar Association.

Sussman, A. (1971). The confidentiality of family court records. *Social Service Review, 45*(4), 455–481.

Swan, P. (1976). Privacy and recordkeeping remedies for the misuse of accurate information. *North Carolina Law Review, 54,* 585–621.

Swift, L. (1928). Can the sociologist and social worker agree on the content of case records? *Social Forces, 6*(4), 535–538.

Sytz, F. (1949). Teaching recording. *Journal of Social Casework, 30*(10), 399–405.

Tarasoff v. Regents of the University of California, 17 Cal. 3d 425, 551 P. 2d 334 (1976).

Tatara, T. (1987). Information systems: Client data. *Encyclopedia of social work* (18th ed., pp. 931–937). Washington, DC: National Association of Social Workers.

Taylor, A. (1953). Case recording: An administrative responsibility. *Social Casework, 34*(6), 240–246.

Tebb, S. (1991). Client-focused recording: Linking theory and practice. *Families in Society, 72*(7), 425–432.

Telephone Consumer Protection Act, 47 U.S.C. § 227 (1991).

Templeton, M. (1986). The psychotherapist-patient privilege: Are patients victims in the investigation of medical fraud? *Indiana Law Review, 19,* 831–851.

Testa, M., Fuller, T., & Rolock, N. (2005). *Conditions of children in or at risk of foster care in Illinois: An assessment of their safety, stability, continuity, permanence and well-being.* Urbana: Children and Family Research Center, University of Illinois at Urbana-Champaign School of Social Work.

Thomas, E. J. (1978, Winter). Research and service in single-case experimentation: Conflicts and choices. *Social Work Research and Abstracts, 14,* 20–31.

Tice, K. W. (1998). *Tales of wayward girls and immoral women: Case records and the professionalization of social work.* Urbana: University of Illinois Press.

Timms, N. (1972). *Recording in social work.* Boston: Routledge & Kegan Paul.

Tomm, K., & Wright, L. (1982). Multilevel training. In R. Whiffen & J. Byng-Hall (Eds.), *Family therapy supervision: Recent developments in practice.* Orlando: Academic Press.

Toseland, R. (1987). Treatment discontinuance: Grounds for optimism. *Social Casework, 68*(4), 195–204.

Toseland, R., & Rivas, R. (1984). *An introduction to group work practice.* New York: Macmillan.

Towle, C. (1941). *Social case records from psychiatric clinics.* Chicago: University of Chicago Press.

Trabin, T. (Ed.). (1996). *The computerization of behavioral health care.* San Francisco: Jossey-Bass.

Turner, J. (1987). Confidences of malpractice plaintiffs: Should their secrets be revealed? *South Texas Law Review, 28,* 71–91.

Tuzil, T. (1978). Writing: A problem-solving process. *Social Work, 23*(1), 67–70.

Uniting and Strengthening America by Providing Appropriate Tools Required to Intercept and Obstruct Terrorism Act (USA Patriot Act) of 2001, P.L. 107-56, 115 Stat. 272 (2001).

Urbanowski, M. (1974). Recording to measure effectiveness. *Social Casework, 55*(9), 546–553.

Urbanowski, M. L., & Dwyer, M. M. (1988). *Learning through field instruction: A guide for teachers and students.* Milwaukee, WI: Family Service of America.

Urdang, E. (1979). In defense of process recording. *Smith College Studies in Social Work, 50*(1), 1–15.

U.S. Department of Health, Education and Welfare, Secretary's Advisory Committee on Automated Personal Data Systems. (1973, July). *Records, computers and the rights of citizens.* Retrieved July 17, 2007, from http://aspe.hhs.gov/datacncl/1973privacy/tocprefacemembers.htm

U.S. Department of Health and Human Services. Institutional review boards. Retrieved May 30, 2007, from http://www.hhs.gov/ohrp/irb

Van Dyke, C., & Schlesinger, H. (1997). Training the trainers. *Administration and Policy in Mental Health, 25*(1), 47–59.

Velasquez, J. (1992). GAIN: A locally based computer system which successfully supports line staff. *Administration in Social Work, 16*(1), 41–54.

Video Privacy Protection Act, 18 U.S.C. § 2710 (1988).

Vogel, L. (1985). Decision support systems in the human services: Discovering limits to a promising technology. *Computers in Human Services, 1*(1), 67–80.

Volland, P. (1976, Spring). Social work information and accountability systems in a hospital setting. *Social Work in Health Care, 1,* 277–286.

Warren, R. V. (1995). *Merging managed care and Medicaid: Private regulation of public health care.* Washington, DC: NASW Office of Policy and Practice.

Watkins, S. (1989). Confidentiality and privileged communications: Legal dilemma for family therapists. *Social Work, 34*(2), 133–136.

Weaver, D., Moses, T., Furman, W., & Lindsey, D. (2003). The effects of computerization on public child welfare practice. *Journal of Social Service Research, 29*(4), 67–80.

Weed, L. (1968). Medical records that guide and teach. *New England Journal of Medicine, 278,* 593–600.

Weed, L. (1969). *Medical records, medical evaluation, and patient care.* Cleveland: Case Western Reserve University Press.

Weick, A., Rapp, C., Sullivan, W. P., & Kisthardt, W. (1989). A strengths perspective for social work practice. *Social Work, 34*(4), 350–354.

Weisberg, R. (1986). Child abuse and neglect: The high cost of confidentiality. *Stanford Lawyer, 24*(3), 24–25, 74.

Weissman, J., & Berns, B. (1976). Patient confidentiality and the criminal justice system: A critical examination of the new federal confidentiality regulations. *Contemporary Drug Problems, 5*(4), 531–552.

Wernet, S. P. (Ed.). (1999). *Managed care in human services.* Chicago: Lyceum Books.

Westin, A. F., & Baker, M. (1972). *Data banks in a free society: Computers, recordkeeping, and privacy.* New York: Quadrangle.

Wheeler, S. (Ed.). (1976). *On record: Files and dossiers in American life.* New Brunswick, NJ: Transaction.

Whiting, L. (1988). *State comparison of laws regulating social work.* Silver Springs, MD: National Association of Social Workers.

Wigmore, J. (1961). *Evidence in trials at common law* (Rev. ed.). J. McNaughton (Ed.). Boston: Little, Brown.

Wilcznski, B. (1981). New life for recording: Involving the client. *Social Work, 26*(4), 313–317.

Wilke, C. (1963). A study of distortions in recording interviews. *Social Work, 8*(3), 31–36.

Wilson, D. (1974). Computerization of welfare recipients: Implications for the individual and the right to privacy. *Rutgers Journal of Computers and Law, 4*(1), 163–208.

Wilson, G., & Ryland, G. (1949). *Social group work practice* (pp. 70–77). Boston: Houghton Mifflin.

Wilson, S. (1978). *Confidentiality in social work: Issues and principles.* New York: Free Press.

Wilson, S. (1980). *Recording—guidelines for social workers.* New York: Free Press.

Witt, J. C., Daly, E. M., & Noell, G. (2000). *Functional assessments: A step-by-step guide to solving academic and behavior problems.* Longmont, CO: Sopris West.

Wodarski, J. (1986). The application of computer technology to enhance the effectiveness of family therapy. *Family Therapy, 13*(1), 5–13.

Woolfolk, C. (2003). *Presentation on cultural issues to DCFS supervisors.* Urbana: University of Illinois at Urbana-Champaign, School of Social Work, Training Partnership.

Yalom, I. (1986). *Psychotherapy with groups.* Paper presented at the National Conference on Clinical Social Work in San Francisco, CA.

Yaron v. Yaron, 83 Misc. 2d 276, 372 New York S 2d 518 (1975).

Young, D. (1974a). Computerized information systems in child care: Techniques for comparison. *Child Welfare, 53*(7), 453–463.

Young, D. (1974b). MIS in child care. *Child Welfare, 53*(2), 102–110.

Zuboff, S. (1983). New worlds of computer-mediated work: Paying heed to staff resistance can help managers. *Public Welfare, 41*(1), 36–44.

INDEX